BAMBOOZLED!

Besieged by Lies, Man Never a Sinner

How World Leaders Use Religion to Control the Populace

ISBN-13: 978-1461063599
ISBN-10: 1461063590

BAMBOOZLED!

Besieged by Lies, Man Never a Sinner

How World Leaders Use Religion to Control the Populace

Timothy Aldred

Also by Timothy Aldred

Why They Gagged My Daughter:
What Big Publishers Don't Want You to Know

This Book is Dedicated:

To Dr. Samuel Noah Kramer, who has provided a wealth of life-long knowledge for many generations to come; and to the other authors and sources cited in this work.

To my beloved wife, Pearl, who stood with me like a brave soldier in fierce battle.

To my daughter, Nadine. Thanks for your encouragement and linguistic help, your patience with my slow learning, and for all of the technical assistance you contributed to this book. Without you, it wouldn't be possible.

To all of my brothers and sisters, of course, they're too many to name, with the exception of Joseph, who has offered personal attention and gives encouragement to help boost my interest along the way. However, I appreciate the influence and indirect support of all my siblings.

And to my friends, Lorenzo and Michael. I am very gracious to the both of you for your factual and logical embrace of the world that history delineated.

One man can't stand alone, and so I am most joyful to have all of you in my life. I wish you all blessings that last forever.

CONTENTS

PREFACE

⚜

I am not a proper writer, just a guy with a lot to say. I am an unlikely source for the information I provide in this book. The fact that I am writing a book is a miracle, and you should be prepared to experience some intense sensations brought on by my teasing logic; it will be like a loving invasion of the most precious portions of your mind, areas you may not have tapped in a long time, if at all.

My daughter, Millenia Black, is a young novelist, author of *The Great Pretender* and *The Great Betrayal*. If you have not heard the name Millenia Black before, I'm sure it won't be very long before you hear it again. Her reading fans rave over her talent as a storyteller, of which I am really proud. It is wonderful to know that my only child has such ability.

Honestly, I am not a storyteller, but I have a propensity for investigation and conversation. Now, I can only carry on about what sustains those proclivities, which is consistent, non-fluctuating, intense reasoning. My daughter has given me some grammatical lessons, because she came along and found her dad academically challenged, so set yourself in a mood to do some slow substantive deliberation with me, because I am presenting something that I believe you will find highly interesting. My spirit inspires me to write this book in the same way I would speak to my companions in person, and that sounds good to me.

As to my background, I was brought up a Christian, and that experience is at the heart of some of the troubling things I aim to have a conversation about. The issue is clearly matters concerning, in my view of it, a cultural bamboozle—man has never been a sinner. I am about to disclose facts that intimate that we are all in serious trouble, though some of us are affected in different ways. For anyone who has not picked up quickly on where I am headed with this, the volume of it is ahead herein.

I became curious about an attempt to write this book, because of the outcomes of conversations I'd had with various people. When they heard what I had to say, I noticed that they grasped an enlightenment that instantly changed their attitude. Their eyes were opened like never before.

I have a tendency to challenge conventional thoughts, and I seek to engage the cream of the crop—those well learned. I reach out to theologians with PhDs to harvest their views; I have even deposed a lawyer and a federal judge.

If you think of yourself as being in my shoes, then welcome to the club of slow readers, but far from shallow in reasoning. I want to do my best to communicate my ideas here so that at the end you may be benefited by my inspirations. I have a fire deep down in my soul; it's boiling and churning. It pains me to see the current human state of affairs. There is subversive undermining of societies around the globe, and I know that there are many people waiting to have their attention drawn, and that most people do not know what has been going on; but this is an issue that directly affects everyone's lives.

An article appeared in the 2008 Reader's Digest edition. It featured the honoring of about seventeen renowned personalities for their work to help change other people's lives. I went through the article with interest and excitement, to learn what magic or wisdom had been used to affect these people. I must confess that people's lives were really changed, and the credit going to the honorees was well deserved. But my expectation was not really met because these people had only received piecemeal change, not the basic fundamentals required to effectuate change based on an objectively broad worldview. All of the mentoring took place on domestic and economic turf and never attempted to go beyond that horizon. The change lacked a global vision. None of the mentors broached any essential elements of the two most dominant issues affecting people around the world today: religion and politics.

In my view, the failure to confront these intrinsic aspects of society at large keeps you at a lengthy distance from reality.

Accordingly, I write this book to raise the flag of enlightenment, and maybe a war of reason over the dignity owed to a person, which has been stolen for centuries. A governmental regime should not have the audacity to commandeer generations of people by means of hoodwink and bamboozle. Unequivocally, that is what I will show the Roman Empire has done to a sizable portion of world society.

I do understand why people savor the idea of wanting to worship a loving God, it is part of my experience. I have been affected by the same stories, but it was before I had a chance to know anything about the history of the world. It would be fine if what the Reverend Joel Osteen, Billy Graham, T.D. Jakes, Joyce Meyers and Creflo Dollar, et al., are preaching had one element of truth. But it is an indisputable fact that the subject of their biblical text is completely false, and is based on blind belief, blind faith and assumptive reliance. While we follow our commonsense in doing daily chores, government has historically used religion as a convincing device, telling us that assumption is more valuable than certainty, and best used in place of facts.

I am not presumptuous. I will not go so far as to say there is no Creator, or maker of the cosmos. I am sane enough not to do that. But I would not accredit a religious scheme of ideology, devoid of virtue, wisdom, knowledge and understanding to such a majestic being or beings. We make no sense when we demand that important things in our lives be performed coherently and logically, while exempting things pertaining to the bible from the same rules.

I think the bible should be coherent as a tool that purports to lead souls to God. But to the contrary, I've discovered the bible to be replete with disjointed allusions of unproven occurrences, symbolisms, distortions, parables, dreams and revelations, none of which, in my opinion, can take one into a progressive direction. There is not one preacher of the gospel who has personal knowledge of the things that they are teaching people as fact. Are we to only take their word for it that Adam caused a curse on mankind?

The words "faith" and "belief" fuel the religious hypnosis that is Christianity. With these two words, everyone who accepts the gospel gets turned into dysfunctional, harebrained characters. From this state of mind, believers are taught to rejoice in the hope of glory, by accepting concepts that are ridiculously impractical and hopeless. As such, religious leaders are able to deceive people into believing the fantasy of scripture, which in turn yields them large financial benefits of pledges, tithes and offerings.

Some unwitting believers are so zealous to prove that God will bless a cheerful giver, they offer up almost everything they own to the church, which in the end yields them fierce poverty. The God of their bible has let them down time after time, but still they fail to suspect that the gospel is a farce. All of this happens simply because the church taught us to believe and not question anything written in the bible, along with theological interpretations, of course. Yes, just believe and have faith.

Do not pass over this without taking strong note of the trick being worked with these doctrines. The whole motive is to keep people from questioning the things that make no sense in the bible, which would quickly unravel the church's role in society. But if we would take the time to acquaint our senses with the presentation of the biblical text, we would find that the initiators must have known these stories weren't true.

An introduction to the "so called" faith can be found in the book of Jeremiah 31, verses 31-34. It contradicts what preachers say and do as they claim to be God's servants. Since they say God inspired men to write the scriptures, we must apply logic to its messages. From the authoritative verses of Jeremiah, it is told that a time would ripen when God makes a brand new Covenant with Israel and Judah. This New Covenant would not equal the covenant made with Israel after the Egyptian deliverance, but would be formulated on a much higher premise: God would place his law within man by writing the laws in their hearts; He is man's God, and men become his people.

The next saying is also noteworthy for the value it places on the whole scheme of salvation's plan: "And they shall teach no more every man his brother, saying, know the Lord: for they shall all know God, from the least of them unto the greatest of them, says the Lord, I will wipe out their iniquity and I will remember their sin no more."

You look carefully at what the bible says God will do under the New Covenant, and it does not say that God would use spiritual leaders, as he used Moses to speak to the children of Israel in sundry times, but that he would write his law in each individual's mind, and be their God and they become his people. That is clear enough. And added to that is a New Testament text that corroborates God's inclusive association with individuals who believe and accept his laws.

In the First Epistle of John 2:27 states: "When the anointing resides in the believer, it would teach them all truths, and since the truth is no lie, they would not need any man to teach them." If this text is truly being held as the law of the Christendom land, then why isn't this verse shining as high tower of light? Instead we have "teachers of the gospel," founders who torture and kill people to accept their dogma.

For me this all means that our dignity is at stake. I am writing to my fellow human brothers and sisters to stop being suckered into this convoluted belief system, arranged by a corrupt regime with men in white robes, who swung smoke lanterns around like imbeciles while calling upon Holy Mary mother of Jesus. I am flabbergasted. Wake up and shake off the religious habit. Together we can recognize real history instead, and see this bogus biblical narrative of empty myths for what it really is.

If at all there is a heaven prepared for man by God, we should be able to use our God-given intelligence to get there, right? Why should anyone blindly accept a religious leadership that has used blackmail, intimidation, and brute force or sequestration of people under duress, as done to the Jewish people? Basically forcing them to accept Christianity, which is contrary to the Judaism faith.

Have Christians really considered the blatant lie Rome tells? How Jews rejected Jesus Christ, their promised Messiah? The messenger of the New Covenant God made to Israel and Judah? Yes, the Jewish faith did expect fulfillment of Messianic scriptures designating someone who would deliver them from their oppressors, as Rome had been. But Jews are angry because they were kicked out of their country, and because Rome invented a counterfeit Messiah, in the image of incarnate God, which was contrary to the Messiah they were expecting. It does seem peculiar that the Jewish people would suddenly reject God's man of deliverance. Are we mindlessly accepting the notion that God ordained Jews to reject their long awaited Messiah? Would this not be an egregious sin?

And how are we to believe that God caused Judas to commit such a damnable sin by betraying Jesus into the hands of sinners? It is not rational for anyone to absorb the incredulous notion that the Roman, Pontius Pilate, knew Jesus to be the incarnate of God at the time of the crucifixion, but turned him over to hostile hands to be killed.

Ladies and gentlemen, I propose that before you believe in Jesus Christ as your Lord and savior, take a deeper look, brake the cycle of gullibility. Verify the story to see whether it can be unequivocal fact worthy of your faith.

Can the Genesis account of Adam and Eve be proven true? I think the mere reading of the story gives one a feeling of discomfort, with the tale of how the wisest of all the animals God made tricked the world's first woman, Eve, into eating forbidden fruit. I don't believe any such thing actually occurred—it is flat foolishness. And because of the falsehood, we have one giant leap to make in proving that a sinful debt is owed to God, and must be paid via a cosmic act—a virgin must bring forth the incarnate of God. Well, look closer. You will find that it is easier for a mule to go through the eye of a needle than for anyone to be saved by the so-called "blood of Jesus."

At least Jews know the story is not true. I am told that some Jews become Catholic priests to make their lives prosperous economically, and some resort to calling themselves "Jews for Jesus," because the Romans are still working to pressure society to accept the icon of an historic Jesus as the Lord and savior of sinners.

But the man Jews knew in Palestine over 2000 years ago was one who dubbed himself a Messiah, but not in the context of dying to atone for sin, but to set Israel free from oppression. And in that instance Rome exaggerated the character of the real historic Jewish Messiah into an imagined "Jesus Christ." This is the reason why there is religious commerce, many suffering people, and the reason I express such strong umbrage against it.

When I did not know about real history, I had no alternative thoughts, but the instant I gained the knowledge of the truth, I awoke completely from the spell of the religious bamboozle. Why should anyone continue living a mockery? When I think about the scope of this brainwashing, and the years I spent believing in it, my heart grows extremely sorrowful, and I even get angry all at once. I accepted Jesus as my Lord and savior at the tender age of seven. So I gave fifty or more years of my life, wasted in this absurdity.

My advice is that people open their eyes and reject the erroneous story of Rome's counterfeit Jesus Christ, and instead seek and find the true information that points to the reality of life. The presentation of this book is without apology to anyone, unless they can provide authentic proof of their position.

I am writing this book because the next generation of human beings should know that the Adam and Eve story is an outrageous hoax. You will see the word "bamboozle" used in this literature many times. Please understand that I do not use it to walk in the red shoes of vain repetition. Whenever you see it, it stands for: poisonous religious deception; a holy ponzi scheme.

If we were living in earlier centuries, the Roman Inquisition or the Crusaders could very well have killed you and me for not at least pretending to believe in Jesus Christ –all done under the auspice of Roman Catholicism. Many Christians don't know about the contrivance that took place at this period in Israel. But it is this same fraudulent Jesus story that gave rise to Martin Luther's fight with the Catholic Church, bringing the Protestant and Lutheran Churches into being.

If you ask me, I believe that one way to remedy this situation is to withdraw the bible from publication, or at the very least, have it republished without the proven misrepresentations, since it contains some Books of probative value.

As you read this book, you will be shown how the Christian faith is one of the biggest obstacles in our society, and how it is an object of hatred and violence among races and ethnicities. Wherever the terms Jews and Gentiles were first derived, the use should not be accepted in any religious context, because they are misnomers in the application of spirituality. Rome has found it convenient to use the designation of "Jew" and "Gentile" as though it was an unseen God who created these words.

In the advent of correct understanding, it is with great delight that we welcome the knowledge of ancient Sumerian history, which reveals the truth of human origin. This is great because it provides clarity, an unbroken history that puts the Jew and Gentile classifications into context.

It's certain that no unseen God decreed religious terminologies, but rather they were borne out of the chaotic human imagination in a manipulative attempt to foster their own brand of spirituality, much like the way they formed derivatives of Pharisees, Sadducees and Essenes. They are all formations of ancient Palestine, first appearing in 2nd century B.C. And there is no need to think that the identity of these sects were of divine origin. In fact their very existence operated by dislike, separation and challenge.

Arnold A. Rogow pointed out the un-artificial seismic effect in his book, THE JEW IN A GENTILE WORLD, to which this author asserts, is so-called Gentile-Jewish relations. He speaks of the traumatic experience Jews have long suffered, and how political and civil emancipation didn't reach them until 1791 in France, and 1860 in England.

With an emphases on the attributes which singled Jews out from the vast Gentile world, the aim of his book was to help set the record straight on the root of the relationship between Jews and non-Jews. He says, in part: "The ancient world saw the Jews as separate and unique, and the sense of separateness and uniqueness, whether it was based on any reality, has been the view Gentiles have of the Jews throughout history." He pointed to an observation that no one seems to be able to agree upon exactly what particular qualities make Jews "different."

Because nothing from the past provides even one scintilla of evidence that some divine authority inaugurates any sects whatsoever, Rogow does not accept the designations of "Jews" and "Gentiles" as containing spiritual meaning. And in this case, it's imperative that we don't accept or apply any serious meaning to the Gentile and Jewish titles. They are political devices that reek havoc in the human arena, by fostering false nobility and inferiority.

Since both sides have assumed the name of Gentile and Jew as meaningful classifications, bequeathed by divine purpose, it becomes a self-inflected historical quandary that one must pick apart in order to discover how it all happened. Since it is widely believed that Jews are God's chosen people, and that he gave them land by covenant, Rogow asks why God allows them to be kicked around more than any other people, and why they need political emancipation from evil governmental bodies? These are compelling issues that warrant adequate answers, which will solve lots of problems. They are issues with global impact, and they require the attention of all people. The purpose of this work is to help in the advancement of credible global knowledge, so that with understanding the confusion around us will disappear from our view.

One needs to perceive why this confusion was planted. It's because powerful people of the past were motivated to use the most effective means and methods to subtly hoodwink and bamboozle the average individual, through psychological fermentation.

Many readers may find portions of this book strange, so I earnestly direct your attention to the evidence, which provides clarity and illumination.

For example, I will point you to take a deeper look at commonplace fixtures that rule your life, such as the "B.C." and "A.D." calendar. The significance is so heavy and brazen that I can hardly believe it has eluded us for so long. Many people do not know this, but history has made no secret of the fact that it was the regime of the Roman Empire that orchestrated this calendar for a very specific purpose. They created it as a paradigm to repose their proprietorship of Christianity. And you will see how establishing such a calendar was an act directed at disrupting and disconnecting people's consciousness from the realities of the past.

Rome established itself as the God of most of the planet, and so it does as it pleases. Under its intimidating influence, the Sanhedrin caught Joseph's son, crucified him, and then implicated Jews as the culprit who killed their Messiah. The man never thought of himself as Jesus the "Christ," but Rome would nonetheless turn him into an imaginary Christ. Do you doubt this is true? Then ponder for a moment why Jews don't wear the cross of Jesus around their necks, but rather identify with the Star of David? And there is much more irrefutable evidence that we have not been paying attention, but they have been staring at us for a mighty long time, waiting to be seen.

It is clear to me that Rome's mission has been to obscure the super important truths, such as the fact that the invisible, cruel and murderous God of Genesis did not miraculously create man. People should continue to blindly believe that Christ died at Calvary for their sins; an imaginary Devil was tossed down to earth from a place called heaven, and that he is fighting against God to deceive people and take them with him into hell. And then there is the allegorical scripture of God's request to have Abraham sacrifice his son, Isaac.

The end result of the brainwashing is that we believe in a concept that says we are under a curse and need a savior to deliver us from eternal hell. I find that to be akin to being buried alive, not in the literal sense, but psychologically. It is so because that is exactly what false premises do when one assumes wrongly about anything. Whatever you believe has the power to create a reception to certain things, which then allows unreasonable power to be exercised over you. In this case, the belief in a man-made God, original sin, Satan, and a Christ sent to redeem you from condemnation, reroutes one's ability to imagine, to reason, and to distinguish correctly.

One's intellectual power is thwarted when they blindly accept the interpretations of others; thought processes get plugged into the wrong frequency. To me, that is equal to being buried alive.

So do not be afraid of the truth. This book is forthright. Think of it as a sort of whistleblower on many basic fronts, uncovering the story that Greco-Romans have imposed on an unwitting populace. Jesus is an imaginary impression much like burlesque, an adventure used in Rome to bring much gain once it got off the ground. The most difficult part for Rome was to shift the deep-seated beliefs in paganism to monotheism, and have it bud and blossom. They figured out how to do it: use violence. Torture and murder people for however long it takes for them to lose track of the former convictions.

To our benefit, one of the more insightful scriptures, Luke chapter 12:3 says: "Therefore whatsoever ye have spoken in darkness shall be heard in the light; and that which ye have spoken in the ear in closets shall be proclaimed upon the housetops." Take a look at modern society from every angle. The evils of the past are the ingredients of the many contradictions that plague our lives today. You can see the way the populace is treated. Political geniuses know how to exploit the populace, controlling the collective thinking and making us their prey.

For those who understand the realities in the history of religion, we can see how strongly people have always aligned with their religious beliefs. Let it be fully understood that the use of spiritual tenets to control entire colonies of dwellers began in ancient Egypt. As Arnold A. Rogow points out in his book, THE JEW IN A GENTILE WORLD: "It started out in early times after life was established there, under the gods and heroes. A man by the name Mneves, was first to persuade communities by use of written laws—which were attributed to divine beings like Zeus, and Apollo. The idea got popular in Egypt and from there great numbers of colonies spread from Egypt to the inhibited world under the same frame of mind.

A certain instance of migration to Babylon was headed by one colonists leader name Belus, with a claim that he was the son of Poseidon and Libya, settled on the Euphrates River and once he established himself appointed priests, called Chaldaeans by Babylonians, and were exempt from taxation."

Now from the 21st century, we esteem to perceive divinity in Mr. Mneves actions in ancient Egypt. But in this writing, I will help you to see how this system was the impetus of the mass bamboozling. Today the Catholic Church takes credit for conveying this (hoax) tradition to our times. Nothing has changed in the concept that started in these ancient times. In every division of modern-day churches, countless men of the cloth are asserting themselves as messengers of God, anointed and sent to preach the word of the Lord, offering righteousness to everyone who believes.

"Thus it is recorded that among the Arians Zathraustes claimed that the Good Spirit gave him laws, among the people known as the Getae who represent themselves to be immortal Zalmoxis asserted the same of their common goddess Hestia, and among the Jews Moyses referred his laws to the god who is invoked as Ioa. They all did this either because they believed that a conception which would help humanity was marvelous and wholly divine, or because they held that the common crowd would be more likely to obey the laws if their gaze were directed towards the majesty and power of those to whom their laws were ascribed." –**The Jew in a Gentile World by Arnold A. Rogow**

Why continue reading if you're devoted to your religious teachings? I think that it would be a waste of your life to continue following religious rituals when this book more than makes the case that it's all bamboozle. So I cordially invite all of you readers to join in with the academic knowledge we have today and glean the understanding of the ancient people. Take back the power you inadvertently gave away. Life is no longer a mystery, as church ministries have taught us. Extricate your mind from religious bamboozle.

You may find this book has the ability to enlighten portions of your mind that have been hypnotized by falsehoods. If the light goes off in even one person's mind, I will rejoice greatly! You may be taking actions this very day based on deceptions that have been stored in the recesses of your mind over the course of your life. Such programming doesn't go away easily, you've become a slave to those beliefs. We must take a look beneath the surface that we are walking on.

Wisdom is a power broker to our freedom. It gives a preemptive strike against the ignorance that inhibits our ability to maneuver correctly and resolve or avoid problems, preventing unnecessary stress. Realize that in this world you are always on your own when it comes to sound reasoning. It does not matter how many friends and family members you've got around you, it is your knowledge and understanding of the way of things that counts in the end. The less truth you know, the greater the advantage others, and negative situations, have over you.

CHAPTER ONE

LITERAL HUMAN ORIGIN

It rocks my brain when I think of the awesomeness of the human body. Have you ever thought about how your body functions? Take a moment to contemplate the invisible, but ever-present, process that takes place from conception and birth to growth and old age.

At the time of our birth, we know nothing at all, and it takes years before a toddler develops some sense of self to rely upon. We come into a world where things like cultures and languages, the notion of God, heaven and hell, right and wrong have already been established, and are waiting for us. We find out later that we are not comfortable in life, but we don't fully understand our lack of happiness, until somewhere along the way we realize that this is a wicked place to be.

A deeper look at life may reveal that there is not much one can do about what needs fixing in the world, because you are born into a controlled environment of fixed governmental laws and cultural indoctrination.

From observation, I think the birth of newborns represents two dynamics: an emergence from the unknown, and an entry into the sphere of human consciousness.

Settle Down

As our biological and mental faculties develop, we learn how to settle down on earth, adjusting to various challenges as they are posed to our senses. We see buildings, trees, mountains, valleys and the beautiful ocean, and we see the sun shining ever so brightly as it seems to make its daily east-west appearance. Then we come to find ourselves engaged in many of the unavoidable nuances of human existence. Among the host of earthly requirements, there is one that stands out uniquely in a class by itself—the obligation to have sex, nature's vehicle for progeny.

Human life is kind of funny; there are so many variations that affect the things we do. Life as a whole is found to be generally tough, especially when faced with situations that call for personal knowledge. Because these types of impediments exist, those in power have always effectively exploited earth's newcomers. The new settlers have no choice but to follow the course of their parents and community. Perhaps it can be dubbed "automatic conditioning."

Our preliminary orientation in human society features a good and bad side. The process teaches some very essential habits, both in word and in deed, such as proper sanitation and health care, and ethics. While on the other hand, they also learn to form bad habits like smoking, intoxication, false worship and a host of other evils. However, time and maturity always grants opportunities for individuals to expand their senses in great measure, and to become informed beyond the perimeters of the status quo.

So we develop unique thought structures, which enable the art of observation, analysis, distinction, judgment and deduction, and then life takes on a characteristic of dimensional value. At this point only the curious, visionary mind will seek to restructure the initial philosophical paradigms, but such an awakening has only happened to a slim amount of people. Why hasn't this illumination affected us all? Well, we don't know why, but at the very least, it is safe to say that everyone should be blessed with exposure to this providential enlightenment.

Researchers have said that a person's individual thought patterns, proclivities and attitudes develop between toddlerhood and adolescence, though we can be born with some genetic predispositions. In my early childhood, I recall that I spent a lot of time pondering and trying to perceive what else may exist besides what I saw around me. I remember staring up into the sky, hoping to find something that would satisfy my curiosity. Now, I am apt to sound simple-minded here, but I used to think that the circumference of the country I was born in embodied the whole wide world. And I believed that for a long time before I discovered it was not so.

In my youthful states, I did feel like something was missing, but I had no clue what that was. Now, I do understand how crucial that primal yearning for basic information was.

In our formative state of mind, any impressions that omit essential truths, or inserts lies, are bound to have long lasting and dreadful ramifications on our future conduct. One of the most potent impressions one can receive during the formative years is the concept of "God," as it has a radical affect on the psyche. Once the word "God" gets into our innocent, unconditioned minds, it stays there and creates a finite assumption that there is a separate, imaginary object "out there" that regulates and governs everything we do throughout our lifetime.

The most important thing to note here is that this conception of God is impressed upon our minds at a time when the mind is not exposed to any other points of view or possibilities. And by the time one's mind is able to master reasoning, there are high walls of subjectivity and biasness already formed towards a bizarre sense of "God" and against commonsensical thought. And what's worse? We are taught that we do not need logic to have faith in God.

Once folks have settled down on the initial indoctrination of a man-made "God," they can no longer discern or identify beyond this scope—and so the status quo, with all of its incorrectness, has its way. Because this is such a commonplace occurrence in the human experience, I see it as an attack on our psychological upbringing, and it makes me very unhappy. This should not be happening. It is really exploitive of our newborn minds, at a time when we are void of all information and have virtually no knowledge of anything; we are basically at the mercy of those in authority and dependant on their examples for our learning.

The collective body of information we learn determines the success of our whole autonomy, marketability and overall usefulness for a lifetime. So the information that we are exposed to along the way really matters, since it seriously impacts the way we contain our motions and assimilate in society.

An Important Realization

Except to say that everyone is born with a level of inquisitiveness, there had to be a reason why, as a child, my imagination was always searching the unknown for significant dynamics. I wanted to imbue my spirit, to feel virtuous and wholesome. And even now, at the age of sixty-three, I am still curious.

It was not too long ago, perhaps five or so years, that I made a finding that I had never heard anyone mention before. And boy, oh, boy, this discovery has really made a majestic impression on me. This finding is not farfetched for anyone to comprehend, but it is nevertheless a bit remote, you are not likely to discover it by accident. Are you aware that your age is directly related to the perennial revolution and rotation of planet earth?

To those who are highly skilled thinkers, you may not find this to be a big deal, but for those of us with slower understanding, discovering the knowledge of how and why we exist is therapeutic and uplifting.

It is such a wonderful thing when people cultivate and maintain razor-sharp observatory skills, and an independent judgment that breaks up ambiguities, which makes ongoing orientation and progression less flawed. I can say with great assurance and conviction, that the human world is hardly ever perceived for what it really is. And when we start off on the wrong track, having not been taught basic concepts, we are vulnerable to the false persuasions that are ever prevalent in society.

Earlier on in my life I developed an interest to think on my own two feet, I began to pay earnest attention to the details that are conveyed in messages, slicing, dicing, and mitigating matters to find the truth in things. Yes, I sharpened my proclivity to stay focused and intensely driven to find details.

Beginning with my inner circle of family and friends, whom I love dearly, I never forgot the principles required for maintaining logic, and so I would always view their words to me along the lines of distinction. For me, information should not be received and interpreted under the influence of biasness or favoritism, but rather it must be allowed to sift through your mental refinery, where its elements can be seen for exactly what they really are—seriously!

I trained myself to hold people accountable for what they say by applying pertinent linguistic principles to their words. Learning to command sensory activity is a glorified attainment, and when we are unable to exercise a close scrutiny of things to discern accuracy, the failure and agony of defeat will forever threaten our progress.

So while showing love and due respect to people, we must remain fully assertive with a well-dignified sense of control on issues; this is the right position of integrity to hold, it benefits everyone. Mind you, though, however mild and generous one may come across in communication, there may be those who reject your cogent poise, and understandably so, for they have yet to see logically as I explained earlier.

Some people will view you as an elitist or a "know-it-all," things like that. That must never be a problem, for the real concern is whether or not the issue is based on the reasonableness of evidence, rather than on inappropriate assumptions. You are likely to discover unique things that disprove the false myths imbedded in colloquial or world orientation.

And even when hardly anyone agrees with it, the irresistible principles of language and probative evidence always come to the rescue, these never fail. The assertion of the meaning of words, their contextual value and connotative arrangements, are also vital to an equitable position on issues. I have learned not to compromise anything when it is inappropriate to do so, because you could be giving away the lifeblood of yours and others.

Self-preservation lies in personal dignity and it can only be preserved when we cultivate an independent ability to investigate and analyze the factors that are presented in various issues. Failure to protect the mind and belongings allows folks to take unfair advantage of you. I urge and promote self-reliance, which enables one to exercise basic defenses, to guard their interests. This does not mean that you need to attend any particular school to learn the necessary skills, because by simply paying attention to words (the conveyors of advantage or the detractors of it) you can assert their powers in arguing merits.

Somewhere along the way, I discovered the realization that I have the potential to do common investigations, something I realized when I took an exam for a state paralegal certification. If a person never develops enough understanding to do basic self-defense inquiry when situations arise, they will lose out on advantages to safeguard their interest and ward off unwelcomed attention.

Your life belongs to you and mine belongs to me, so there is a certain level of selfishness in all people, which tends to interfere with fairness. But when learning to make good distinctions, a healthy degree of selfishness is a good thing. And like everything else, overdosing and becoming condescending and arrogant will always cause problems and run counter to your purpose. I think our senses are tools given to us to take care of our own interests, in ways no one else can. Respect for oneself is first, equally to respect of others. I don't want to overstate the concern for self-preservation, because such importance is hard to overstate.

When we speak we either give something away, or we receive something, so it is the individual's duty to be thoughtful about the words they use, and about those used by others to the individual. I think people need to become highly word-conscious, to be very sensitive and responsible in how they receive messages, and in how they deliver messages to others.

If you are feeling very comfortable with the way you are living now, and you think that the world is treating you kindly, then that is wonderful, but be mindful of the fact that it does not mean all is well with one's standing in life. It is important to take your psychological pulse and do logical self-examination just to make sure that your situation is as good as you believe it to be. Sometimes a moment of introspective scrutiny can surprise you.

The way our society is now organized, with the false worldwide consensus about God and spirituality, people can't help but be dysfunctional in their individual make up. So much so, that even in view of the most potent evidence left behind by the ancient civilized world, people resent and cough at the very idea that such things exist. Some even think that anyone who recognizes their authenticity is crazy.

The obvious truth about human life can never be gleaned through dreams and visions, but rather from the human cradle on the African continent, and in Mesopotamia. It is the governmental bamboozle that has deluded the global populace for thousands of years, diverting people's cognizance from knowing the certainty of life. This is an alarming and lamentable situation that has reached epidemic proportion, and has our society standing on its head, instead of walking on its two feet.

People have been taught to rely on the contrived sources of apocryphal biblical writings, or Darwin's theory of evolution, rather than on the right information of the ancient civil world. Though I believe that both Darwin's and the King James Bible's version (KJV) of scripture offer some degree of worthwhile information, in that they have a little relevance to the historical truth about human origin, they are nevertheless deliberate misrepresentations, used in lieu of the complete, congruent account of literal human origin.

There seems to be a consensus among people around the globe about whom God is, the worshipped, man-made image based on patently false information, not plausible history. And people are unified in the belief that this imaginary God dwells in the sphere of the skies. Where? A direction designated by pointing above our heads. They think a God is up there somewhere in space, but is too lofty to speak with men directly, and thus he remains unidentifiable.

Ancient governments created a well-organized scheme, under the guise of the church, as an independent spiritual entity, working for the unidentifiable and false government-created God. These churches are wired to manipulate our psyche with the tantalizing energy of a promised salvation, which is emotionally contagious and lures folks into the excited anticipation of the grandiose things this false God has promised. For this reason, the bible was fictionalized and shaped to portray the role government has fashioned for the character of God.

Now you can understand why I am so adamant about individuals being equipped with commonsense and logic. The scam is a cleaver arrangement, and its influence is heroic enough to make people disregard the wonders of Stonehenge, and the physical relics on every continent; and even to view Dan Brown's book, THE DA VINCI CODE, as wasteful art.

Watch out, because the biblical maze has been used to convert millions, and induce the belief and feeling that there is no other way to live. Giving up on the intimacy of the relationship with this imaginary God you grew up believing in doesn't feel like an option. These thought patterns are imbedded in our minds along with the devil in hell that will get you if you do not believe. It goes without saying that no one wants to be condemned to a burning, eternal hell; to face off with a big red beast holding a pitchfork, right? And therefore the government drugged us with fear of another man-made entity - Satan.

Yet, Satan is a figure those with governmental power seem to escape, as they commit all manners of evil deeds behind closed doors. There is an infinite lesson to be learned in this volume, and going forward in this chapter and beyond, it takes courage and intestinal fortitude to deprogram your own mind from the years of make-believe.

Take the following scripture, Psalms 19:1:

> *The heavens declare the glory of God*
> *and the firmament shows his handy work.*

There are many other maxims throughout the Old and New Testaments of the King James version of the bible that are designed to convey and support the idea that an invisible God is in charge of human life. Along with the idea that this divine God established present-day religion with a church body that has unquestionable authority. It is very important that everyone understands the exact reason why this scheme was purposefully orchestrated in the first place.

'Monotheism' is defined as the "doctrine or belief that there is but one God." It is a concept that was designed to lead civilization away from the knowledge of its actual human origin, for the purpose of monolithic control. Since its inception, the concept of monotheism has spread throughout the world like wildfire, and today it has become ever so natural, as though the cosmos has personally told us it is so.

I understand that some of the people who read this book will be very disturbed to hear these views about God, and may consider people who have such views to be out of their mind. But never say never. When religious beliefs are accepted without any personal verification of any kind, how can you be sure that what you think you know is the truth? When the creed says that salvation is given to everyone who believes, and you believe this, isn't that just a belief? How can you know you should believe it? How do you know it is absolutely true?

Bear in mind the origin of the word "god," the nation and tongue from which it was derived is the early Sumerian Greek and Hebrew civilizations. I discovered that throughout the ages, its usage has been modified to mean different things. We need to be clear on this, so there is no confusion. But clarity in anything demands an informative process, and one cannot expect to receive an education by choosing not to attend school. As such, I affirm that it would be foolish not to believe that there is a great intelligence behind the existence of the cosmos.

I believe that there is a creator of the world, and I acknowledge that planets have been around for an exhaustive amount of time. Based on the ancient history that has been made available to us, there is no authentic evidence that shows that such a creator of planets has at any time or another established contact or alliance with humans. No evidence is found to substantiate the likelihood that earth and mankind was initially made by a joint purpose, as the biblical story of Genesis purports.

Of course, this explains why blind faith and belief are mandatory prerequisites in order to gain acceptance within any church organization.

What Are Fallen Angels?

In accounts of ancient history that I have read, I believe there is strong evidence to support the idea that life migrated to earth from another planetary body, or bodies.

Along that vein, the ancient people tell us that heavenly hosts, actual super beings, literally came to earth for the purpose of harvesting gold. Sound strange? Yes, I think so. Especially in light of what we have been taught in the bible about the rebellion in heaven, and how God threw Satan down to the earth with his many renegade angels. But to the contrary, they were alien individuals called *Anunnaki,* who were mere administrators and laborers.

According to Sumerian history, a mutiny erupted among these alien laborers digging African goldmines, resulting in the creation of "black-headed" humans. The historical account says that it was the need for additional help in the goldmines, that prompted one of two brothers heading their habitat, a great scientist, to initiate an experimental genetic hybrid, designed to be slave workers in the mines.

Whether one believes this account or not, I think it supersedes the biblical narrative by light-years. Compared with what the bible tells us, it is extremely plausible, because it sets forth a literal human origin with pragmatic and commonsensical detail, as opposed to an apparitional model. The account gives us historical details of times, locations, and the names of individuals for authentication. But I don't see anything in the form of proper place, name or time given in the ghostly, biblical account.

The Only God Man Knows Are Celestial Ancestors

There was a period of time called the dark ages, when paganism reigned, but it should be noted that the dark ages relates to a period in the human era.

The darkened time period came on the heels of extremely high intelligence, which our extraterrestrial ancestors bequeathed to humans, who once created as laborers, struggled to develop. To make some sense of the situation, man's alien creators, subsequently known as the *olden gods*, apparently co-existed with them for a time, teaching men many things until the day came when man was placed in charge and given dominion over all of his affairs.

The Babylonian Epic of Creation, *The Enuma Elish, Tablet VI,* has this to say:

> *Four black-headed ones are among his creatures;*
> *Aside from him no god knows the answer as to their days.*
>
> Then *Tablet VII* says the following:
> *Without fail let them support their gods!*
> *Their lands let them improve, build their shrines,*
> *Let the black-headed wait on their gods.*

Let's not be made a fool here. The fact is clear to me that in the historical records, humanity began with a mixture of peoples—some with full human DNA, and others were a cross between human and aliens. The aliens were the gods, the Creators, and were worshipped by humans. (For the sake of relevance, please see the 6th chapter of Genesis in the bible, which shows that the text was drawn from these ancient records, as it cites an account of alien interbreeding with humans.)

Accordingly, those of the alien bloodline have always controlled society, using elected leaders as the middlemen between themselves and the populace. A good biblical example of this can be found in the book of Jeremiah, the 44th chapter, where *Yahweh*, God of Israel, uses Jeremiah as his spokesman. In this fashion, humans worshipped these higher alien beings, these "gods of old."

I view this account of our beginnings as the unshakable facts of history, and have seen no evidence to disprove this version of events. To me, it is declaratively set forth that the human adoration of these superior creatures ushered in what is called 'polytheism' today, which is defined as many gods. (I will elaborate on this later.) Instead of continuing on in progressive knowledge, once left to govern themselves, humans ebbed into ignorance, which, in time, led to the period now called the *dark ages*.

The Renaissance, and the subsequent New Age then followed the Dark Ages. But let us first make the connection clear, for this is the area where the church leadership shifted the historical timeline and facts. They began labeling certain views: paganism, polytheism, monotheism, which means 'one God' and represents Christianity.

The new Christian design was intended to get individuals to self-govern, through a multilayer of assumptive beliefs—in hyperboles, conjectures, and metaphoric representations. First, the populace had to be willing to believe the one-God theory, a God who is inscrutable to humans. The one-God concept was simultaneously engineered to beguile one's mind into a sense of solid spirituality that basically revolved around the *idea* of God.

Let me firmly establish here that my views are not meant to bash religion; I have no ulterior motive. I know how painful it is to hear arguments that criticize the faith we love to the death and have grown up with. Everyone has different abilities and plays a different role in life. Seeking and speaking the truth is my calling.

I have the deepest respect for the readers who may be hearing these things for the very first time and find the information challenging. And if you happen to be such a reader, please view this as a test of your character, judgment, eloquence, intelligence, and, in addition, a test of your resolve.

There is a saying that goes like this: "If every truth is to be known, there would be no peace." And another saying: "The truth hurts." And yet a third saying goes like this: "The truth shall set you free." So goes the truth about human origin and its connection with paganism.

It may seem unlikely that monotheism could be reversible, but intelligence is a very powerful thing, and as such, I have faith that whenever people come to their senses, it is certain that the metamorphosis of modern-day monotheism will disappear. Monotheism is pure superstition and belongs to people so psychologically impaired that they are unable to discern the abnormality.

Let's take a tip from the many mysterious and unproven acts said to be done under divine influence. Prophets working miracles; beasts devouring false prophets; birds feeding the hungry; a widow having her last measure of wheat flour multiplied; and Moses parting the Red Sea. Blind faith allows people to believe all of these things, for many years, based on the simple notion that God can do anything. But do we have even one piece of evidence to show the authenticity of the entire God idea? There is no evidence that I know of, at least not yet. Zilch.

There are many accounts of miraculous conversions under the scheme of monotheism, especially of the Christian persuasion. One of the most outstanding of these conversions relates to a man named St.

Paul. He was a Jew, a member of the Sanhedrin; a supreme council, and highest of the ecclesiastical and judicial tribunal of the ancient Jewish nation. The story is recorded in the book of Acts of the Apostles.

And then there are the vast numbers of high profile individuals of modern times, who have professed to have their share of born-again, conversion experiences. These accounts are usually of a psychic impression, and occur in the absence of any eyewitnesses, yet Catholicism utilizes them to advance the incarnation of God and everything alleged concerning the birth, miracles, and resurrection of Jesus Christ. But once these accounts are well investigated, the results carry a bizarre impact, as they are without probative foundation or growth.

Today the landscape of our societal worldview concerning god attributes different types of names, such as: Allah, Yahweh, Elohim, Jehovah, God Almighty, God the Father, et al.

When the one-God theory is looked into, using relevant history, it becomes paralyzed and simply doesn't check out. A reader may want to investigate history further to identify whether or not a non-local God wrote the bible; whether He inspired any human to write it, or whether or not Rome, or others, wrote it and dubbed it *God's word*.

Jewish people's claim of the land is based on the argument that their forefather Abraham gave it to them, and that the communication came straight from God in heaven. But can any of this be proven? Have the Jews themselves been hoodwinked and bamboozled also about this one God? It seems like that's exactly what happened to them, too. If there is proof of such a grandiose act—God dealing so prejudicially with Abraham—then Palestinians and all people of the world should capitulate to such a divine gesture, out of necessity.

To have a better understanding of the underlying truth concerning the difference between polytheism (Paganism's many gods) and monotheism (Christianity's one God), there are many reliable resources around for investigation into the ancient Greek, Roman and Jewish gods. This volume's aim is not geared toward exploring the "gods of old" in further depth. Its aim is to simply point to the connections between the ancient Gods and the human ancestors who were worshipped by their subjects.

CHAPTER TWO

❖

EVIDENCE OF OUR LITERAL ORIGIN

Dr. Samuel Noah Kramer earned his PhD in 1929, and in his autobiography he tells of his experience studying at the University of Pennsylvania alongside one brilliant scholar, a guy named Ephraim Avigdor Speiser. He became one of the world's leading intellectuals in Near Eastern studies deciphering cuneiform tablets of the late Bronze Age, dating back to circa 1300 B.C. In this field, Kramer devoted his studies to the cuneiform writing system.

In his 1986 biography, he further tells of contributions to the restoration and deciphering of cuneiform tablets, and disclosed some areas of specialty as follows:

> *"First, and most important, is the role I played in the recovery, restoration, and resurrection of Sumerian literature, or at least of a representative cross section...Through my efforts several thousand Sumerian literary tablets and fragments have been made available to cuneiformists, a basic reservoir of unadulterated data that will endure for many decades to come. Second, I endeavored . . . to make available reasonably reliable translations of many of these documents to the academic community, and especially to the anthropologist, historian, and humanist. Third, I have helped to spread the name of Sumer to the world at large, and to make people aware of the crucial role the Sumerians played in the ascent of civilized man."*

Unlike many people of the past, we here in the twentieth century have been blessed with the fortune of having a highly recognized work of probative value, which tells us in great details how we *Homo sapiens* came about.

So here we have it, the first known civilization of beings, called the Sumerians, gives an account that takes us far deeper into the things we got mere glimpses of in the bible. They documented how the 'alien Lords' descended from the sky to earth, and started our present intelligent life. The many parallels with the accounts recorded in the King James Holy Bible makes this account most compelling! But only when we get into the nuances of the Sumerian life story do we appreciate the many symbolisms borrowed for the creation of the biblical scriptures.

For example: Did anyone ever find out who the beguiling serpent was? And how about the forbidden fruit? And even the six days in which God made the heaven and the earth? Were those Jupiter or Saturn days, or was it earth days counted at a stage before it was fully developed and making full rotations? Wouldn't it be interesting to find out what planetary jurisdiction these 'six days' made referenced to?

What about The truth of the 'all of man' in the Garden of Eden? The sons of God? Noah's flood? The tower of Babel? All are spelled out clearly in the compelling accounts of Sumerian civilization.

The Sumerians' rendition of human history shows that after millions of years passed, a slow evolutionary period went by, which brought forth nothing but a few uneventful species. Then, suddenly, a society of well-equipped, intelligent people appeared. But it all happened subsequent to the advent of the heavenly visitors known as *Anunnakis*, who the bible calls *Nephilims* in the 6th Chapter of Genesis.

Bear in mind that this is the real history of the Sumerian civilization, and all of this information is reportedly sitting in the British archives. The Sumerian account of humanity precedes even the *birth* of all supposed prophets, Moses and the other authors of biblical scripture. Isn't that revealing, to say the least?

The Arrival of Heavenly Lords

The Sumerian account of how humans came into being shows that in 445,000 B.C., Enki, the eldest son of Anu (one of the oldest Gods in the Sumerian pantheon), and his half-sister, Ninhursag, Chief Medical Officer, headed a mission to Earth, with other alien companions. Under Enki's directives, preliminary settlement ensued, during which time the earth's climate mellowed, and additional workers (referred to as 'fallen angels' in the bible) arrived on the earth by 430,000 B.C.

Thousands of years passed where things seemed not to go well, and this prompted yet another group of aliens relocating to earth. On or about 416,000 B.C., as gold production faltered in the mines, Anu arrived on earth with his youngest son, Enlil, the apparent heir to Anu's legacy. At this time, some different planning went into effect regarding the production of gold, and a decision was made to mine in the area of southern Africa. Of the two brothers, Enki and Enlil, Enlil won command of the original settlement, and Enki was relegated to the new one in Southern Africa.

On departing earth, Anu was met with a challenge by one of his counterparts, Alalu the King's grandson, Kumarbi, back on their home planet, Nibiru. This speaks to the biblical "war in heaven."

Enki and his brother Enlil had very strong and bitter feelings between them. At the heart of their conflict was the fact that although Enlil was the youngest, he was the heir, while Enki, the eldest, enjoyed less authority. As expected, the rift between them was handed down to their offsprings.

The study of these mighty Lords is too intriguing to ignore, especially when viewed alongside the biblical accounts of Jesus Christ and his nemesis, Satan the devil. There is a compelling parallel in the Sumerian story that would compare Enki to the Jesus Christ of the New Testament. More specifically, in the book of St. John, Chapter 1:3, it says: "All things were made through him, and without Him was not anything made that was made."

While on the other hand, the Sumerian history describes Enlil as the one who hates humans, and therefore he is comparable to the image of Satan the devil. He doesn't like human beings much, and so seeks to destroy all of the good work, plans, and the will of God, according to the bible.

However, under the order of their father Anu, the purpose of the brothers' mission to earth was to harvest gold and transport it back to Nibiru. And to this end, servant workers were engineered, and heavenly helpers brought along to earth to fulfill the task.

The time came when the alien laborers working in the goldmines staged a strike, which presented the Lords with a serious labor dilemma…Let me pause here to say that I know those who are strongly rooted in the Christian faith may find what happened next in the story hard to believe, because of what has been written in scripture concerning the creation of man. But the Sumerian version is just too poignant for anyone with a thinking, intelligent mind to leave alone.

While the Lords pondered the crisis of the strike at hand, Enki entered the council room of the elders, and made a startling announcement. He told the audience that he could procure a viable workforce to perform the tasks the mutants failed to do. He said: "I have the basis by which this can be done."

After the ruling council reviewed Enki's proposal, it was decided upon that it would be something of a win-win situation, and therefore the plan won easy approval, and the go ahead to make human helpers was given.

To tell the truth, I have been quite anxious and excited to get into this portion of the biblical text, and I believe you'll find this fascinating as well. Here comes the celebrated moment that we have been reading so much about in the bible; the familiar words spoken by the ancient Gods of the ruling council:

> *And God said, Let us make man in our image, after our likeness: and let them have dominion over the fish of the sea, and over the fowl of the air, and over the cattle, and over all the earth, and over every creeping thing that creepeth upon the earth.* - **Genesis 26**

Also in Genesis 3:22, the singular term 'God' is speaking locally, with other collegiums, and it would appear that they were standing right by his side, at close audible proximity. Listen to what follows:

> *And the Lord God said, Behold, the man is become as one of us, to know good and evil, and now, lest he put forth his hand, and take also of the tree of life, and eat, and live forever; There the Lord God sent him forth from the garden of Eden, to till the ground from whence he was taken.*

The historical rendition that the Sumerians have given has coalesced with portions given in the biblical language. Now it is evident from the quote that one individual is conversing with others, as in a group, and it can be logically deduced that they are of the same living entity. When we ask our theologians to explain the meaning of the latter verse, they typically say: "Almighty God has one Son, and then the Holy Spirit, which just happens to be a by-product of both."

They say this in the context that suggests God has only one son, but are we not taught that Satan was His son as well? Yes, the churches have presented us with a mixed bag of interpretations for who these characters are. In one part it purports that God is in heaven working, and communicating with men by apparition, and on the other hand, he works in some kind of semi-literal way that suggests that He is partially on earth with men. It is virtually impossible to make any sense of an unseen God using telepathic means to do business with humans on earth.

Only with the blindfolding advent of religious faith will one exalt these psychoneurotic statements of supposed Truth. I see clearly how they were only meant to confuse readers so that they do not gain knowledge about the *actual* creation, and know the conditions under which human life began on earth, and whom bears the responsibility for our being here.

Genesis Extracts and Parallels: Biblical Follies Exposed

Only when one reads the Sumerian cultural history will he come into the knowledge of the duration of time it has taken to actually perfect Man. You will not read about this in the bible. My purpose is to create an effective "main street" enlightenment; enough to capture the attention of even the most hardened faithful believer. Yes, I think very strongly about this issue, because I know how it feels to have the veil of assumption removed from the mind.

Get this: Enki and his sister, Ninhursag, a medical scientist, set out to produce mankind as prospective slave workers. These workers were made, of course, in their image and likeness, just as stated in Genesis. We are now learning the practical truth of how Lord Enlil, Commander in Chief over the mission to earth, gave consent to make man. This is worth remembering because of the connection with the many things built upon that explanation, especially the unforgettable events in the Garden of Eden.

Next, we are at the place in time where man's development qualified him to serve the intended purpose of the alien gods. Let's get some perspective as to how Enlil and Enki are situated. Remember, Enlil, the younger brother, won control over the earth mission, he then took over the residence that Enki had previously established and occupied as chief at Earth Station number one, in Eridu. This was the intended spot for the mining of the adjacent areas of the Persian Gulf. Enlil assigned Enki to South Africa, causing the sibling tension to fester.

In 300,000 B.C., pre-deluge time, Enlil (depicted in the bible as Satan) removed all the *Anunnakis*, the alien workers who revolted, from the African mines and replaced them with none other than human beings. He also brought the humans into Eden to perform personal work for himself. It appears that Enlil did not merely dislike the humans his brother and sister had created, but many accounts show that he thought of Man as lower in esteem than animal pets. In Enlil's pomp of arrogance, he gave humans a stern warning not to frolic or mess around with their genitals, because if they did, there would be dire consequences.

Apparently Lord Enki (the human creator) had greater appreciation for the human hybrid when he perfected their bodies. And contrary to the inexplicable riddles of Genesis, it was Enki who paid a visit to Eden. Upon meeting Eve, Adam's wife, he broached the question by asking her something like: "Have you guys tried to have sexual pleasure yet?" Eve then explained that their Lord, Enlil, instructed them not to touch their private parts, for they would die. I am sure that this makes perfect sense in explaining the Adam and Eve controversy.

Enki was wroth upon hearing what Eve said. So he then began to enlighten her. He said: "Your Lord is lying to you. Because he is well aware that when Adam takes away your virginity, you would both become equal with him and the rest of us aliens, knowing right from wrong, and no longer will you be lower beasts. Those words sent all sorts of chills up and down Eve's spine, and she was very enticed by what she heard. She went quickly to see Adam and share the good news with him.

It appears that Adam had an instant arousal of his manhood, and nature called. Before they knew it, they were both swept away by an everlasting erotic sensation. When it was all over with, Adam remembered Enlil's instruction not to do the very thing he had just done. He knew that Lord Enlil did not care much for them and braced for the worse. He and Eve sewed fig leaves together and made aprons for themselves, then they waited in the garden for Lord Enlil to appear.

In the following, see if what happens is indicative of acts you would expect from an invisible God out there in heaven, or if it is in line with a literal figure right here on planet earth:

Based on Genesis 3:8 (Paraphrased):

> *And they heard the voice of the Lord God walking in the garden in the cool of the day; and Adam and his wife hid*

themselves from the presence of the Lord God amongst the trees of the garden. When in audible reach, Enlil, the Lord God called out to Adam and said, "Where are you?"

Adam replied nervously, "I heard your voice nearby and I'm so afraid to let you see that I'm naked."

Enlil responded by saying, "Who told you that you were naked? Have you had sex with your wife, Eve, against the order that I gave you not to penetrate her private part, because severe consequences would follow if disobeyed?"

Poor Adam said, "I could not overcome my wife's irritable charm, my Lord, I don't know what really happened to us."

Enlil just could not resist his own emotions of wrath, and he issued a categorical curse that landed Adam and Eve beyond the comforts of Eden, to fend for themselves.

Human indulgence in sexual pleasure would continue to flourish for many years to come, and the escalation of this enthralling pleasure caused their downfall. Under unavoidable romantic strains, of course, the human population grew tremendously well, and above everything else, their sexual ambition overwhelmed all other day-to-day activities.

At 100,000 B.C., in pre-deluge time, Enki the inventor of the humans was a man of pleasure, a sex maniac basically, and he was quite pleased with his handy work. The population of mankind thrived. But Lord Enlil grew angry at man's egotistical conduct. Men were on top of the world, flaunting their sexual gifts, showing off industrial skills by building their own city, and even erected a tall commercial tower. To their surprise, this was not acceptable to some of the *Anunnaki*, so a decision was made to sabotage the humans' ability to carry on with the building program.

As the project continued and was well underway, Lord Enlil decided to pay a visit to see the progress of the city and tower, but his intention was to create a linguistic chaos among men. So it really came to pass that the tower called *Babel* could never be built, because men could no longer speak a common language.

Along the lines of man's sexual agenda, it was one thing for them to enjoy themselves with their own kind, but when the human girls ventured off into having inter-species relationships with the heavenly *Anunnaki* boys, that was the proverbial straw that broke the camel's back, at least that was the way Lord Enlil viewed their sexual conduct.

The Lord Enlil was an avid meteorological weather god, so he hatched a plan to wipe out Enki's humans by keeping them oblivious to an impending killer weather system.

To ensure that no human flesh would survive, he used his supreme rulership to handout an executive order to all members of the alien council, and other relevant parties. He decreed that under no circumstances should anyone divulged information of the coming weather bane to mankind.

We have now come to an occurrence of colossal biblical importance. Concerning the alleged tower sabotage, the Roman scripture purports that the invisible God is responsible for doing it. As justification, they say God can do anything, and while I would agree with the sentiment, I have to put it in its right context, which limits the kind of things an all-knowing, wise and holy God would do. So I object to the notion that God would breach his own purpose and mission as it relates to mankind. Would this God of heaven have set man up to fail, then wipe him out with a vicious flood? Does that sound remotely plausible? But it makes complete sense as the Sumerians have it.

It was Lord Enlil here on Earth who agreed to make human slaves, but could not stand their ever-increasing vulgar population and intractable attitude, so he decided to do away with them.

The Sumerian account presents praxis as opposed to the borrowed biblical theories. No more should anyone go about lost in bewilderment, because there is no more confusion, when the many years of religious mysteries are simplified, the mystiques all disappears.

Now Lord Enlil gave the decree for all human life to be extinguished by the fierce flood. Enki and Ninhursag grieved over the decision to extinguish the hybrid adventure they had come to love. So Enki sought a cleaver plan to save at least some of his human products, one household that would prolong his legacy on Earth.

This takes us into the biblical story of Noah and the Ark. And we shall keep in mind that the bible was not the first literature, as the church would have us believe. Quite to the contrary, the Sumerian history came first. The bible was, and still is, an extracted and intentionally misapplied presentation. In the Sumerian history, it was Lord Enki, the leading creator of man, who acted in subtle defiance of Enlil's order and transmitted by code to a man named Ziusudra (known in the English translation of the King James Bible as Noah),

Enlil's plan of disaster, giving him instructions on how to make a boat for their survival.

Enki subverted Lord Enlil's decree, and that is the only reason all of humanity exists today. Enki is truly the savior of the world, as the Sumerian relays, which bible pushers echo with a bamboozled arrangement called 'Jesus.' Enki's love and mercy for the people he created initiated a simple plan that worked beautifully under such terrible circumstances. His act was so discrete and covert that Enlil got no wind of it, and no doubt could have hindered the operation of saving Ziusudra.

Do you wonder where the *Anunnaki* went during the flood? Sumerian history says that they orbited the earth in their spacecraft and witnessed the horrific death of many helplessness humans as they drowned. I offer thanks, praise, glory, majesty and honor unto our Lord Enki, for all of his marvelous favor toward mankind.

So Rome would have us believe that God killed humans in Noah's flood while thinking: "Oh, I will have to send my only begotten son to die for their sins later." As I have said, and will always maintain in the context of my constructive revolutionary view, what intelligent God with the purity of characteristics the bible describes, would carry out the administration of such disdainful and corrupt conduct on helpless humans? I think it is well said: "We worship and know not of what we do."

After the Deluge

After the flood, in 11,000 B.C., Enlil was displeased because the very situation he had sought to get rid of had survived. However he understood that he should show some respect for one of the most admirable innovations his elder brother, Enki, had created on earth. Enlil could still savor his efforts to rid the earth of the undesirable humans—only eight or so of the bunch remained. And so he decided to help out with the programs that would provide amenities for man to rebuild their living accommodations. He provided seeds and other useful things, while Enki worked on domesticating animals.

In 10,500 B.C., Noah (Ziusudra) and his lineage were given certain regions for habitation. Joining in the process of restoration was Enlil's prized son, Ninurta, who dammed mountains and drained rivers. Naturally, the children of Lord Enlil and Lord Enki were allotted precincts that they controlled. These offspring inherited the conflict between their fathers, similar to how families of today might fight for territory. These descendants of Enlil and Enki have been embroiled in an ongoing bitter conflict for years over places like Egypt, Mont Moriah, Nile Valley, and the Sinai Peninsula, to name a few, and in 8,670 B.C., a second Pyramid war broke out between the *Enlilites* and *Enki* people. Enlil's son, Ninurta, won that conflict in which he emptied the Great Pyramid of all its contents.

On or about this period, an administrative ruler ship occurred, when the Dynasty Ra/Marduk, Enlil's eldest son, was transferred to Thothe, and at that same time, Heliopolis was made into a substitute Beacon City. In 8,500 B.C., the *Anunnaki* maintained outposts at the gateway to the space facilities; Jericho is one of them. There was ongoing war between the extraordinary heavenly creatures, but interestingly, they had among them those with hearts for peace. Accordingly, in 7,400 B.C., there was a time of prolonged peace, and the *Anunnaki* granted mankind new advances. It was at this point in time that the Neolithic period began, when demigods (half-God, half-man) ruled over the land of Egypt.

Urban civilization commenced in the summer of 3,800 B.C. when the *Anunnaki* reestablished their "Olden Cities," beginning with Eridu and Nipur. Now, as I read about the factual representations of times, places and actual beings that existed and constituted the beginning of our life, some itching questions and observations start to buzz in my mind. I wonder: Are all these things literal facts? And if they do represent our incipient life on earth and the geographical spot of the human cradle, why isn't this being taught in every corner of the world?

This knowledge belongs in every educational system, and there is no justification for why it is not a part of the United States history curriculum.

After a time, the noble Lord Anu came to earth on a visit because the city Uruk (Erech) was built in his honor. He then made a temple the abode of his beloved granddaughter Inanna/Ishtar. Remember the name of Anu's granddaughter, because I shall make a special presentation concerning this alien lady and the roll she plays in Jewish history.

Kingship Came to Earth

Our alien parents brought all enlightenment to earth, and there was a special period in time when they introduced man to a thing called *Kingship*.

Following the corrosive reasoning I have illustrated, there is no limit to which government and other entities will go to use the channel of religion to establish societal norms—for their own power and aggrandizement. If keen observation is made, of both the government and the religious communities, the evidence would show that these bodies want the populace to accept that an invisible God placed human beings on earth.

Britain, which is one of the staging headquarters for religious bamboozle in the western hemisphere, used the bible in years gone by to teach people that earth was 6,000 years old, though they only got so much mileage out of the deception.

But by programming people to think that the earth is so young, the manipulators have undoubtedly achieved a substantial goal. Because having that kind of an understanding diverts attention from an otherwise logical focus. It offsets correct observations, analysis, calculations and findings about all planetary existence. The subjugation of people to this type of narrow psychological outlook on the world is very wretched, and unforgivable on the part of those responsible for the scam.

They wrote in the bible: "Beware lest any man spoil you through philosophy and vain deceit, after the rudiments of the world, and not after Christ." But to whom was that statement directed? This is taken from Colossians 2:8.

The principal aim of a corrupt government is to have people's minds buried in the dependence on a God who is invisible, for by believing in the influence of an imaginary spiritual object, one is likely to stay faithful to good conduct, and not be quick to suspect or judge anything. Meanwhile, the manipulators maintain their power and can indulge in all manner of abominable aberrations from behind the scenes, while the believers wait for God to intervene and change things. It is designed to keep the world in good behavior, in prayer and hope, and endlessly seeking to become closer to a God they have not seen, but still believe in fervently. As such, intelligence now demands that appreciation be given to coherent history, and people must tighten their belts and brace themselves for right change, so long as it carries evidence with it.

And as olden times moved along, the *Anunnaki* thought to upgrade the status of man's life with Kingship. After the inauguration of that eventful moment, history shows a series of civilizations and different administrations, featuring many legendary personalities came into being and passed away.

Kingship

In 3450 B.C., there was a change of Primacy that took place in Sumer, when the transfer of power went from Nannar/Sin (a Sumerian God of the Moon and son of Enlil), to Marduk (Enki's first-born son), who proclaimed Babylon the 'Gateway of the Gods.' Around this period of time, mankind accumulated much knowledge, learning from the *Anunnaki* gods, and their ambitions resulted in great innovations. It is the burst of understanding received from the alien parents that would cause man's attempt at building the Tower of Babel. This is one of the rare instances in which the bible comes pretty close to telling the plain truth, because it is written in Sumerian history that, indeed, the "Anunnaki confused Mankind's languages" at the Babel tower when they attempted to establish the enterprise at a place called Shinar.

I want to remind you that the bible serves as evidence of the Sumerian history of man, not vice versa. I give a large degree of credit to the account written in the King James Version (KJV) of the holy bible. It is pretty accurate since it actually says that the Lord confused man's language. One of the revealing points made in the bible is the inclusion of the plural transliteration of "us," where one Lord speaks to other companions on earth.

Looking at this portion, the way it is presented, it does not give the impression that the author of the bible was out to mislead anyone. Especially when it in no way, shape or form suggests that the Lords were somewhere other than earth when events took place. The biblical rendition becomes ludicrous, however, when it brings in the doctrine of monotheism. It is a silly rendition because the plural and singular terms that address the same object lose their synchronization and value.

In 2650 B.C., the status of Kingship deteriorated, and once again Lord Enlil got near to the end of his patience with the human population. In the interim during these times, the great Lords and their offspring held the predominant rule. There were hot conflicts among these heavenly beings. In 2316 B.C., Sargon, an ancient Mesopotamian ruler, set aim at ruling four regions, he removed sacred

(Sargon)

soil from Babylon, and an inactive conflict flared up again between Marduk and Inanna. It would end after Nergal, Marduk's brother, journeyed from South Africa to Babylon and swayed Marduk to depart from Mesopotamia.

After a number of administrations came and went in the region, power changed hands many times, by usurpation.

An interesting period came about in 2220 B.C., when Sumerian civilization ascended to a new elevation under the progressive rulers of Lagash. Thoth assisted King Gudea in erecting a ziggurat-temple for the noble one, Ninurta. Thereafter, and down the line, the historical timetable of 2193 B.C., gives us Terah, Abraham's father, who was born in Nippur into a royal family.

As far as this is concerned, it offers more proof that the bible is extracted material and presents issues taken from sources written in earlier earth history, as opposed to through subliminal mediums like sporadic revelations from God.

The era moves along, finding Egypt divided in 2180 B.C. Those following Ra/Marduk held on to the South, while the Pharaohs opposed to them gained control of the lower part of Egypt. The Central authority deteriorated in Mesopotamia in 2130 B.C., because Lord Enlil and Ninurta were away often, and this influenced Inanna's attempt at regaining the kingship.

Abraham In Sumerian History

Now anytime you mention the name of Abraham, all eyes light up. I won't hold back from revealing that mine do. In the minds of many, his name represents the one who provides humanity with the primary link to the God of heaven and earth, whether or not there is any truth to the symbol.

According to the King James Bible, God pronounced a special blessing upon Abraham and his progenies, and established a significant spiritual earth-post, comprised of him and his offspring. Anyone who respects the authority of the bible understands that the Jews in Palestine are direct heirs to promises God made to Abraham. They are the conduits through which the world attains redemption through the messiah, Jesus. Unlike any other nation in the world, by and through Abraham, Jews have intangible rights to lands; they have

God-given power to evacuate other people from their property, at their own choosing.

I was excited to find information about Abraham that went beyond the abbreviated mentioning in scripture. The enlightenment one stands to gain from further knowledge concerning this biblical patriarch is priceless. It really is, because Abraham's introduction to the world was something of a mystique. Unabashedly, the biblical production of Abraham as a man with an invisible connection to an unseen God is comparable to a grand scam, equivalent to Bernard Madoff's fifty billion dollar Wall Street ponzi scheme.

I am very sorry for my fellow Christian friends who have failed to read up on history, go beyond the biblical gimmicks and into knowledge of the real world. They will always be thinking that the character of Abraham had an intimate relationship with an imaginary God. But the Sumerian precedent of Abraham is the Alpha and Omega of what the world is to know of him and his life. Unfortunately the bamboozling of Abraham inextricably inculcated the generations that preceded us, and can surely continue to affect countless others yet to be born.

Now, the following sequence of events is real, and they are earthly dramas, not something that was communicated by telepathic means, as biblical commentators would direct our minds to believe.

From Sumerian history, we now understand that Abraham was born in Mesopotamia in 2123 B.C., at a place called Nippur, in Lagash, a notable location that, once upon a time, was regarded as the foremost religious center for the Sumerian and Akkadian people. Approximately ten years after his birth, Lord Enlil assigned Lands of Shem to his son, Nannar, and declared Ur of the Chaldees the capital of a new empire. Nammu ascended to the throne and was named Guardian of Nippur. Interestingly enough, Abraham's father, Terah, was a Nippurian priest, and under assignment he relocated with his family to Ur, as a liaison with the royal court system. In 2096 B.C., Nammu died while fighting in battle.

People believed his untimely death was a betrayal by Anu and Enlil. Terah made another move, leaving with his family for Harran.

Then in 2095 B.C., Shulgi of Urim, the second king of the Sumerian Renaissance, rose to the throne of Ur and reinforced colonial ties. And as his empire flourished, he plummeted under the glorious charms of Inanna, a Mother-Goddess, and become her lover. More conflicts would erupt in 2080 B.C. Theban princes allied with

Ra/Marduk and pressed northward in support of Mentuhotep I, a local Egyptian prince. Nabu, son of Marduk, gained enthusiastic adherents for his dad in Western Asia.

What happens next will surely give readers a good perception of something that has always remained puzzling about the spiritual image of Abraham. He was clearly a man of secular warfare. So a pertinent question would be: *Was Abraham working in conjunction with the alien Lords on the ground?* Or was he doing things by telepathy with an invisible God out in the heavens as scripture says?

As the war continued, Nannar, the son of Lord Enlil, gave orders for Shulgi to send more Elamite troops to smother unrest in Canaanite cities. These troops moved forward until they reached the Sinai Peninsula, where the alien Lords had their Spaceport stationed. In 2048 B.C., Shulgi died and Marduk took up residence in the land of the Hittites.

Abraham received an order from Nannar to carry an elite corps of cavalrymen to South Canaan. One year later, Amar-Sin, known in biblical literature as Amraphel, (this is found in Genesis 14: 1-9), became King of Ur. Abraham traveled to Egypt for a five-year stay, and then returned with more troops. On or about five years thereafter, circa 2041 B.C., under the guidance of Inanna, Amar-Sin structured a coalition of 'Kings of the East', and embarked on a military expedition to Canaan and the Sinai, with Elamite Khedor-la'omer as commander. But Abraham blocked their advance at the entry leading to the Spaceport.

Shu-Sin replaced Amar-Sin's seat on the throne of Ur, as the condition of the empire ebbed.

In 2024 B.C., Marduk led his followers in a march on Sumer, and then he assumed the throne in Babylon. The fighting proliferated into central Mesopotamia, and the Nippur's 'Holy of Holy' was defiled. Enlil exacted punishment for Marduk and Nabu, but Enki objected. And then in a strange twist, Nergal, son of Enki, took sides with his uncle Enlil.

Up to this point, earth had never seen tensions rise to such a level, particularly with what subsequently developed through the lineage of Enlil and his brother Enki. But things got very hot, and, as you will see, the fallout brought a horror of a different proportion into being; the likes of which wouldn't be forgotten for generations to come.

At this time, Nabu was determined to take charge of one of the most important and valuable pieces of real estate in the region. So he positioned his Canaanite supporters to capture the Spaceport. The stakes were really high, therefore the great *Anunnaki* approved the use of nuclear weapons to protect their interest. Nergal, Enki's son, then defected to fight on the other side.

Using their high technological capabilities, Nergal teamed up with Ninurta, Enlil's son. Together they destroyed the Spaceport, including some delinquent Canaanite cities. This was a miserable catastrophe and a bad precedent. This disaster took place sometime in 2023 B.C. Winds carried radioactive mist all over Sumer, causing people to experience appalling deaths, innocent animals took their last breath, the water supply was poisoned, and loam became sterile. The great civilization of Sumer was consumed and lay face down.

The heritage that remained passed to Abraham's seed, Isaac, the legitimate heir.

On the question of truth, take a moment to get introspective about this situation with Abraham. Did Abraham really have an invisible call at all, or was he coexisting with the alien ancestors/parents?

Have we seen anything that suggests an invisible spirit in the heavens gave Abraham unfettered rights, and as an assignment borne for his children, unquestionable rights to kick Canaanites, Elamites, Amorites, or any of the Mites or Rites off of their lands in the name of almighty God, maker of heaven and earth?

Yes, we know about the argument that God can do anything, but if God acts in ways that gives impunity to some human beings, while subjecting innocent ones to cruel and unusual punishment, that cannot be the act of a unbiased creator.

True

CHAPTER THREE

✤

CATHOLICISM CONTRADICTED

Introduction to Genesis Review

The collective image presented on how heaven and earth were formed, according to the KJV bible, is clearly one that suggests that the God making them must be grossly disoriented, unstable, unmerciful and lacking in foresight. Certainly not one who is all-wise, loving, or easy to deal with as we are led to expect of such a God, as depicted in many places of scripture.

Secondly, there are too many vague descriptions in the text that we cannot relate to with any degree of commonsense. One comes to believe the inscrutable explanations when one is at his lowest point in the knowledge of world awareness. And shall we place our trust in a cruel regime like the Catholic Church, an organization that imposed the iniquity of slavery, and the use of the Inquisition to torture and kill people they labeled as spiritual heretics?

How about the priests swamped in pedophilia, etc.?

How does it come across, and how must we feel, when we read or listen to sermons about an omnipresent, omnipotent and all knowing God, who made so many blunders in the undertaking of human creation? Come with me now, for a collegial, commonsensical review of the Genesis account, a foray into the most revered story: 'The God of human creation.' We shall begin at the very top, until we have had enough and are full to the point of reclining.

Genesis Chapter One: Moses' Role Examined

This is a compelling story of gigantic proportion in the arrangement of human history, and I want to explain it simply and not botch it.

It is said that Moses wrote the book of Genesis. Therefore, we must believe the notion that God told him of these events by a telepathic medium, through visions or mind revelations, etc., and then

Moses put the information into words for all people. It was conveyed to us that Moses was a resident of earth, and not one of the alien Lords who migrated to the planet, and must have been here when these communications between Moses and God took place.

Is it important for us to know where God was when he told Moses these things? I suppose that it really is, and will proceed with the investigation in this context. One of the gravamen affecting Moses' power play in the KJV constellation is the time history shows he lived. He was around in the neighborhood of 1450 B.C.

I was very surprised when I tried to find Moses' place in the St. Matthew 1 genealogies, and did not see it recorded there. It seemed like the bible producers had a lapse in memory, since he was left out of that chronology of events; granted he was made out to be such a patriarchal symbol. The flint observation that moves Moses forward in this intriguing exploration is that he lived under 2000 years, before the alleged Jesus Messiah that he and other holy men prophesied about.

I find it very odd that even at this stage in the game, the invisible God was still dealing with mankind ever so intimately; by telepathy in the eyes of many people. And in addition to this, Moses was supposedly living at the time when the alien gods ruled in the historic land. He lived in a place we all know today, that flourishes in times of yore, relics. And the names that identify most of the inhabited ancient lands were named by and for some of the alien gods. Even the roads Moses must have walked upon were prepared and named under the sponsorship of the alien ancestors.

For example, the main road between Canaan and Egypt passes along the northern coast of Sinai, and a number of Biblical figures undoubtedly traveled this road, which is known to the Egyptians as "the Way of Horus." And who is this Horus?

Wikipedia Encyclopedia offers some good facts on this individual called Horus, saying: "Horus is a god of the ancient Egyptian religion, most commonly known by the Greek version *Horus*, of the Egyptian Heru/Har. Horus was an ancient and important deity. He was also the son of Isis and Osiris." Well, if you could have seen how this formation lit up my face! It makes it crystal clear why Christianity is such a hard sell in that part of the world. I remember how a good friend of mine, after visiting places like Egypt, bade adios to the biblical idea of the Lord Jesus.

If you should begin to feel nauseous, take a break until you are able to compose yourself again. I encourage a 'hang in there' attitude.

Don't waste this opportunity to attain rewarding knowledge. And hey, I almost forgot to mention an important element as to why I think no mystical transactions took place with Moses and the imagined divine: Why would God allow the holy laws given to Moses for the good of his chosen people and for the benefit of nations to be trampled by the Gentile government?

Why allow his chosen ones to be shoved around here and there by dogs? Leaving their offspring to depend upon manmade military might, rather than upon divine protection? What happened to the heavenly protection that worked for them at the Red Sea, and in the vanquishing of their attacking enemies? Who exactly was it that wrote on tablets, giving them to Moses for distribution? Was it an alien Lord or an invisible hand, as the bible would have us believe?

Moses served as political ruler over Israel, and at one point his father-in-law advised him to appoint others to help in the daily running of operations. It should also be factored in as well that Moses started out as a murderer on the run. With these outstanding thoughts in mind, better analysis can be done.

The style in which it is said God appeared and talked with Moses should be well noted, and Exodus 33: 9-11 gives us an excellent example of how these occasions supposedly transpired:

> *"And it came to pass, as Moses entered into the tabernacle, the cloudy pillar descended, and stood at the door of the tabernacle, and the Lord talked with Moses.*
>
> *And all the people saw the cloudy pillar stand at the tabernacle door, and all the people rose up and worshipped, every man in his tent door.*
>
> *And the Lord verbalized unto Moses face to face, as a man speak to a friend..."*

I believe that an unbiased reader can realize from this that Moses did not likely receive this information by telepathic communication, but rather person-to-person. A sensible analysis of the Genesis text cannot be handled as though Moses wrote these things. There are too many disjointed portions and twists and turns for first authorship. The presentation is consistent with the sculpting of a ghostwriter; with the aim of achieving an awe-inspiring effect, and capturing people's attention.

Genesis 1:1 opens by saying that in the beginning God created the heavens and the earth, and thereafter, he made more things in six days' time. It appears that God made all living creatures after their types, and mankind on the sixth day. Then the all-knowing God took a good look at the man he had created and affirmed His creation was good. This concise portrayal of God doing so many things in so little time makes the God of the bible seem like He can do anything.

In the past, these sly expressions were overlooked; the curious minds that spotted them either kept quiet or were silenced when they spoke out.

How do we assess the six-day duration God is said to have taken to create everything? Every planetary system has its own time, and some of their days would swallow up many earth years, not to mention six earth days. Earth has to rotate one full cycle in order to have one day, how then are earth days used when calculating the time spent for making not just earth, but the heavens, too?

Following the biblical theory that God can do anything, I guess we're not supposed to worry about it. It is also impractical to believe that the sun could be made in one earth day, because it is the sunlight that gives day on earth and the lack of its light that gives us night. So if heaven and earth were made simultaneously, how does one calculate time? Yet it is written that the celestial God had a physical day's rest from the job.

Now, the 26th verse of Genesis is extraordinarily interesting, because it involves some thoughtful elements that I want to single out. God said, "Let us make man in our image, after our likeness." Note the two plural pronouns used, which indicates that whoever God is, and wherever he was, he was not alone. He was also acting in concert with others of the same group similarity.

The narrative goes on to say: "God created man in his own image, in the image of God created he them." Again, we have the use of a pronoun but this time it is the singular term "his." I have concluded that a stipulation is being made, and it is a clear presentation that man was not only made in God's image alone, but in the image of those in his company as well.

And what name would be given to God's companions? Surely they would be gods just as how we would refer to a group of human beings, yes, because it is said that the word 'God' is just a title. So logically, the pronouns 'us,' 'our,' and 'his,' as used to address the group God was speaking to, would apply the title of 'god' to represent them all.

Readers are smart, and the biblical use of semantics is simply a mind game technique to cunningly transfer one meaning to something else. I see that on this particular point, a shift has moved the identity of multiple gods to one God, which was laying the groundwork for the concept that would replace the role of the aliens in human life, and have people focus on one imaginary God.

Genesis Chapter Two

Whenever there are no answers, there is freedom to draw any conclusion. So I am asking you, the reader: Where was the Lord when he blessed the seventh day and took a day of rest? Was He on earth, or was he out in the unknown heavens? There are crucial issues at this juncture to be resolved.

The supposed six days of work with an additional seventh day for rest takes the first link out of the chain of events. This means that the first building block was not produced, and we are therefore unable to lay a second block. What follows next are laconic statements that appear like bones without meat or sinews.

Genesis verse 7-8 says:

> *"And the Lord God formed man of the dust of the ground, and breathed into his nostrils the breath of life; and man became a living soul.*
> *The Lord God planted a garden eastward in Eden; and there He put the man whom He had formed."*

No one can deny the existence of the planet, with the fullness thereof; the sea, land, trees, men and animals—these things are tangible. God made trees grow in the midst of the garden that he thought was pleasant to the sight and good for food. He put a tree of life, which contained the knowledge of good and evil.

If anyone can explain why God found it necessary to include a tree in the garden that was contaminated with evil, but pleasant to man's sight, I would like to hear it. He made four rivers run through the garden, and then God put Adam there to work for him. Then God lectured Adam, telling him that he could eat freely of every tree in Eden that keeps him lacking in understanding, but not to eat of the one that can make him smart. God calls that special one the "tree of the knowledge of good and evil." Ironically, the fruit tree blended with this mixture of knowledge, if eaten, would cause Adam's death.

Next, God thought it was not a sensible thing to have just one person working in the remote garden. And the place gets off to a good start, for now there are people, beasts and trees. To get the ball rolling, God presented all of his creations to the man so he could get some practice in naming things. God gets around to the moment where he must appropriate Adam with a mate, and how does God go about doing this? He anesthetized Adam and removed one rib from his chest. Adam was brought back to his consciousness, and God brought the most beautiful woman to him, made from his rib.

The Genesis author (said to be Moses) tells us that Adam responded by saying, "This is now bone of my bones, and flesh of my flesh: she shall be called Woman, because she was taken out of Man. Therefore, shall a man leave his father and his mother, and shall cleave unto his wife: and they shall be one flesh." These were the pronouncements of Adam. But there are some issues here.

First, who recorded the words of Adam? Did he leave us a diary, or an autobiography? We are talking about the first individual to walk the face of the earth, aren't we? Yes, that is what the bible says—Adam was the first to walk the earth. Since only two human beings and God were present, logic says that one out of the three passed on the words Adam spoke that day. The bible needs to tell us of the source of Adam's words. Or did God whisper Adam's statements to Moses by telepathy?

The second issue is very irritating, to say the least. The precedent of marriage is of universal respect. So why is it the Catholic Church clergies are barred from themselves marrying by church edict and administrative decree? And it would be remiss not to mention how, over the years, many priests engage in pedophilic acts with young boys, which is more favorable to them because they are prohibited from having conjugal bells ring.

In Miami Florida, recent news reported the closure of many Catholic schools in the area. And it's now close to one year ago that the pedophilia crisis drew many apologies from Pope Benedict, for the violations committed in the U.S. and other countries. This very point raises serious questions about biblical authorship by the church. If Adam was the first man to whom such a command was given, why don't the chief proponent of God's word, the pontiffs, adhere to the biblical decrees?

In the minds of most Christians, it does not matter what Catholic leaders do, they will still follow the bible as the word of God; but they should understand that it is the Catholic Church who authored the word of God in the bible. They should realize that the Catholic Church has used the bible to horde people together for centuries. This biblical analysis is worthwhile to expose the con job, and to build the right character for one's self. To have the right 'world freedom,' we cannot throw the baby out with the bathwater.

Genesis Chapter Three

This chapter is going to take you on a wild ride—fasten your cognitive seat belt.

For the first time, you may get a fresh realization of things you have been reading over and over again for years, yet they remain unfathomable. Think of how Adam and his beloved wife have been placed in this garden, where it is assumed that God built them a cottage on the premises where they worked. Up to this point it may be assumed that they are both in their worst state of delinquency, very ignorant, because God did not allow them to eat of the tree of knowledge.

Here comes an intruder. The serpent came into the garden that the bible depicts as the wisest beast that the Lord had made, equipped with speech, but crawls on its belly…how about that? Let us not forget at this time, Adam and Eve were the only intelligent beings walking on the earth. Other biblical representations present the serpent as Satan who traverses between heaven and earth, a brilliant angel who rebels against God. Bear in mind as well, this is the only known incident KJV has given that causes man to fall from grace with his maker, to being under a curse.

So what is it then, a beast made from the ground or an angel who zooms around the deep skies? Whatever the confusion, one thing is made clear by the biblical narrative: the serpent had a lot of inside knowledge about God and about communications that took place between God and Adam, and was passed on to Eve. The exchange between the serpent and Eve leaves no doubt that this could not have been a mere earthbound beast, as we know them to be today. Besides, it is not likely that at that stage Eve would possess the psychological mindset that would accommodate a crawling animal speaking in such an intimate way.

But, again, to faith believing people, God can do anything. Whatever it was, according to the account, the serpent was on a mission to mess up God's plan, and God did not prevent it. Here is the spooky description of what happened between Eve and the serpent:

> *Serpent's Question: "Yes, has God said you shall not eat of every tree of the garden?"*
>
> *Eve's Answer: "We may eat of the fruit of the trees of the garden: But of the fruit of the tree which is in the midst of the garden, God has said, we shall not eat of it, we must not touch it, lest we die."*
>
> *Serpent's Reply: "You shall not surely die: For God knows that in the day you eat of it, your eyes shall become opened, and you shall be as gods, knowing good and evil."*

It went on to illustrate how adept this beast was at human conversation. Eve was enamored and moved into activation by its words. She was convinced God was being very unfair in withholding such enlightenment, so she ventured off into unknown exploration. This entire scenario is shocking, because only in this case has a snake done such marvelous things.

I find that the biblical people made a mistake in writing the exchange between Eve and the serpent. In my judgment, the entire exchange really exposes that none of this information was the product of telepathy. What the serpent said could not materialize from an invisible host, and there is the mention of the plural term 'gods' instead of the monotheism one 'god.' As a matter of fact, the entire Eden episode is totally inconsistent with reciprocation, involving corporeal and incorporeal entities. Only the Sumerians history can tell us the truth of this serpent story.

One thing is certain, Eve proved the beast was correct, and she was glad she listened. Today, some even believe that the serpent had sex with Eve, because there is indication she experienced sensations from tasting the forbidden fruit. Were we to stay within the context of the story, it is reasonable to see something like that taking place.

What enhances the notion that she probably enjoyed romance for the first time, in that sex talk, is the fact that Enki, the Sumerian's human hybrid creator, was himself a sex maniac. Enki was alleged to have intercourse with his daughters and even granddaughters, not to mention that among the alien gods it was normal to wed half-sisters.

The bible says the woman first tasted the fruit by herself, and finding it delicious, she introduced it to her husband. And after that experience both their eyes were opened to new dimensions of themselves. According to KJV, they ate a literal 'forbidden fruit' and then their perceptions changed. But as we have now learned from the authentic source of earlier Sumerian history, the KJV authors created symbols to hide the truth of what really happened.

I am sure thinking Catholics do not want to identify with these absurd things written in the bible. And the Vatican is depending on the blind faith, and their men in white collars to keep hope alive in their institution. If those we have discussed thus far were brought to trial, there would not be one scrap found on planet earth to corroborate the things the scripture represents. Since then, nothing shows that digesting any fruit can cause such an alteration of mind.

The story continues, and suddenly veils were removed from Adam and Eve's eyes and they discovered their nudity. They sewed fig leaves together to keep their genital parts private. But this story gets even more ridiculous. On or about the time their aprons were made and fitted, in the cool of the day, they heard the familiar voice of the one they knew as the Lord God walking in the garden. So they hid themselves among the trees of the garden. Something is not right, because the Lord had no problem seeing them upon arrival before, but this day, they were nowhere to be found. So the Lord called out, "Where are you, Adam?"

And Adam replied, "I heard your voice as you were walking in, but I am undressed and feel afraid for you to see me."

The Lord knows that this guy is not supposed to be sensitive to nakedness, so he asked him, "Who told you that you were naked Adam? Have you eaten from the tree I cautioned you not to take of?"

Adam, only so wise, knowing not what to say, threw his wife under the proverbial bus, saying, "It is the woman you gave to be with me, she brought the fruit, it was irresistible and I devoured it."

Then the Lord God said to Eve, "Why have you done this thing?"

Eve replied, "It is your beastly serpent that enticed me into tasting it, Lord."

Now here God confirms that it was an animal that spoke to Eve, because he addressed the serpent that must have been standing, "You

Serpent! Because you do this to her, you are cursed above all cattle, and above every beast of the field..." This was followed by curses upon Adam and Eve that would affect the rest of their lives. And it was God himself who made them proper clothing...The same God who did not want them to have knowledge and things that were good, now admitted that humans had become as one of 'them,' knowing good and evil.

Now, do any of these events come across like God was flying to earth on business trips to visit the real estate of Eden?

Next based on what happened, why didn't God want Adam and Eve to find out that they were naked? Did he intend to keep this level of knowledge about their bareness a secret forever? And what about giving them garments to protect against weather conditions? Now, as long as we attribute these acts as things our God in heaven has done, it is not possible to prosecute him on anything. The rift here is over a clear fact: man has manipulated history so that subsequent generations accept what has been contrived to be true about God.

You can't hold that God is all knowing, is everywhere at the same time, loving and forgiving, all wise, among other high attributes, and also accept that he behaves opposite to those proclivities. What do you make of the scripture where God reserves the right to have mercy on whomever he will, love some people while hating others, and is just an arbitrary God? I don't see anyone who would like to live in heaven with a God who behaves in such contradictory ways.

The God depicted here does not seem to know what happens when his back is turned, or how things will go after he sets them in motion. So he reacts as ignorant humans would. To me, it seems like everything that would enhance Adam and Eve's wellbeing, this God pre-empted their having it. At first He deprived them of the knowledge of good, and now he doesn't want them to have life.

For what reason, then, did he decide, before he made the world, that Jesus Christ would die for the curse He placed on Adam and his fallen progeny? Was it not to give them all the same life that he took away in Eden? Come on now my Christian theologians; see if you can unravel this, because I don't see it coming through with anything life changing.

They were evicted to the street side, with no forgiveness or revocation from this status until Jesus Christ made an appearance. Adam was then treated like a hardened criminal, who then lived under a heavenly injunction that barred him from re-entering the premises.

The Lord God placed special cherubim guards and a flaming sword, set in every direction just to deprive these fledging people of long lives. This scenario is extremely disturbing to me; it is very offensive. This cherubim stuff is nothing more than a contrivance.

Genesis Chapter Four

Something very interesting happens in this chapter. According to this scripture, Adam and Eve were the only two people on earth. The first verse here says, Adam humbled (had sex with) Eve and she conceived and gave birth to a son they called Cane. Eve also had another baby boy they named Abel. Things did not go well with these brothers.

In looking at Cain's divergent behavior toward Abel, and the Lord's intervention, I do not get the impression that the boys were ever interacting with a Lord God who resides in heaven. Clearly this is an earthly person-to-person interaction. It raises the question as to who was acting as the Lord, mediating Cain and Abel.

Verse fifteen is the part I am most excited to talk about. After the murder of his brother, Cain left the residence his father Adam was given by the Lord God, and came to the land of Nod, on the eastern side of Eden. Wait a minute—this guy found himself a wife and started a family. This is a dramatic contradiction because the bible's author said Adam and Eve started the first family on earth. Where did these *other* people come from, living on the east side of Eden, outside of this family tree? That is bunk, isn't it?

I am not trying to be biased against a true God, but this biblical narrative speaks for itself. There is no theologian to clarify such controversy. It makes no sense to say Adam and Eve, taken from the dust of the earth, were the first two people to walk the land, and then suddenly bring other people from out of nowhere. This is a blatant denial of the idea that the alien Lords started human life. We have signs of them everywhere, yet here in the bible stories, Rome will do anything to keep people in the dark and maintain control. This is how we've been hoodwinked and bamboozled.

You might want to take a little break. This has been another rocky ride, and there is much more just around the bend.

Genesis Chapter Five: The Genealogy of Adam

This is the book of the generations of Adam. In the day that God created man, in the likeness of God made he him; male and female created he them; and blessed them, and called their name Adam, in the day when they were created. And Adam lived an hundred and thirty years, and begat a son in his own likeness, after his image; and called his name Seth….

We must not forget these terms 'image' and 'likeness' because it is a significant parallel, as we shall see. Genesis 1:26 says: "And God said, Let us make man in <u>our image,</u> after <u>our likeness</u>." Watch this. Man was made in the image and likeness of God, and after that, until this very day, all human descendants came bearing the same characteristics of God.

Question: What 'image' did man receive from God? Is the image a symbolic, incorporeal one? Or is it totally corporeal? To those who believe that Man/God image is only spiritual, would they be able to confirm what the image and likeness is? And can they explain how God shows the characteristics of himself in Man? These are some very, very interesting points.

The 'image and likeness' reference is one of the things the bible author(s) did not change when extracting from the Sumerian history. As to be expected, there is hardly ever a perfect crime, and I think it's because this is what people call a sticky situation. Have you ever tried to separate the cream from the coffee?

Since the birth of Seth, Adam begot sons and daughters in the image and likeness of both himself and God. Then he lived to a ripe age of nine hundred and twelve years, and died. Seth's progeny consisted of several patriarchs to the time of the deluge, ending with the guy, Noah.

Reflect upon the many sons and daughters that have been born unto the generations from Adam to Noah. Do know that they transferred the image and likeness of God to one another? Based on Sumerian history, I would have you believe that the God referenced here was not spirit or imagination, but was implicitly physical and visible to the human eye. And as humans began to reproduce, before the deluge, the sons of the Gods began falling in love with human girls…

But while the male Gods had easy access to the beautiful human girls, human boys could not enjoy the same freedom with the celestial female deities. This may be a strange story to some. I shall cover it in more detail later.

Genesis Chapter Six: The Deluge

Theologians today try to turn the sons of God into sons of Seth. The portion of the narrative that presents Seth and his offspring makes no allusions to the fact that they had produce children who were giants in the land. The birth of the children, who became giants, did not happen until the sons of God married and copulated with human women, and from their union sprang forth giants in the land who were men of renown. (It has even been purported that angels had come down from heaven, and had sex with human girls.)

As we learned earlier, according to Sumerian history, it was interspecies marriages between the deity bloodline and the subordinate human bloodline, coupled with human rebellion, which infuriated a senior alien God. The bible text is extracted from this portion, with, in my opinion, the use of the following type of language to convey an invisible, spirit as God: "My spirit shall not always strive with man, for that he also is flesh; yet his days shall be one hundred and twenty years."

This is a contraption. Don't you see the avalanches of glaring evidence to the contrary? The alien Gods and Lords have been made into one God. In verses five and six, God reached the end of his tolerance, as though he had no idea things with mankind would turnout this way. He announces: "I am sorry that I made man on the earth." Further, he says, "I will destroy man whom I have created from the face of the earth; both man and beast, the creeping things and the fowls of the air; because I regret making them all." Again, the truth here is, the God who said those things, according to Sumerian history, was the youngest of the two alien brothers who had supreme earthly control— none other than the human-hater, Lord Enlil.

I discovered something else that goes unnoticed in the Roman manipulation game, and there is good reason for readers to think about it as we go over these observations: Do you remember the story of Dr. Jekyll and Mr. Hyde? Over 2000 years ago, the Roman regime terrorized Israel, kicking them out of their homeland, prohibiting them from returning, but allowed Christians in. They harvested the materials necessary to spread the Jesus ideology around the world with torture and murder.

Once Rome was successful in taking the gospel of Jesus Christ, the man Pontius Pilate supposedly crucified, to the world (which is really a gratuitous Roman command written in St. Matthew chapter 28: 18-20), they allowed Jews to return to their homeland. A picture emerged showing the Roman Vatican to be nothing but Dr. Jekyll and Mr. Hyde. Do you see it? Well, when they killed Jews and threw them out to go settle in desolate places, Rome was Dr. Jekyll.

And now, after 2000 years passed, what do you see? Rome wins. Jesus has become the sweetest name in most ears around the world, the biggest merchandizing machine. And what picture do you see of Rome today? Rome is calm and pious, cool as a cucumber—the brilliant image of Mr. Hyde.

It is not right for the Vatican to represent a regime of annexation with torture and murder, and then shrewdly become the universal vicar of Jesus Christ. Welcome to Mr. Hyde, the most merciful, this should give us a refreshed look at what we see in these chapters.

Genesis Chapter Seven

In this chapter, the KJV continues its delusion, by not identifying which of the brothers (God) told Noah to save himself and his family. If it is the same all knowing God who ordained the purpose of man and set their destiny, then turned around and killed them, I think he must have lapsed into psychosis by this point.

The mind of the true God just cannot possibly be so fickle, as to flip-flop at anytime regarding the good things he ordained to take place. So which God spoke to Noah? Again, Sumerian history says it is not the one who wanted to kill man. Rather, it was the elder, unwed brother, Enki, who tried to save at least one family from extinction and avoid losing the entire human hybrid venture. He was the 'Lord God' who introduced and undertook the project of creating man, as I have shown.

This is the KJV bamboozle as presented to us, starting at verse one:

> *"And the lord God said unto Noah, come thou and all thy house into the ark; for thee have I seen righteous before me in this generation. Then he instructs him to bring into the ark by*

sevens, clean beasts, male and female mates. Of fowls of the air by sevens, male and female to keep seed alive upon the face of all the earth. For yet seven days, I will cause it to rain upon the earth forty days and forty nights; and every living substance that I have made will I destroy from off the face of the earth. Noah did accordingly, unto all that the Lord commanded him.

Noah was six hundred years old when the flood of waters was upon the earth. Noah went in, and his sons and his wife, and his sons' wives with him, into the ark, because of the waters of the flood. Of clean beasts, and of beasts that are not clean, and of fowls, and of everything that creep upon the earth, there went in two and two unto Noah into the ark, the male and the female, as God had commanded Noah. And after seven days as the Lord said, the waters of the flood were upon the earth. And they that went in went in male and female of all flesh, as God had commanded him: and the Lord shut him in.

The flood was forty days upon the earth; and the waters increased, and bare up the ark, and it was lifted up above the earth. And the waters prevailed, and were increased greatly upon the earth; and the ark went upon the face of the waters."

Now, the nineteenth verse to the twenty-forth is summarized this way: "The waters prevailed exceedingly upon the earth, to the covering of the highest mountains. All people, creeping animals and flying birds, were summarily perished, by the merciless and all encompassing flood."

To refresh: the Lord God Enlil, who stated that he was sorry he created man on the face of the earth, and that he will destroy man, beasts and fowls, was sovereign over the earth. He gave an executive order to all of the gods, including his second in command, his elder brother Enki, and placed them under the oath that the plan to wipe man from the face of the earth must not be made known to man. But his brother, Enki, second in command, broke the oath by advising Noah to make the ark, so that his precious invention of man would not be a total loss.

This explanation is very essential to unraveling the confusion of the KJV's presentation. To an intelligent person, the bible makes not a drop of sense here; something has to be wrong. Here is why: It is not logical that only one family would be righteous enough and more deserving of mercy. What about children, and other harmless people who would never crush an ant? It is clear that Enlil ordered every soul in existence be destroyed, and it would have surely been done had Enki not taken action to save one family. Enki is credited with the creation of human beings, and the one by whom mankind still lives today.

Genesis Chapter Eleven

I now fast-forward the narrative through to chapter eleven, bypassing a series of pedestrian interactions between God and men, and some notable genealogies. It is worth remembering, though, that we are proceeding with the ancestry of Noah's family after the flood, and their reproductive explosion.

Again, together we will consider this chapter with careful observation and then decide whether to put our faith in what the KJV presents. Accordingly, based on this chapter, we are to believe that God is in heaven monitoring the conduct of men, as opposed to these great beings living on earth, whom inferior man call Lord and God. I assure you that the events of the following chapter will shake up a lot of deep emotions, because it deals with seismic spiritual activity.

Two worlds are about to collide, so I must give a caveat with love. One world belongs to people who have read the narrative under the influence of religious faith, and the other world is for those who read the same thing under the influence of common logic.

> *"And the whole earth was of one language, and of one speech. And it came to pass, as they journeyed from the east, that they found a plain in the land of Shi'nar; and they dwelt there. They said one to another, let us make bricks, and burn them thoroughly. And they had brick for stone, and slime had they for mortar. And they said, Go to, let us build us a city and a Tower, whose top may reach unto heaven; and let us make us a name, lest we be scattered abroad upon the face of the whole earth."*

I have no aversion with the above verses, one through four, because it is consistent with Sumerian history. But now we shall see where the contraption starts. You can just expect Rome's God to do a bunch of unsavory things to mankind—he always does.

> *"And the Lord came down to see the city and the tower, which the children of men built. And the Lord said Behold the people is one, and they have all one language, and this they begin to do: and now nothing will be restrained from them, which they have imagined to do. Go to, let us go down, and there confound their language, that they may not understand one another's speech. So the Lord scattered them abroad from thence upon the face of all the earth: and they left off to build the city. Therefore is the name of it called Babel; because the Lord did there confound the language of all the earth: and from thence did the Lord scatter them abroad upon the face of all the earth."*

The above paragraph ends with verse nine. This author would like to know where the Lord came from to see the city and tower. I reject the notion that this is all telepathic action. The KJV wants us to believe that God who resides in the heavens, approached men in an apparition, and spoke to men from nebulous cloud formations. It also wants us to believe that God brought other spirit beings with him to earth to execute these changes.

But why would the God of heaven, after expelling man from the Garden of Eden, take pleasure in sabotaging human progress? To me, life is more complex and difficult with different languages, because more often people find themselves among others who speak a language that they cannot understand. This is a situation that pressures people to become bi-lingual, and it is not really easy for some of us to learn a new language.

From a commonsensical point of view, though, no one can deny that it was an enterprising venture that man had engaged himself in at Babel. It would be interesting to have someone to step forward, after looking in hindsight, and give a sensible reason for why God would confound their language, stopping the City and Tower from being built. The venture of the tower was noble and commendable, and it is befuddling as to the attitude this God had for destroying human resources, time, effort and unity.

To tell the truth, there is stark similarity between the destruction of the Babel Tower and the destruction of the Jerusalem temple in 70 A.D. The only explanation given for God's muddling up their language and scattering the people from Shinar, is that He had some fear the roof of the building would reach too high into the sky.

Commonsense tells us that could never have been the cause for the disruption of their lives; it had to be something sinister. Likewise, we may never have known why the hostile Roman regime destroyed the Jerusalem temple, except for the use of logic to discern it. We now know that it was for the purpose of creating fermentation, ushering in the Virgin Mary/Jesus, the incarnate of God, era. What's the difference between these two events? It must be said that this kind of behavior goes against the concept of unity espoused by the KJV scriptures, which is the Lord's supposed desire for men.

Another pertinent question to be asked is this: why would God, who is light-years away in heaven, be afraid of a tall building? Could the almighty God really fear men building a high tower? Why would He find fault with primitive man's ability to erect buildings and skyscrapers? That makes no sense at all. In modern times, we have made great accomplishments along these lines.

We have set many satellites in the skies, some two thousand miles above the earth...and what about the New York towers, and hundreds of thousands of towers in many urban and suburban areas around the globe? I have to wonder what their God really thinks about man's boldness to walk on the moon, since he supposedly regards this area as off limits to man. So does Rome's God still care about man venturing out of his jurisdiction on earth?

Over the many years that I took the KJV to be the inherent word of God, these observations had never entered my mind. And why? The answer is simple: *I believed.*

Let's continue. We have come to a small segment of genealogy in verse twenty-four. It could be a little boring, but it is part of the intrigue so just hang in there. Please meet one of the most important patriarchs (and I will have to admit that I am not too familiar with his name but I am familiar with his offspring).

> *"And so it was that Nahor lived nine and twenty years, and begat Terah: And Nahor lived after he begat Terah a hundred and nineteen years, and begat sons and daughters. Terah lived seventy years, and begat Abram, Nahor, and Haran and Haran begat Lot. Haran also died before his father Terah in the land of his nativity, in Ur of the Chaldees. Abram and Nahor took them wives: the name of Abram's wife was Sa'rai; and the*

name of Nahor's wife Mil'cah, the daughter of Haran the
father of Mil'cah, and the father of Is'cah. Now Sa'rai was
barren; she had no child."

The narrative goes on to say that Terah took all of these family
members with him, including Abram and his wife Sa'rai, to go into a
land called Canaan; and they came unto a place named Ha'ran, and
they dwelt there leaving their native land Ur of the Chal'dees behind.
And Terah died at a ripe age of two hundred and five years, in the land
of Ha'ran.

Genesis Chapter Twelve

For the sake of distinguishing between the fake and the genuine, based
on the Sumerian account, I believe that Abram was a real person from
Mesopotamia, Ur of the Chaldees. I'm convinced that the truth people
are to know about Abram is subverted in the Genesis account, to
protect the advancement of falsehood. Look at the way they have
turned Abram into a supernatural agent.

The issue that we have going forward is to explore how
discussions took place between God and Abram. Having offered my
sagacious sparkle on this, let us move further in the pursuit of
integrity, honesty and certainty in what Abram had to do with
authentic human history.

According to the bible, the God of heaven spoke to Abram by
telepathy, saying: "Abram, Get thee out of thy country, and from your
kindred, and from your father's house, unto a land that I will show
you. I will make out of you a great nation, and will bless you, and
make your name great; and you shall be a blessing: I will bless them
that bless you, and curse him that curses you, and in you shall all
families of the earth be blessed."

Those were the words spoken by God, according to the KJV. (You
may notice that I made some changes, like 'thee' to 'you,' etc., to
make it sound more modern.)

So God spoke to Abram, and now its time for him to respond to his
Lord, so let's see how he handles telepathic instruction:

"Abram departed, as the Lord had spoken unto him, and Lot
went with him: And Abram was seventy and five years old

when he departed out of Hā'ran. He took his wife Sarai and their substance that they had gathered, and the souls that had gotten in Haran; and they went forth into the land of Canaan. Abram passes through Sichem, into the plain of Moreh, a place occupied by Canaanits. The Lord appeared unto Abram, and said, 'I will give this land unto your seed.' And Abram build an Alter unto the Lord, who appeared to him."

Now, which seems more logical? Is God way off in the blue skies interacting with Abram? Or was it a supernatural superior, of which he was seemingly a close interracial bloodline?

Verse nine through twenty covers an interesting saga of Abram's continued journey in a southern direction, which eventually landed him into the hands of lethal adversaries. He ran into a life-threatening situation of famine. The alien gods always blessed Egypt with plenty of food, so Abram decided to take a stint there.

Now if you know what an exuberantly beautiful woman looks like, that is what Abram had for a wife. Customarily in those days, all extraordinarily beautiful women technically belonged to the rulers of territories, and more especially to the King. So much so, that even Abram foreknew it as the rule of the game.

Knowing that he could lose his wife, and even his own life, hunting for food, he prepped his wife, Sarai. In reality, Sarai was Abram's half-sister. So he told her something along the lines of, "Listen, when we get into Egypt, they may want to separate us and perhaps even take my life because of your beauty. If they make that move, then tell them that you are my sister." And bingo! Just as he thought, when Sarai came into view she was ordered before Pharaoh.

Now we are getting into a segment in verse seventeen where there is implication of divine intervention to save both Abram and Sarai from rape, and possibly murder. The bible uses Abram's natural life to stage the assumption of a subliminal connection between God and man. Here it depicts how the great faith of Abram caused God in heaven to look down and see Abram's plight. God then responded with plagues as a nuisance to Pharaoh. Remembering the literal Sumerian history of Abram's ancestry is the only way to understand this contraption.

As profound as this scam is, reasonable people have figured out the maze, and this instance with Abram is a jolting point where anyone can open up to realization. I don't believe there was any miraculous, divine intervention in Abram's situation. Again there is nothing provable in history that stands with these alleged superstitious acts. The essence of life is lost when we believe that Abram was a spiritual port, socket, switchboard or heavenly ambassador, because it is ridiculously untrue.

Genesis Chapter Thirteen

Without going into every little detail of Abram's nomadic movements around the promise land, I think the most important thing worth showcasing are the encounters between him and God throughout.

Something that I think may be worth taking note of, is that the Lord did not tell Abram to take anyone else along with him when he was instructed to relocate, except that we should assume that his wife Sarai was considered to be the better half of Abram, and therefore definitely allowed. But it seems the inclusion of Abram's nephew, Lot, may not have been intended for the trip. Though one should take this with a grain of salt, it may be innocuous to add reasonable conjecture. There is no just cause for the will of their almighty God to create a conflict between Abram and Lot, in maintaining an equitable coexistence with their servants and cattle.

Abram ended the conflict by offering an open-ended option for residence unto Lot, who took what is considered to be the most fertile of the land available for feeding the cattle. While it is considered an unfortunate situation for Abram, down the road in time, Lot's conduct proved to be a bigger misfortune for him, his family, and the herd servants. Abram's alleged problems with this ungrateful nephew, is not in my pursuit, but it should not hurt to give a little salute to the gracious character portrayed by Abram, if any of it is true.

In a quarrel between Abram's herd-men and those of Lot, it seems that Lot was willing to have a standoff with his uncle over the issue. But in verse eight we read: "And Abram said unto Lot, Let there be no strife, I pray you, between me and you, between my herd-men and your herd-men; for we are brethren. Can't you see all the land lying before your eyes? For peace sake, let us be separated. I am giving you the choice. If you are pleased to go in the left direction, then I will take the right and vice versa, it's all up to you.

Well, Lot lift up his head and look around, there he had a panoramic view of the plains of Jordan that it had water everywhere, before the Lord destroyed Sodom and Gomorrah, even as the garden of the Lord, like the land of Egypt, as you are coming into Zoar." Oh boy, this was absolutely too irresistible for Lot, and so he chose all the plains of Jordan, and took off in an eastern direction.

And so it came to be that Lot, without any reservations, separated himself from his uncle Abram, and forgot who brought him to the location. To me, this incident with Lot shows at least two significant things. People should not be ungrateful to those who are gracious to them, and they should cleanse their heart of greediness. Abram was pleased to settle in Canaan, while Lot chose to dwell in the cities of the plain that looked toward Sodom.

Having now been in this distasteful state of separation from his beloved brother's son, Lot, the Lord (you can hear me say 'what Lord' right?) reaffirmed his promise to Abram. He said to Abram, "Now I want you to look from where you are, in all four directions, because every land that your eyes can see will I give to you and your seed forever. I will make your seed be as the dust of the earth; so that if someone can number the dust on the ground, only in such a case could your seed be counted." (Still on the table is the issue of where the Lord is as he speaks to Abram throughout all of these chats, on the ground? Or in the beyond, light years away?)

The Lord continues to tell Abram, "I want you to walk through and familiarize yourself with the length and breadth of the land, because I will surely give it to you." Having once again received assurance of great blessings, Abram took up his mobile tent and came to reside in the plain of Mamre, which is in Hebron, and in this place he built an alter for the Lord...It makes perfect sense here to think that alien ancestors gave Abram land without any problem, because they were the first to occupy the earth.

Genesis Chapter Fourteen

> *"And it came to pass in the days of Amraphel, king of Shinar, Arioch king of Ellasar, Chedorlaomer king of Elam, and Tidal king of nations; that these made war with Bera, king of Sodom, and with Birsha, king of Gomorrah, Shinab, king of Admah, and Shemeber, king of Zeboiim, and the king of Bela, which is Zoar."*

These events are presented in the context that an invisible God above is directing the ways of men, and an evaluation of this segment proves rather interesting. Four kings went up against five other kings, and the five got their butt whipped. Verses three through seventeen relay the triumph of King Chedorlaomer and his comrade over all the kings of Sodom, the capture of Lot and the seizure of all his substance, Abram's victory over the kings and the release of his dear nephew, Lot.

Now after Abram performed a sensational feat by slaughtering the kings and freeing Lot, verses eighteen through twenty-four contain extremely vital information that deserves very close attention. Dissecting this biblical production to find divine handling is imperative. According to the KJV, amid man's vileness on earth after Adam's fall and curse, God placed cosmic value on man's soul, and overshadowed his life. We have been scouring the biblical landscape for anything that may suggest the idea is true. Whenever such things are found, I will gladly confirm that the bible is correct.

After Abram's extraordinary victory over the kings, a priest whose name is Melchizedek (Měl-chĭz´e-děk), came forward with bread and wine to congratulate Abram on his conquest. He was not just a priest, mind you, but rather the King of Sā´lem, and a priest of the most high God.

So here are some of my first questions: Who is the Most High God that Melchizedek was assign to give priestly service to? And what kind of process ordained him to be such a decorated priest? The repeated account of God conversing with man often leaves a vacuum that never gets filled. This corona needs to be sledge hammered.

And indeed readers of the bible have never been given any logical explanation about how these things actually happened…Oh, I just remembered that believers are not privileged to ask for practical answers of when and how they happened (it is against the Roman Catholic rule of bamboozle). Just accept it by faith.

Verses eighteen through twenty provide the sparsest of biographies concerning this important king/priest personality. While this is the only in-depth disclosure on Melchizedek, there is one other Old Testament and one New Testament reference to him. The latter reference concerns me the most because it poses a serious problem—the New Testament reference makes claims that are not in the Genesis biography of Melchizedek.

To be specific, the author of Hebrews wrote this in the seventh chapter: "Without father, without mother, without descent, having neither beginning of days, nor end of life; but made like unto the Son of God; abide a priest continually." The latter contribution was used to support the concept of paying tithes to the church under the Leviticus priesthood, and to elevate the great gospel of Jesus Christ.

Throughout my years as a Christian, I was taught that Abram paid tithes to the great Melchizedek. But for the first time in my entire life, while doing research for this book, upon reading Genesis chapter fourteen, something caught my attention. I even called my friend who used to study the scriptures and visit different churches with me (we got arrested at a famous Fort Lauderdale church years ago), and I drew his attention to what I'd begun to see in Genesis fourteen, verses eighteen through twenty.

First, I confirmed what we had both believed about this passage all along. We agreed that it was Abram who paid tithes to Melchizedek, not the other way around. So I asked my friend to read the text once again to see if it really says that Abram was the individual paying tithes to the priest, and not the priest paying the tithes, bread and wine to Abram. We read over the chapter and scrutinized the verses. My friend thought that it was just as we have always known it to be.

Using tools of linguistic context, I began to poke holes into our old interpretation. The story can be kind of confusing, but we followed the text closely. Now we managed to distinguish which kings were fighting and the problem was found at verse twenty. The last line of verse twenty shows that Melchizedek, Priest of the most High God, and King of Salem, paid tithes to Abram! My friend and I ended up with a consensus that the political king/priest, gentleman Melchizedek, was the one who came bearing gifts with the sole purpose of offering them to the valiant war man, Abram.

Now the Kings of Sodom offered Abram the privilege of taking as much of the commodities as he pleased, but the proud worrier declined. Abram had no interest in reclaiming control. Therefore we find no linguistic logic to support the tenth part of the spoils Abram is said to have paid King Melchizedek. Rather, he insisted that possessions be restored to those taken captive during the war, and to his nephew, Lot.

So, as you can see, Rome wants people to believe the bible is the inspired word of God, yet for the sake of money, they wrote lies into the conflation that makes up the New Testament. And this is quite interesting, for even though the New Testament doesn't advocate paying tithes outright, the misrepresentation that Abram gave tithes to Melchizedek is used as the foundation upon which they argue the fairness of paying tithes under the concept of a new covenant.

Now we have seen the twist, there is now conclusive evidence: Melchizedek was the one giving of his church tithes to Abram! We are finding out that the scriptural writing must never be blindly assumed, and that our stereotypical way of believing that every word in the bible is true, no matter how absurd and ridiculous, needs to discontinue.

Melchizedek and Abram are two biblical icons, and they are like drive shaft, universal joints, providing motion between differential engines, and the truth about their lives is without question a matter of high stakes. If they were to be withdrawn from the biblical pantheon, everything would automatically be pronounced dead. For me this story has fallen apart and has been dead a long while now. If there were no apocryphal elements to scripture, no suspicion, there wouldn't be any need to question the audacity that places these men of nobility off limits, but every test has failed. All of the characters are fictional, because this is a Bethlehem of Judah, Roman bamboozle.

This presents a great danger to all people, because these men are specifically utilized to form a sort of divine coupling, which dovetailed the Old and New Testament.

We have come to the end of a revealing chapter.

Genesis Chapter Fifteen

The Pulitzer Prize worthy fabrication used throughout scriptural scenery probably reaches its summit in this chapter. You are bound to get your heart pricked when the facts meet your attention.

Let's consider the Sumerian account that explains the interaction between Abram and the Gods of his day. It is nothing more than a literal face-to-face conversation with Abram and the great heavenly inhabitants of earth, to whom many different names and titles are attributed. Names and titles used to identify alien Lords are commonly used in the annals of ancient history, and in biblical topography. 'Lord God' is a term that has been used in Sumerian history, but not in the bamboozled context of Rome's theological design. Their version does not direct anyone toward an imaginary God up in the blue skies.

And as I've read the bible over the years, in all honesty, I always had a funny or unfulfilled feeling over the parts showing God and man having telepathic discourse. The real truth is, when we read these portions, it makes perfect sense within the Sumerian context, but has no coherency in the KJV. But we never had much access to a different interpretation, because Sumerian history hasn't been given equal exposure.

The first verse of this chapter starts out by depicting Abram dealing with a spirit God, while quite to the contrary, it was an ongoing relationship with living beings on the ground. In the same manner, one can imagine the sons of the gods having sex with and marrying human women on the ground.

I have noticed something in the opening verses here, where God is stimulating the mind of Abram in a way that seems to suggest Abram is not sure of what God is doing in his life, and is seeking to know. But since Abram had just defeated many mighty armies in battle, supposedly by the help of God, what other affirmation could he have needed?

Can you see and feel the difference it makes when the same text you may have read over countless times suddenly appears more radiant than ever? Because now you have historical enlightenment!

Now, let us see how the following is going to play out…

> *"After these things the word of the Lord came unto Abram in a vision, saying, Fear not, Abram: I am thy shield and exceeding great reward. And Abram said, Behold, to me though hast given no seed: and, lo, one born in my house is my heir. And, behold, the word of the Lord came unto him, saying, this shall not be thy heir; but he that shall come forth out of your own bowels shall be thy heir."*

Verses five through seventeen sum as follows: God entreated Abram by having him appreciate his mighty power. God said to him: "Man, look up at the stars. Can you count them? That is how many I will make your seed be." The Lord further gave Abram more confidence in Him with this reminder: "I am the Lord that took you out of Ur of the Chaldees to give you this land."

But Abram was apparently still behaving like a doubtful Thomas. He said: "Lord God, how am I going to know that this land will be mine?"

Do not laugh, my readers. In verse nine, the Lord God's reply was: "Get me a heifer that is of three years old, and one she goat three years old, and a ram of three years old, one turtle dove, and one young pigeon."

Now if you have taken keen notice, you see that the Lord did not require the pigeon to be three years old like the rest of the meat. We've come to a very cute part with this portion, because Abram did not prepare the pigeon and the turtledove as he did the other meats. I believe that the Lord God came down like a ton of bricks on Abram, because he was not diligent in the preparation of this divine meal. Therefore, the Lord caused a malevolent depth of sleep to overtake him and tormented him with a curse on his offspring.

Readers, do you remember that it was not long ago that the Lord God was nursing the faith of Abram? Telling him: "I am thy shield and exceeding great reward." So what could Abram have done to warrant such a surge of vitriolic denouncements by the Lord? He found fault with the preparation of food? Come on! The theologians have said that God can do anything, and that is all right, but who is this God that is telling Abram to prepare a meal for him? If we follow Rome's KJV, it must mean that an apparition would come light years down to earth to enjoy human food, eh?

The relationship between God and Abram continued despite the umbrage that affected their association. So it is written from verses eighteen to the end of the chapter that the Lord made a covenant with Abram, saying: "Unto thy seed have I given this land: From the river of Egypt unto the great river, the river Euphrates…"

There is indication in these later verses that God in heaven telepathically bequeathed to Abram and his seed some ten lands, occupied by other nations of people. The territorial conflict between Israel and the Palestinians in the Middle East seems to link back to Abram and the land some God gave to him and his descendants.

Now, if this is all about the virtue of God…What God? And where is He? One has to keep wondering why our loving, heavenly father dealt so prejudicially and cruelly with so many of His innocent children.

Is the bible making any sense?

Genesis Chapter Sixteen

This chapter has too many jaw-dropping dramas, and by viewing the inscrutable events, we can see clearly that someone designed them to deceive us. The story is intriguing, but at the same time, demoralizing. If Sumerian history hadn't come to our rescue, revealing the falsity and audacity of such a high magnitude of mystery, mankind would be doomed to perish in the awe of ignorance.

Now let us examine what the KJV authors and theologians would have us believe in this portion…

The saga continues with a phenomenon of childbearing difficulties—watch carefully: Abram's wife, Sarai, who had trouble conceiving, cared not how Abram made love to her. Now, since there was nothing hidden from the Lord God, and given the buddy-buddy, telepathic relationship Abram had with God, he would be blessed with offspring. Most readers know of this legendary story. Sarai was barren and childless. She seemingly had more bravery than today's women, since she consented to Abram having a conjugal relationship with her maid to conceive a child.

So this shows us how cultural values can persuade the unlikely; in this case, it was for the sake of removing the stigma of childlessness. On the other hand, I question Abram's sense of reason. I don't believe that a real man should make the maid of his house equal to his wife; that seems immoral. Especially when the wife is his half-sister, it is too close a bond to insert romantic love with strangers.

The other factor to consider is that Abram was not an ordinary fellow, but a man who had diplomatic ties of hierarchy, not to mention telepathic relations with God Almighty, the maker of heaven and earth. How could he descend into such degrading despair? The cosmic alliance with God of heaven supposedly brought him blessings. God did not like Abram's situation, so He promised to give Abram offspring.

Abram had absolutely no idea how God could make it happen without lowering their dignity. But as it turned out, the ill-fated plans of Sarai, Abram and the maid was a no-no. God should have been consulted about it, but was not. So then everybody had to pay a price for impatiently taking matters into their own hands.

If we do a little musing here, we can see some similarities between Abram and Adam, after God warned him not to eat of the tree of the knowledge of good and evil. These two men allowed their women to lead them astray. Adam, likewise, had no recollection after Eve came to him with the same lovemaking thing. Eve's argument caused a block-out in Adam's consciousness—all he ever wanted was for his eyes to be opened, to become wise, to hell with death.

Under those kinds of precedents, how can you blame President Bill Clinton for the love affair with the intern, Monica? Or Senator John Edwards for his secret sex with his campaign staffer? No matter how hurtful that may have been to Mrs. Elizabeth Edward, his wife.

The point here is very convincing: men are far less than divine, fleshy from the start. And what we are seeing in the case of Abram and Sarai is the enthralling, predestined sexual desire of man. I would expect that a man of Abram's stature (shown to have a higher destiny) should have spotted some danger in the desperate reach for his wife to have a child. Abram should have known that having a child with the maid was a bad idea from the start, something absurd. And shouldn't the issue of having children have been discussed in his prior 'radio frequency' conversations with God?

I can never understand why the God of the Roman bible sat by and allowed libidinal energies to destroy the credibility of His trusted men. The course of history was changed right under Abram's watch, despite a high-fidelity lifestyle with the majesty of heaven. Now historical data proves that, regardless of man's stature, when it comes to sexual temptation and opportunity, they never willingly back down. Why did God permit this anomaly to strike the first family?

Rome has styled the bible to adopt the inevitable nature of man as a sinful concept. But they have never been able to show where the imaginary God actually cleansed anyone of that sin. In the case of the first man of faith, Abram, there should be a power cleansing guidance that the perfect Lord would offer to his children, but none of that is seen here. And why not? Who needs the purging and cleansing of sins more than all the pedophilic Catholic priests?

No sooner than the 'honeymoon' between Abram and Hagar (the Egyptian maid) was over, she had conceived Abram's baby. Things then took an unfavorable turn, a twist Sarai probably never anticipated. Hagar now felt herself to be the true first spouse, and that her mistress, Sarai, being old and unable to produce a child for her husband, was no longer significant in the house. "Get out of here, you old bag," she may have thought to herself. But guess what? She had something coming, and would soon find out who had the autonomy in the residence.

Hagar's impertinent conduct toward Sarai is not all that surprising; it's petty human nature by both parties who seemed too immature for the experience. Sarai complained to Abram, who then drew a line, which didn't solve the problem. It was like he patched one section of the tire but left a gaping hole unattended. Given Abram's failure to ask God about these matters, he took what he considered to be manly action. He said to Sarai, "Look, remember that Hagar, our maid, did what pleased you. So please let nothing come between you and me, my darling."

Nonetheless, things got really hot in the house between Sarai and Hagar, and the latter just could not take the heat, and so she ran away.

While Hagar was on the run, she supposedly had an apparitional experience. An angel of the Lord found her by a cascade of water in the bushes, a place called Shur. This angel offered her some advice. Hagar learned that fleeing was not in her best interest, and that returning and humbling herself unto Sarai would be more beneficial for her fate. The angel then handed down some unflattering news from an astrological point of view. Now, wouldn't it be nice to be in Hagar's shoes? To be blessed by divine company amidst such demeaning bad luck and heartache?

She learned her baby would be a boy child, and she received heavenly instructions to name him 'Ishmael.' The angel told Hagar that the progeny would be exceedingly multiplied; that the baby would be a darn wild man, against others and others against him. This is not sounding good at all for Hagar. In this type of situation, though, you have to ask: Where did the angel of the Lord appear from to find Hagar at the water spring?

For one thing, the narrative makes it out to be a literal, supernatural happening. I say it had to be that one of the alien God's, being privy to Abram's life, intervened, serving as a mediator in the conflict. Doesn't that make more sense? There are questions about how this saga was preserved for posterity. If a spirit indeed spoke to Hagar, did she write down all of these things we now read in the bible? Or did God reveal the incident to Moses thousands of years later?

I find it fruitless to think that God would abandon Abram, his designee, and allow all of these ill-fated experiences into his life, only to have an angel show up out of the blue to help refurbish Abram's home life.

Rome should have written a more intelligent narrative to sell their spooky tales. Case of divinity dismissed.

Genesis Chapter Seventeen

Caution! In this chapter one has got to retire all constructive reason to read the intellect-eroding, incongruous illustration, herein, as with the previous ones. Do you see how the bible seems to insist that we accept that, for unexplained reasons, God in heaven deals with man in unnatural ways, and has elected one special person and his seed superior overall. And He makes certain that no one can judge the biased choice of this individual, bestowing special sovereignty, with wealth and multiplication of his seed. He is the premium human, through whom redemption comes by covenant to all sinners. It will not be surprising if your faith is seriously challenged after a thorough review of this sweeping 'heaven and earth' tale.

In the first verse, the Lord appeared to Abram when he was ninety-nine-years-old. But this time, it does not say he appeared in a vision, and we are not permitted to assume that it is a vision, either. However, God tells Abram: "I want you to walk perfectly before me, I will make a covenant between you, and me and I will multiply you exceedingly." Then Abram fell on his face and God talked with him, saying the following: "My covenant is with you, I will make you father of many nations, and I am changing your name. You shall no longer be called Abram, but your name, as of now, shall be Abraham, I will make you very fruitful, nations and kings shall come of your loins. I will give unto you and your seed the land where you came in as a stranger, all the land of Canaan, for an everlasting possession; and I will be your God."

Now I have to make an important observation: Since a decree from heaven surpasses man's will and purpose on earth, it is inevitable that the promise God made, giving the land of Canaan to Abraham and his descendants, would remain visible until this very day, for all eyes to bear witness of it. In that vein of understanding, the appropriate question is: Where is this God-given land of Canaan? If Canaan can be located, with proper identification, this would surely solidify the authenticity of Rome's KJV rendition.

And since the Jews have been kicked about the planet, an explanation is definitely due. God in heaven is all-powerful and whatever he does, man is not permitted to mess with it, right? Unfortunately, it must be a coincidence that Rome occupied Israel and destroyed the place and people, while acting as the host for the gospel of Jesus Christ.

At verses ten through fourteen, God fashions a major covenant with Abraham, and for the first time, God imposed a ceremonial ritual on him. And it is on this occasion that God allegedly initiated the doctrine of circumcision.

As part of the heavenly covenant with Abraham, God changes Sarai's name to Sarah. (I think we should all ask God to change our names and see what happens. Has God changed anyone else's name? If so, for what reason, and how is it executed? I wonder if maybe Rome's God is still around doing things with people in our population via U.F.O.)

The Lord promised Sarah's old age would be blessed with the birth of a son, making her the mother of a lineage that produces kings. But when Abraham heard God say all of those flattering things, he could not help but burst out in laughter! He thought to himself, *Could I have a child at one hundred years old, with Sarah, who is ninety?*

Nevertheless he asked the Lord to protect his illegitimate son, Ishmael, the son Hagar bore him.

The Lord said to Abraham, "You have nothing to worry about, because Sarah your wife shall bear you a son, and you are to name him Isaac: I will institute an everlasting covenant with him as well, and with his seed after him." As for Ishmael, the Lord said, "I heard of your concern for him. I will work things out on his behalf by making him fruitful, and will multiply his seed exceedingly. Twelve princes shall he begot, and I will allow him to produce a great nation. But listen to me Abraham: I am going to do something special with Isaac, the son Sarah shall produce for you about this time in the next year."

After the Lord made all these disclosures to Abraham, he went on his way. So this conversation is apparently not by telepathy, but rather person-to-person. Verses twenty-three to twenty-seven explain how Abraham wasted no time in circumcising himself, his son Ishmael, and all the male servants of his household.

Genesis Chapter Eighteen

This chapter takes us into happenings that are very exciting, to say the least! Although the bible's author made special efforts to camouflage the literal communication between alien and human beings, there are some areas where it's impossible to veil. And in this portion of the narrative, nothing is left to the imagination regarding Abraham, as you shall see.

> *"And the Lord appeared unto him in the plains of Mamre: and he sat in the tent door in the heat of the day; And he lift up his eyes and looked, and, lo, three men stood by him: and when he saw them, he ran to meet them from the tent door, and bowed himself toward the ground, And said, my Lord, if now I have found favor in your sight, pass not away, I pray you, from your servant: Let a little water, I pray you, be fetched, and wash your feet, and rest yourself under the tree: and I will fetch a morsel of bread, and comfort you your hearts; after you shall pass on: for therefore are you come to your servant. And they said, so do, as you have said. And Abraham hastened in to the tent unto Sarah, and said, Make ready quickly three measures of fine meal, knead it, and make cakes upon the hearth. And Abraham ran unto the herd, and fetched a calf tender and good, and gave it unto a young man; and he hasted to dress it. And he took butter, and milk, and the calf, which he had dressed, and set it before them; and he stood by them under the tree, and they did eat...."*

Beginning with verse nine: *"And they said unto him, where is Sarah your wife? And he said, behold in the tent. And he said, I will certainly return unto you according to the time of life; and, lo, Sarah your wife shall have a son. Sarah heard it in the tent door, which was behind him."*

Now, Sarah was about ninety and Abraham closing in on one hundred—a very old couple. Having children was outside the realm of possibility for Sarah, and for that very reason, when Sarah heard one of the men (the Lord of course) predict she would have a baby, she burst out laughing. The men wanted to know why Sarah chuckled and ask Abraham.

Of course, it was self-explanatory. She was far too old to believe she would have a baby. The Lord replied and said, "Is there anything too hard for the Lord to do? Listen to me, Abraham, at the appointed time, I will return unto you according to the time of life, and Sarah shall have a son." When Sarah heard this affirmation, she got timid, and denied that she had laughed at all. The point was not pursued any further. But the men (God) told Abraham, "You need to know this, especially because you will become a noteworthy man, producing nations. We know that you will command your children to follow in your footstep with the discipline we have taught you." They went on to say, "We have received some complaints, and thus we go to Sodom to investigate whether or not these reports have merit."

Abraham had a premonition of hot wrath concerning the vileness in Sodom and Gomorrah. So he began pleading with the men. He emphasized to them the importance of saving the city if even one righteous soul lives there. Starting at fifty righteous people, he reduced the bid to ten. An agreement was struck, and the men consented not to destroy Sodom and Gomorrah if at least ten righteous people were found.

Genesis Chapter Nineteen

From the previous chapter, we know that three real men visited Abraham in the plains of Mamre; he had a meal with them, in the usual manor that people do. When those gentlemen left Abraham's presence, they were on a mission to Sodom. And now, in chapter nineteen, we see two of the men approach Lot. The problem is, these men are called 'angels,' and technically they are, for the simple fact they came to earth from another planetary body—but that is the gist. You shall see that Abraham and Lot greeted these Gods similarly when they approached as visiting men.

Verse one:

> *"And there came two angels to Sodom at evening, and Lot sat in the gate of Sodom: and Lot seeing them rose up to meet them; and he bowed himself with his face toward the ground; and he said, behold now, my Lords, turn in, I pray you, into your servant's house, and tarry for the night, and wash your feet, and you shall rise up early, and go on your ways. And they said, no; but we will stay in the street all night. And he pressured them to stay; and they turned in with him, and entered into his house; and he made a feast, and did bake unleavened bread, and they did eat. But before they went to bed, the men of the city of Sodom, scoped the house round, and*

they were all sorts, both old and young, and from just about everywhere of the city."

The saga went on to say that the men of Sodom called Lot out of his house demanding that he bring the male visitors out to them, so they could have sexual intercourse with them!

It appears that back in those times, these men would have intercourse in front of people as dogs would, without blushing. But Lot seemed willing to satisfy their sexual rage, saying to them, "Look guys, I have two daughters inside my house who are virgins, allow me to bring them out to you, and you can use them as you please. But you shall not harm my guests, they are under my roof, and I must keep them safe from any discomfort." When they heard what Lot said, the men went crazy, almost to the point of total insanity. These brutish men said to Lot, "You get your ass out of our way right now.

You just moved into our city recently, no one has made you a judge over us; we will treat you worse than your visitors!" At that point, the men pushed Lot away and got very close to breaking down the door. But Lot's guests opened the door, pulled him into the house, then shut the door and used their magical powers to cast a blinding spell on the pursuers, so that they were unable to find a path to the door.

Around 1970, there was an advent of Sodomy in Miami, Florida. But I just realized that what happened in Florida was modified, the decent conduct by victims of homosexuality compared with those invading Lot's house. I am taken aback by the lack of shame in the behavior the men of Sodom exuded. Do you agree that their sexual throws reached an all-time low in human prurient interests?

Verse twelve:

"And the men asked Lot, who else resides with you? After Lot responds to the men, they said to him, take your son in law, your sons and daughters, and anything you have otherwise in this city out of this place: we have received too much complaints about their behavior, and we now are eye witnesses of their outrageous abnormality, that confirm such allegations made against them. Our superior is highly perplexed over this, and has sent us to destroy it: the only way to flush out their evil deed, is by destroying this place, and that, we intend to do. So

Lot went straightway to his sons in law, who marry his daughters, and said: Up! You have to get out of this place, because the Lord will destroy this city."

But Lot appeared to his sons-in-law like one who mocks what the Lord said. And when the morning was come, the angels told Lot, "Hurry up, take your wife, and your daughters that are here with you; this is serious Lot, do not delay, as that will cause your demise by the iniquity of the city." But remember that this guy, Lot, is a man of apathetic thoughts, not much of a sage character, and his twisted, dishonest thinking caused him to chose the greener acreage of Sodom, away from his uncle, Abraham, landing him in this dilemma. Good for him.

Now Lot seemed to be experiencing some mixed emotions, he lingered and lingered. The sovereign men pulled Lot and his family out of the city and placed them out of the danger zone. The men advised them to run for their lives, to not even look behind them as they left the plain; to try and get into the mountain, less they be devoured by the unbelievable terror about to be launched on Sodom.

After the men directed Lot to make his way into the mountain, he said to them, "I cannot go up there Lord, I know you are being so merciful bringing us to safety thus far, but if I go into the mountain, it may not be secure up there…someone may mug and kill us while we take asylum there." Then Lot made a suggestion to the men, "Look, here is Zoar (Zō´ar), a small city, why don't you permit us to have shelter there?" And the good men said to Lot, "Okay, you may go, it will be safe there, too."

Verses twenty-four and twenty-five are of great significance. This is what they say: "Then the Lord rained upon Sodom and upon Gomorrah brimstone and fire from the Lord out of heaven; (Brimstone is sulfur, used for making gun-power) and he overthrew all the cities, plain, all residents of the city and all vegetations." Now Sumerian history shows that this was the act of physical beings here on earth, not an invisible God beyond the stratosphere. And what is so interesting about this account is the church parishioners' interpretation in countless sermons for hundreds of years, in Christendom assemblies around the world.

It is put forth that God did all of this by mystical technique. He caused literal fire to come from heaven, maneuvered by surgical strikes upon Sodom's cities and plains. Some of the accounts in this disaster are true, and let it be clear that my critique is not to discount any portion of scripture that is true. It warrants repeating that the bible is largely made up of true stories that were manipulated for the purpose of establishing monotheism, the 'one God' theology. The devil is in the details of the translation. So to really understand the secrets of the text, we must take a good look at the big picture, the general message the bible conveys.

So let's continue. It is at this juncture that Lot's wife is said to have looked back on her homeland in Sodom, and she was transformed into a pillar of salt as a result. The next day Abraham woke up very early in the morning, went to the very spot where he and the Lords had stood and looked in the direction of Sodom and Gomorrah. He saw plumes of smoke going up like a furnace.

When this terrible time passed, Lot left Zoar and decided to take shelter with his two daughters in the mountain where the Lords had told him to go in the first place. While in the mountain, Lot's two daughters began doing some thinking of their own, concerned about their progeny. It was clear to them that they may not have men around for some time. So they decided that the only sexual alternative was their old man!

Lot's daughters contrived a plan to exploit their father. The more mature sister told the younger one, "Listen, our dad is old and there is not one man anywhere to give us what we need, you understand what I mean…in the way women and men are lustfully drawn together by the system of nature. Come join me in a cunning venture. Let's prepare some wine for our father, and when he is highly sedated, we will take our turns with him, so that we may preserve his seed."

And so it was, as they planned it: Papa drank wine that night, and the eldest girl went in unto him…and away he went, yeah! And the younger sister went with him the following night at her sister's encouragement. Their father, on consecutive nights, became their romantic lover, and he had absolutely no idea what had transpired!

And so it came to pass that both girls conceived after their one night stands with dad. The eldest daughter bore a son and called him Moab, from which the Moabite people sprang. And the youngest daughter had a son she called Ben-Ammi, and he became father of the Ammon people. As I see it, most women live in denial when it comes to needing sex almost as much as men do. Why do so many put forth a pretext, as Lot's eldest daughter, saying they needed to preserve the seed of their father? I look at it this way: Their father was old, but he was a man with elements of youthfulness, so he could have been the one to express concerns about the importance of leaving his seed behind—but he did not. So I just do not buy into the girl's reasoning. She apparently felt the throws of sexual passion roaring within her soul, and wanted to satisfy the urges.

I believe that beneath any obligatory sense to preserve their seed, there was some desire for pleasure too. I do not mean to trivialize the importance of producing offspring, the issue here as I see it is whether or not it's merely conscious thought that triggers sexual moods, or the power of hormonal secretions that prompts thoughts and emotions into action.

Genesis Chapter Twenty

After the devastation of Sodom, Abraham journeyed to other venues. Once again, we are confronted with the main concern of this book. We have been tracking the areas of the biblical narrative that sabotage the literal truth written in earlier Sumerian literature. And so in this chapter, we will focus on areas that purport that God above is watching every step Abraham makes, intervening on his behalf, in dreams.

The chapter starts with Abraham in a place called Gerar (Gē´rär), and his wife Sarah's beauty became a serious problem for her husband once again. Unlike today's more civilized society, back then customs allowed people in political power, such as a king, permission to seize a man's wife, if he desired. This is the exact problem Abraham had when he faced King Abimelech (Ā-bǐm´e-lěch). But as you may recall, according to Abraham, he and Sarah had a mutual agreement about how to deal with the sexual demands of the powerful: Sarah agreed to pretend she was Abraham's sister whenever they encountered this situation.

Upon arrival at the King's province, Abraham introduced Sarah as his sister. Well, no one thought of killing him, but his wife was swept away from him by order of the King. Now think with me on this 'soap opera-like' saga between the King, Abraham and Sarah. The king had Sarah under his complete control, with one sole objective in mind—to devour her. The king made a big mistake, though, by procrastinating, and would therefore lose out. Guess what? Sarah had divine protection. Here comes God in a dream rebuking the king for his salacious pleasures! Can you believe that the divine actually told the king he was a dead man because the woman was His servant Abraham's wife? In the dream, the king defended himself to God, saying, "Look Lord, I did not even come close to touching her, much less to make love to her. In any case Lord, she is his sister. Am I not a righteous man who has consistently preserved my integrity in hands of innocence? Shall I be faulted in all of this, and will you destroy your people for doing what is fair?" The rest of the dream is quite revealing.

Verse six. "And the Lord said unto him in the dream, "Yes, I know that you did this in the uprightness of your heart. But I am the one who has manipulated and induced the chemical power in your brain that defers your desire from her. By all means, restore her back to her husband; he is a prophet. Any failure on your part to see that she is restored with her husband will result in your death, and those belonging to you."

See, when people are allowed to spread the idea that God in heaven works in these ways, and other people believe it, it deadbolts generations of people into assumptions, speculations and conjectures, resulting in an artificial faith/belief/lifestyle.

Now, when King Abimelech woke up early the next morning, he gathered all his people and told them of the hell he'd gone through the previous night, and the people became afraid. The King wasted no time in calling for Abraham.

Upon seeing him, he said, "My good man, what have you done to my people and me? And what wrong have you observed that I have done to bring all of this evil upon my kingdom?"

Abraham replied by saying, "I did not believe this was a God-fearing place, and was surely afraid for my life because of my wife. However, I have not lied to you: she is my blood sister, the daughter of my father, but we are not from the same mother. And she became my wife. When we pledged together in our native land, I knew she was a pretty woman, so I asked that she say I am her brother when we travel to strange places."

As the king listened to what Abraham had to say, he put much thought into responding conciliatorily enough to provide satisfaction for the Lord. He gave gift offerings of great wealth: he restored Sarah to Abraham untouched and gave them collections of sheep, oxen, men- and women-servants. And to further advance his effort of good faith, the king said to Abraham, "Listen, my friend, you may reside wherever your heart desires on all my land." After delivering all of the gifts to Abraham, the king apparently still felt a little insulted, because no one should make a king look ridiculous—especially not over an exuberant woman. So he could not help telling Sarah: "See, I have given your brother a thousand pieces of silver. I realize he is just covering the eyes of those around you." He was basically saying: "Sarah, you are very lucky." He knew she was being spared from scores of sexual encounters with men such as him. Abraham put an end to the king's mania of his wife by praying for him.

Now back in those days, a marriage between half siblings was allowed to take place; it was normative of the alien culture for men to bed their half sisters. But under the New Testament it was no longer considered a moral or spiritual thing to do. Yet we have the practice with the British royal family.

See, except for Sumerian history, we would never have known there was something noteworthy about Abraham's marriage. In the ancient account, it is shown that Abraham and his father, Terah, lived while our alien parents still populated the earth. And for these alien beings, close family weddings such as between half siblings and first cousins, was the rule rather than the exception. In fact, it was the prized way to produce heirs…such as Sarah giving birth to Isaac in her old age.

We can see that there was real value placed in close family unions. And by looking at our society worldwide today, where everybody hunts for a mate who is unrelated by blood, there can be the assumption that it allowed for people to become more violent toward each other…whereas, with close relatives there would be a more natural love and tenderness to bind. And perhaps the world would not have become so excessively vile.

Genesis Chapter Twenty-one

The three men had promised to return in one year's time, when Sarah had conceived and had her first child.

As it happened in the first visit, three men visited Abraham a second time. It was on a hot day, as he stood in his tent door, he saw these three men and went to meet them. Yes, he called the men "Lord," as we are accustomed to the imaginary God being addressed. Now once again, let's note how the bible exploited these visits, turning them into 'moments' that display the enigmatic ways of an imaginary

God. It does not say that one, two or three men visited, but that the "Lord" visited with Sarah regarding having a child, as the three men promised. All right, after that, Sarah had her radiant boy child, named Isaac.

Abraham fulfilled God's command by circumcising the boy on his eighth day.

Now, pay special attention to Sarah's umbrage against her nemesis, Hagar, and her son, Ishmael, who was a toddler when Isaac was born. Abraham was eighty-six years old when Hagar had Ishmael. After four fleeting years, a royal birth celebration was made for Isaac…We are about to discover something brewing in the hearts of both Sarah the mistress of the house, and her maidservant, Hagar, with the illegitimate boy she bore for the great Abraham.

The problem came afloat when Abraham gave an affluent feast honoring the day Isaac was weaned. Isaac was showered with royalty while, by contrast, Abraham had not done anything similar for his concubine son, Ishmael. Big mistake! And this made a recipe of everlasting envy and strife.

Sara observed Ishmael mocking their merrymaking for his brother, Isaac. Clearly the lad was old enough to notice the inequality of attention and gifts. From the way the boy behaved, he was apparently well programmed with jealousy and biasness toward his younger brother, the legal heir. Since Ishmael could not have possibly known the background on his birth, it seems fair to say that his mother Hagar ingrained her son with this negativity. And I think Ishmael had to be somewhat precocious to comprehend that level of information.

I also have qualms about the mentality of these supposed God blessed people, Abraham and Sarah. The question has to be asked: Would God consent to this kind of conduct? To masters and mistresses imposing disparaging treatment on their servants? To have sex and bear children for their purpose? Judging from the way Sarah instructed Abraham to lie with the maid—actually handing her over to Abraham—it all seems to be beyond the scope of morality; more like slavery, where a slave master humbles his female slaves.

The bible shows God to be the protector, sustainer, and inspiration of the lives of Abraham and Sarah. And in the United States of America, the founding fathers, who were called 'Puritans' and 'Pilgrims,' were all bible-believing Christians, yet likewise, they too ravished their female servants. I do not think this is the way a universal God of love works.

Ask yourself why the bible, a sacred work that is supposed to represent ideal living, shows the God of the universe working so closely with such unsavory, yet privileged people? Why didn't Abraham refuse to have sex with the indigent maid, Hagar? And in the midst of the in-house conflict, here comes God to comfort Abraham.

Isn't it funny how God never counseled Abraham or Sarah in prevention of any of the problems that occurred? But he sure appeared in the midst of a bad situation, or amidst the wreckage. This from a reliable God who sees everything before it happens, and who knows your thoughts before they come?

In church, we always hail the God of Abraham, of Isaac, and of Jacob—oh, he is a great God. He said to Abraham: "Don't let what is going on between Sarah and Hagar bother you, because Sarah is right about one thing: in Isaac shall your seed be called. I will also see that Ishmael, your bondwoman son, begets a great nation, because he is your son." Should any of these apocryphal, purportedly divine words be taken seriously? I say that it is an 'in your face' farce, too indigent to be believed.

On the kind advice of God, Abraham woke up early the next morning, loaded some bread and one bottle of water on Hagar's back, along with the boy, and sent them away. Now this cruel treatment of Hagar and Ishmael was bound to make any parent sick to their stomach. Instead of giving Hagar and the child a dignified home, they were railroaded off to wander the wilderness by a brother-sister/wife-husband team.

When the bottle of water was spent, the boy got dehydrated and Hagar placed him under a tree for shade, then sat a little distance away so as not to witness his death (where is the invisible God to prevent this time of need?), and there she wept under the weight of Abraham's desertion. As in previous instances, the story then takes an incoherent turn—apparitional and corporeal interaction ensue. This time God dispatched His angels to comfort, saying, "Why are you crying, Hagar? God has heard the voice of your son from where he is lying, just lift him up to your embrace. I will make him a great nation."
This is certainly laughable, isn't it?

The entire span of the book of Genesis is replete with stories designed to inflate the readers' mind with the idea that God is behind the vista, interfering in their lives in a very discriminatory and contradictory manor. I find the dramatization of some of the stories to be unthinkable and absurd. Thinking in such ways destroys the structure of cognizance.

Throughout the battleground of Genesis, there is intentional divisiveness, aimed at hooking people's minds on assumption and belief. And some of those who read this might still fail to grasp the essence of bamboozle that is strewn throughout the storyline.

CHAPTER FOUR

THE NEW SCRIPTURE: Conflation of the Old and New Testaments

Based on what we have covered thus far, it may well be that I am preaching to the choir at this point.

The Old Testament, particularly the Genesis account of creation and early events, seeks to decisively convey a false philosophical view to the world. Earlier accounts are not in agreement with it. Once enough people come to see the deception, a consensus can form, and a different worldview can emerge, with a new breed of thinkers. People are accepting blind faith everyday, waiting enthusiastically for the day of rapture and the judgment of sinners. But what happens when there is literal proof that Genesis, for the most part, is simply plagiarism of the earlier Sumerian text? Well, it appears many believers just don't feel concerned about that. Dedicated to their blind faith and assumptions, nothing can or will change the fermented condition of their minds.

Mankind is that fragile.

Upon the grand marquee of the New Testament sit four rich apocryphal gospels. No one as ever been able to authenticate them, yet millions of saints are fully convinced that every letter of these epistles is God's breath, despite the plethora of contradictions and profuse confusion. Many have even given their lives, ever so willingly, under some of the most inhumane and gruesome circumstances, in the hopes that they will rise in the first resurrection.

Today, great masses of believers are still committed to the faith of Jesus Christ. They believe that as he suffered on the cross for their sins, they also must suffer gladly for his sake, through trials and tribulations. This is a most painful tragedy in the human experience, to say the least.

You tell me this: Since Man was the one who sinned and fell under a curse, Jesus Christ was sent to pay the ransom for the transgression. Why must Man then turn around and suffer for Jesus Christ sake? Do you get it? I surely do not. However, this is the concept that sells. It deserves every discussion.

Have you ever wondered why there are four gospels? As we dovetail through the Old and New Testament writings, ask yourself who was responsible for the canonizing of its contents, known today as the Holy Scripture.

Allow me to draw a parallel I consider appropriate to this scheme: Someone gives you a meal and lists all its nutritious values. On the face, it looks delicious and tempting to eat. But unbeknownst to you, it does not contain the nutrition attributed to it. While you are preparing to eat, flies and dust soil the food, but at the time, it is all you have to eat. Since this is all you have to eat, you cannot throw it away, so you grab a fan, waft the flies from your meal, and eat.

The KJV of the holy bible is perceived as God's divine word, as revealed to holy people who wrote it down whenever His spirit moved upon them. Well, that *sounds* good. But if God implicitly delivered this inspired information for sinful children to be pure, how could the hands of anointed and sanctified servants defile it?

How did God's sacred word get into the hands of blasphemous political rulers? They have given the bible to churches, schools, courts and prisons, saying it is the word of God. And although people have found a legitimate degree of fault in the writings, they cannot summarily put it aside because there is only *one* word of God. Does that not defeat God's redemptive purpose? I think that it does…do you concur?

Believe me, this is a real treat. Look ahead. Have fun.

Matthew Chapter One: The Conflation Examined

This book states that Jesus Christ is the son of David, the son of Abraham, who begot Isaac, who begot Jacob, who begot Judas and his brethren. The chronological genealogy continues from Abraham to King David, spanning fourteen generations.

Watch this. From David carrying away into Babylon, fourteen generations, and from the carrying away into Babylon unto Jesus Christ, fourteen generations. There are two points that do not offer logical congruency in the way human beings identify genealogy.

First, how can David be the literal son of Abraham when there are fourteen generations between them? Second, similarly, how can Jesus

Christ be the literal son of David when there are fourteen generations separating them? Besides those discrepancies, Jesus Christ cannot stand in the biological tree of genealogy, because Joseph, Mary's husband, is not the biological father of Jesus Christ. Get it? All right, for argument's sake, let us assume this is symbolism...how does Christ qualify, in symbolical terms, as the son of David or Joseph?

In a recent criminal court case, a famous defense lawyer uttered these words: "If it doesn't fit, you must acquit." Most people have never given any thought to the details of these representations, because they have been bamboozled by the antiquated idea that all things written in the bible are true; so they don't even bother to check into them. But here and now you can put your fears away, knowing that one is less likely to get hurt when they are informed. There is absolutely nothing to lose, besides an unwitting lack of knowledge.

If God sent it to you, I bet he wants you to understand it. So let's continue to take a look at the ideas of the Old and New Testament, to see if they make sense, and aren't a swamp foundation. Do not forget that the genealogy is used to rip people off. Filling a book with grandiose ideas, such as a heavenly Jerusalem, and talk of everlasting life...oh, it takes my breath away!

Now let us get back to the tactic used in scripture, the bedrock foundation on which all people are to attain salvation, and have a relationship with the Lord Jesus Christ.

Verse eighteen says: *"Now the birth of Jesus Christ was on this wise: When as his mother Mary was espoused to Joseph before they came together, she was found with child of the Holy Ghost."*

This was not acceptable to Joseph, and while he contemplated the predicament, the Lord appeared to him by psychic means, saying, "Joseph, you son of David, fear not to take unto you Mary as your wife: for the baby she is carrying is conceived by the Holy Ghost..." Then a reference is made to a messianic prophecy that ties it all together, saying: "Behold, a virgin shall be with child, and shall bring forth a son, and they shall call his name Emmanuel," which means 'God with us.' (Since none of this is true, they conveyed it in false dream.)

When Joseph was awakened from sleep, he did as the angel of the Lord had instructed in the dream, he went ahead and married Mary. But he could not consummate the marriage until after she gave birth to the heavenly baby, Jesus. The implication is clear: accept that a great deity is behind the vista doing mystical things in these people's lives.

But here is the *danger*—once people began accepting Man's word as messages sent from God, any person could feign being a messenger from God, then use the claim from the pulpit and other venues to preach ideas that are complete rubbish.

One of the most serious dangers mankind faces today is the acceptance of subliminal, dictatorial authority. And with the passage of time, people have been left somewhat helpless, because there is no different point of view available to them. When a false concept is put into place for two or three thousand years, it can easily become an assumed and recognized fact in the twenty-first century. So it is not surprising to see the masses indulging in all types of religions today. And as long people are willing to place their faith in superstitious and unproven beliefs, man-made religions such as Christianity and Islam will control society.

Here is an important clue that speaks ever so loudly, proving that the value of the gospel is non-existent: At every crucial point, when something happened that was a boldfaced lie, they used everything from the Holy Spirit to an angel, a dream, a revelation, a vision, God Himself, and finally, the prophets. In the case of Joseph, they used God speaking to him in a dream to calm his doubts. They know that infinite power lies in keeping people believing in intangibles; the visions from God are paramount, no one would be out of their mind to question an unseen, mysterious, unexplainable God.

Again, to convince people of Jesus' resurrection, they said an angel came down and caused an earthquake. And to make St. Paul untouchable, they made Jesus strike him blind for three days. To give Abraham a connection with God and form the basis for worldwide conversion, they had God appear to him in a vision. They knew very well that once people bit the bait of falsehood, there would be no inquisitive suspicions audacious enough to question the genuineness of the account.

Think of it this way for a moment: What good reason would God have for creating such mischief in the life of one virtually unknown couple? Then resolve the embarrassment in a dream? According to the bible, God has done more absurdities than most mental patients! And because Man's mind is so easily conditioned, whatever they strongly believe, they defend until they die.

One reminder: the saga of Joseph and Mary, who are Jews, was not told by Jews...so by whom? The people who wrote the contraption, conflation, and transliteration of the Old and New Testament scriptures did it. And we know that it was none other than the Roman Empire when they occupied Palestine. There is no Jewish person who would conjure jokes like these and write them down—they are too sickening.

Although the biblical writings give the Jews ridiculous favor from an imaginary God—like the claim that they are Abraham's seed and God's chosen people—the aggregate of the stories result in the mockery of Jews. We can look at this from yet another angle, too. If Rome really respected the Jewish people as God's chosen ones, would Rome have destroyed the Jewish temple in circa 70 A.D.? Woefully driving them out of not just their homes, but also the entire country? See, during this time when the Jews were away, Rome was busily using puppets to conjure up Christianity. Mary and Joseph is 100% a Roman story, intended for evil.

The evidence to support these allegations are reflected in the people who were sacrificed by being burned at the stake, imprisoned, strip of their values, tortured and murdered, so that the bogus story of Jesus Christ would survive to reach us in this era. There it is. The Jews have nothing to do with the plotting of the story that was marinated in visions, dreams, and apparitions…except for those who acted ancillary to Rome.

Do Christians really want to keep hope invested in spurious belief?

Matthew Chapter Two

Getting back on the thread, they say Jesus was born in Bethlehem of Judea, in the days of Herod the King. Wise men came from the East to Jerusalem, asking, "Where is he that is born King of the Jews? We have seen a star that represents him in the East, and we are here to give him honor." Because of this news, perplexity filled the atmosphere. King Herod upon hearing of this strange birth, quickly acquired briefing from experts in the theological business. The chief priest and scribes informed Herod where Jesus should be born.

Upon Herod's finding out the approximate location of where baby Jesus' birth was slated to take place, he invited the wise men to see him. At this point Herod learned that the birth of this male child was the fulfillment of divine prophecy that would give Jews their own governor who would take over and rule all of Israel. That was bad news for Herod, who viewed that as a threat to his job. Herod then inquired of the men what their mission was about and how he could help in their voyage.

Wise as these men were, they had only a symbolic star with very little else to explain what prompted their mission, and guided them thus far. Herod asked them what time the star was spotted, and having been duly informed in the premises, he wanted to be in on the spooky ambiance. He told the men to take the road to Bethlehem, saying, "I want you to go on a diligent search of this infant, and when you have found him, please bring me word, so I, too, may come and worship him." Herod apparently wanted to get in on the show as well, but it may not be in good faith.

The chapter goes on to supply stump events of alleged divine intervention to bolster readers' confidence in what should be taken as God's interest in the souls of men through the birth of Jesus Christ. Some of God's astrophysical insertions after the wise men left King Herod's place worked out against Herod in his pursuit to destroy the Christ child. And in the end, the story shows that God was successful in protecting baby Jesus, which was a fulfillment of prophecy according to Rome, saying: "He came and dwelt in the city called Nazareth: that it might be fulfilled which was spoken by the prophets, He shall be called a Nazarene."

Here is an interesting point that deserves a query: Jews do not believe in the wise men's visit, so conflict exists with respect to who offered and authorized the penning of the story. The bible asserts that prophets foretold the coming of Christ, and accordingly, this was the established communal knowledge among the Jews in Jerusalem and the province of Judea in those times.

Were we to take that seriously, it would be an endorsement by the population of the chief priest and scribes, when they expertly informed Herod of where Christ the Jewish Messiah would be born. And accordingly, the chief priests lay claim to the prophets as being of Jewish heritage. These supposed prophets allegedly wrote down the information that the Messiah would be born among them.

Since this is a cultural understanding among Jews, if the account is true, then it follows that they were expecting Christ, right? Their long awaited lawgiver and messenger of the New Covenant. That being the case, what happened in the interim? What made Jesus Christ a pariah in the land of his birth? And to his own Jewish brethren, who for so long waited in distress and burning anxiety for his arrival?

Matthew Chapter Three

So as not to say John the Baptist came out of nowhere, for all intent and purposes, let's declare that a red herring Old Testament prophecy postured John the Baptist in the narrative scheme. Malachi 3:1-2 says he will be a Jewish gentleman, born to baptize the Messiah just before the earthly mission.

> *"BEHOLD, I will send my messenger, and he shall prepare the way before me: and the Lord, whom you seek shall suddenly come to his temple, even the messenger of the covenant, whom you delight in: behold, he shall come, says the Lord of host."*

Remember: One should regard this persistent St. Matthew account as taking place in an apocryphal climate—nothing has been proven true. St. Matthew is one of four overlapping accounts, securing a concept that is irrelevant and impossible, which had to be the reason they quadrupled it. In that context, Matthew's version speaks out to convince us, and they say he wrote this:

> *"In those days came John the Baptist, preaching in the wilderness of Judea, and saying, repent you: for the kingdom of heaven is at hand. For this is he that was spoken of by the prophet E-sā′ias, saying; The voice of one crying in the wilderness, prepare you the way of the Lord, make his paths straight."*

According to St. Matthew, after feeding on a menu of only Locusts and wild honey, John dressed himself in a unique outfit and then took to the streets to perform his predestined, holy duty. While he carried on his session of preaching, he observed that there were in attendance some nobles of the Jewish community, such as members of the elite Pharisees and Sadducees.

Now one may think that John, being a man of God, would come with a graceful presence, necessary to attract stubborn sinners. But he did not; instead he went across the street as hostile as Rome is known to be. Therefore John the Baptist could not have been a man sent from a God of grace, but rather a bogus character meant to be surreal, befuddling people's minds. Note how John was not equipped with consideration for the people he knew needed salvation. Judge for yourself. I will quote what John blurted out upon seeing the Jewish clergymen of the cloth:

> *"O generation of vipers, who have warned you to flee from the wrath to come? Bring forth therefore fruits meet for repentance: And think not to say within yourselves, we have Abraham to our father: for I say unto you, that God is able of these stones to rise up children unto Abraham. And now also the ox is laid unto the root of the tree: therefore every tree which put not forth good fruit is hewn down, and cast into the fire. I indeed baptize you with water unto repentance: but he that comes after me is mightier than I, whose shoes I am not worthy to bear: he shall baptize you with the Holy Ghost, and with fire: Whose fan is in his hand, and he will thoroughly purge his floor, and gather his wheat into the garner; but he will burn up the chaff with unquenchable fire."*

That message is not one of love, but a combination of harassment, threat and intimidation. It more represents the expression of a tyrant feigning as a preacher, than a meek and mild messenger of a divine who is burdened with compassion.

I must warn you to look out, because the story gets more and more bizarre…and then falls apart.

We have Breaking News in the thirteenth verse: "Then cometh Jesus from Galilee to Jordan unto John, to be baptized of him." But John seemed to be a bit confused, as though God had forgotten to send him a telepathic message, even via a dream the night before to explain things. So he objected to Jesus, saying, "I need to be baptized of you, why come to be baptize of me?" Then Jesus replied, "Suffer it to happen now; for it is agreed upon that you and I, in doing this, fulfill all righteousness." When John heard those words, he yielded and baptized Jesus.

After that ritual, Jesus is said to have walked straight out of the water and the heavens were opened unto him, and he saw the Spirit of God descending like a dove and lighting upon himself. And lo a voice from heaven said, "This is my beloved Son, in whom I am well pleased."

It does not appear as though other people saw what took place with Jesus, because it is specified that this is an experience exclusive to

Jesus' awareness. So how could others have come to know that Jesus had such glorious excitement? Well, of course! Jesus must have communicated the honorable moment of delight to others, because if he didn't tell anybody, how could it end up as the written Word of God?

I question whether or not someone had baptized John in preparation for his ministerial duties, because as I understand the biblical procedure, baptism symbolizes a spiritual autonomy of believers. Why would Jesus Christ, God incarnate, need to be baptized? It suggests that if he had to be baptized before starting redemption work on Man, then by all means, John the Baptist, a man of lower importance, must be baptized, too, as qualification for his mission. In the story, John's response to Jesus was, "I need to be baptized of you, why come to be baptized of me?"

Based on my experience with Christian's attitudes to these unexplained passages, the likely response is something obtuse, like: "Remember that God can do anything, you cannot question him." This type of answer is to be expected whenever troubling questions are posed about scripture that just don't add up.

Matthew Chapter Four: The Fictional Messiah

Imagine that you were a Jewish person living 2000 years ago; in the days Jesus Christ is alleged to have walked the streets of Jerusalem. Imagine you were one of his beloved disciples; let's say Simon Peter, and you were following Jesus, observing him in his maneuvers around the place. Based on the real history (not scripture) of Jewish thinking in those days, what would you have thought about the odd couple, Mary and Joseph? Is there a chance you would have been inclined to believe in their enigmatic marriage, a virgin birth and unofficial resurrection of a doubtful or rejected Messiah?

And if per chance you were one of the parents of Jesus, and he came home one afternoon to report that the spirit of the Lord God, his father in heaven, took him away and led him up into a woody mountain, submitting him to fulfill forty days and forty nights of nonstop temptation—would you ask him what he was talking about? Can anyone make an imaginary motion picture of the Holy Spirit marching Jesus away to fulfill an appointment with Satan?

Well, if I were in Joseph's shoes, as Jesus' symbolic father, the first thing I would think is, perhaps a demonic spirit overcame my son!

Telling me how he had nothing to eat for forty days and nights, and how Satan, the tempter, told him that if he was the Son of God he could command the stones be made bread, and that he preached to Satan, saying, "Man shall not live by bread alone, but by every word coming from the mouth of God."

And then the devil took him into the holy city and set him on a pinnacle of the temple, saying, "If you are the Son of God, cast yourself down." But he countered with his superior logic, and the challenge continued as Satan would not cease his persistence, and again he took my son up an exceedingly high mountain and showed him all the kingdoms of the world, and the glory of them, saying, "See, all of these things will I give you if you just fall down and worship me." This evil spirit would not stop, until Jesus told him to "Get behind me Satan: for it is written, thou shall worship the Lord thy God, and him only shall thou save." If my son told me these weird things I would have had to rush Jesus Christ to the emergency room!

That sums up the gist of what occurred through verse ten, which, again, is an imposition on readers of the bible to accept that a spirit called 'Satan,' an incorporeal entity, intermingles with humanity. The biblical requirement demands that any failure to believe these things are true, forfeits salvation—but that is the hook, the scam. They say God used to deal with men one-on-one, but he has stopped doing so. This leaves a question: if He is still concerned with and attentive to Man's need, what is the modus operandi being use in the twenty-first century?

This New Testament stuff is too good to be true…and because people have believed in it for so long, it will take a lot more effort and energy to burst into realization.

Now…Jesus is once again walking the province, doing his heavenly chores. But he gets some bad news. John the Baptist, second under the New Covenant chain of command, is now locked away in prison. Jesus is the man of deliverance, yet John is there waiting in a cold and dark, claustrophobic cell. To the chagrin of all, instead of the Messiah speaking a Word that would instantly throw open the prison doors—he left the area. Yes, you read that right—Jesus navigated his way out of Galilee through Nazareth and into Capernaum. And why did Jesus do that at a time when John needed him more than ever?

The answer the scripture gives, is that Jesus was destined to fulfill a prophecy; spoken of by an apocryphal prophet name E-saias, who said: "The land of Neph'tha-lim, by the way of the sea, beyond Jordon, Galilee of the Gentile: The people which sat in darkness saw a great light; and to them which sat in the region and shadow of death light is springs up."

Okay, we know that John made a statement that forewarned how he would decrease but Jesus must increase, but even when that is taken into account, I see no justification for Jesus not to pay John a five-minute visit in confinement. But in lieu of a visit, fulfilling a prophecy was more important; a prophecy that would bring light to people sitting in darkness…So what happened to dear John, who needed to be bonded out of a jail cell of darkness? Why was Jesus not concerned about John's life?

This is too incredible for one to believe—that our heavenly father saw it more important to fulfill a prophecy (that could have taken place before John's arrest or even after) and leave poor John forlorn in a prison cell, than to save his own chosen one from the darkness.

This is not the kind of incident one should excuse, while putting faith in it as God's divine will. It is not consistent with the teachings of a God who does wonderful deeds and will save his chosen people. God's pleasure should work for John the Baptist of all people if it works for anybody, shouldn't it? Isn't God about everlasting freedom, joy and security for *all* men?

The rest of the chapter illustrates how, despite the way Jesus abandoned John in the coldest of ways, his prophetic ministry took off in high gear. In the early phase of his evangelism, he recruited some of his disciples; the likes of Simon Peter, and Andrew his brother. The Christ went on preaching the gospel, they say, healing all manner of sicknesses and diseases among the people. Then his fame went abroad, into Syria, and his influence drew followers from several surrounding geographical areas. However, John, the man who baptized Jesus was left to have his head nicked off his body.

In days gone by, when I wholly believed this story, it was pure naïveté on my part—but I am so happy now that I am no longer gullible enough to swallow this without thinking for myself.

Matthew Chapter Five

"And seeing the multitudes, he went up into a mountain: and when he was set, his disciples came unto him: And he opened

his mouth, and taught them saying. Blessed are the poor in
spirit: for there is the kingdom of heaven."

The repertoire of this section serves to advance the Messiah-ship
character of Jesus, and solidify his 'superstar' stature. From the
depictions, it is maintained that Jesus was Jewish. And it didn't bother
him much whether or not Jews liked him as their Messiah. And in the
following, he sets forth a template for his infinite jurisdiction on earth.
Verse seventeen*: "Think not that I am come to destroy the law, or the*
prophets: I am not come to destroy, but to fulfill."

Between verses twenty-one and twenty-two, Jesus shows his
incredible power to change the human spirit. He speaks in a
cosmological, authoritative tone, saying: "You have heard that it was
said by them of old time, you shall not kill: and whoever shall kill
shall be in danger of the judgment: But I say unto you, that whoever is
angry with his brother without a cause shall be in danger of the
judgment: and whoever shall say to his brother, Raca (Rā′că), shall be
in danger of the council: but whoever shall say, you fool, shall be in
danger of hell fire…" And in the end he closes by saying: "Be you
therefore perfect even as your father who is in heaven is perfect."

The scope of the message, as in the book of Genesis, is designed to
address all people on planet earth, without exception. Which means
that the imaginary God called out Jewish people as the apex of all
nations. And that Moses and all Jewish prophets spoke to one
cosmological order of Man's salvation.

This is why I understand how understandably difficult it is for
people who have accepted a blind faith in the Lord Jesus Christ to
awaken from this bewilderment, once they have become enamored by
the all encompassing system of belief. The psychological dominance
that exudes from Jesus Christ's alleged words seem unquestionable
once they are taken literally—which is exactly how they are
interpreted by the religious faith community.

Matthew Chapter Six

"Take heed that you do not do your alms before men, to be
seen of them; otherwise you have no reward of your father
which is in heaven."

Jesus the Jewish Messiah, not acknowledged by Jews as authentic, continued to churn out oracle after oracle to the people.

All men are put on notice: they are born in sin, and under the curse pronounced in the Garden of Eden, but Jesus' word has come for everyone who believes. By not accepting Jesus Christ as your savior when you hear His call, your unbelieving soul is doomed to hell fire. Jesus consistently attached himself to an inscrutable father in heaven; one who he said gave him direct instructions for His lost children on earth.

Some scripture hints that Jesus was on earth as a specter prior to the miraculous virgin birth. A reference can be found in Proverbs 8. Verses 22-23 are particularly enlightening:

> *"The Lord possessed me in the beginning of his ways, before his works of old. I was set up from everlasting, from the beginning, or ever the earth was."*

There are other references as well, and there is one that alludes to how Jesus was the spirit that formed the cloud pillow that followed the Jewish convoy by night as they journeyed through the wilderness forty years.

Now in his stint on earth, Jesus condemned the practice of hypocrisy, most noted by Scribes and Pharisees. He also handed a special prayer key to believers for accessing God's throne—you can speak with the heavenly father by saying the following:

> *"Our father which art in heaven, hollowed be thy name, thy kingdom come thy will be done in earth, as it is in heaven. Give us this day our daily bread. And forgive our debts as we forgive our debtors. And lead us not into temptation, but deliver us from evil: For thine is the kingdom and the power, and the glory, forever Amen."*

Then he gave some clarity to the meaning of the prayer, saying, "If we forgive others of their offense, then God will also forgive our infractions likewise committed against him." He gives many other impressive directives, ending with this one: "Take therefore no thought for the morrow: for the morrow shall take thought for the things of itself—sufficient unto the day is the evil thereof."

Be ye not fooled. (That one's from me, Tim Aldred, not Jesus Christ. I made it up all by myself. ☺) The words of Christ are all axioms that sound divine, but as good as they may sound, their essence is purely to delude people into an adherence to Rome's grand campaign of evangelical ideology.

Matthew Chapter Seven

> *"Judge not, that you be not judged. For with what judgment you judge, you shall be judged: and with what measure you mete, it shall be measured to you again. Why behold thou the mote that is in your brother's eye, but regard not the beam that is in your own eye? Or how wilt you say to your brother, let me pull out the mote out of your eye; and, behold, a beam is in your own eye? You hypocrites, first cast out the beam out of your own eye; and then shall you see clearly to cast out the mote out of your brother's eye."*

There is no way to deny the effects of Jesus' directives—they are too respectful and compelling. Reversing the messianic impression is not going to be easy—and I am well aware that it is very controversial. But we are to become Truth seekers. Observe verses thirteen to twenty-seven:

> *"You must enter in at the strait gate; for wide is the gate, and broad is the way, that lead to destruction, and many there be which go in thereat: because strait is the gate, and narrow is the way which unto life, and few there be that find it.*
>
> *Beware of false prophets, which come to you in sheep's clothing, but inwardly they are ravening wolves. You shall know them by their fruits. Do men gather grapes of thorns, or figs of thistles? Even so every good tree brings forth good fruit; but a corrupt tree brings forth evil fruit. A good tree cannot bring forth evil fruit neither can a corrupt tree bring forth good fruit. Every tree that brings not forth good fruit is cut down, and cast into the fire. Wherefore by their fruits you shall know them.*
>
> *Furthermore not every one that says to me, Lord, Lord, shall be accepted into the kingdom of heaven; but those that do*

the will of my father which is in heaven. As a result, many will walk up to me and say in that day, Lord, Lord, have we not prophesied in your name? And in your name have cast out devils? And in your name done many wonderful works? Then will I profess to them, I never knew you: depart from me, you that work iniquity.

Whoever hears these sayings I give and do them, I will liken unto the wise, which built the house upon a rock: so that when torrential rain and winds beat upon it; and it fell not; because it was set into a rock. But unto those that hear my words and refuse to do them, shall be as a foolish person, which build his house upon sand: and when the torrential of rain and winds beat upon the house; it tilts and falls: Oh, and how great is the fall of it."

Now, take note of this: Isn't it ironic that the Vatican claimed host and proprietorship, even vicar of Jesus Christ, yet the entire clergy has been swamped in direct defiance of substantial tenets taught by Jesus?

By church decree, the Pope and his priesthood cannot marry. So what if the clergy body were to be judged as an example to believers and unbelievers, as they should…what are people to say about their "fruit"? Charges of hundreds, if not thousands, of child molestations! Is that "good fruit"? Remember: no one else said it. The Holy Bible says these are the words of Jesus Christ himself. It is God's commandment that says, "Thou shall not kill." Yet how many people have the Roman regime tortured, imprisoned and murdered because they would not accept the faith of Jesus Christ?

Rome is the only religious entity that brought the historical account of Jesus Christ to modern times. And a careful look reveals that, for the past 2000 years, it has been the Vatican, not Jews, who stand guard over Christianity. So is it too ironic that although the Catholic Church has done many charitable deeds, their most fundamental deeds— fruits— are notoriously evil. <u>And this fact should be taken seriously to the max, because Jesus said trees not bearing good fruits would be cut down and cast into the fire.</u> Where shall the Roman Catholic institution go in this ironic game? What will happen to them, in accordance with their own literature?

The bible asserts that those who heard Jesus' words were astonished by his doctrine, for he taught them with such unwavering authority, and not as their scribe or equal. If such a man as Jesus was around, renowned and well established, aren't you curious as to why there is no official *Jewish history* that recorded the extraordinary power of this great man? Why aren't Jews able to offer any lessons at all from their parents about the marvelous miracles of Jesus? Why are they uncomfortable when you mention the name of Jesus? And if you ask them anything concerning Jesus, they say their parents have never spoken to them about Jesus. However, in gross contrast, Westerners have a favorite hymn that they sing in church. I learned it as a child. It goes like this: "*How sweet the name of Jesus sounds in a believer's ear, it soothes his sorrows, heals his wounds, and drives away his fears; he is manna to the hungry soul, and to the weary, rest.*"

So I reason that while Jesus is purported to have done so many astonishing things in Palestine, the native Jews made nothing of it. Today they sing not one song of Jesus, or own any epithets or relics of Jesus and his twelve disciples to share as proof to their progenies. And what about the hundreds of eyewitnesses who supposedly watched Jesus take off into heaven via cloud?

Why are so many people who are foreign to the land of Israel willing to place their faith in something that its natives loathe? Why does Rome embrace the character of an apocryphal Jesus Christ in a much greater magnitude than any force-ripened Christian Jew? (I use the term 'force-ripened' to define Jews who feign acceptance of Christianity because of the dominance of the Roman Catholicism in the society they live in.) Most Jews disdain the mere sound of the name Jesus. Could there be more to it than Christians care to accept?

Hello, are you still there? I'm speaking to the honesty of your heart.

Matthew Chapter Eight

In this feature, Rome uses Jesus to give credence and congruity to certain Old Testament anecdotes. The book of Revelation, chapter thirteen verse eight contributes to this scheme as well, saying Jesus is a lamb that was slain from the foundation of the world—to restore humans from the nonexistent curse of Adam's sin. Therefore it is in this context that Rome used Jewish individuals to conflate, as it were, old sayings with new.

What Rome left out of their fictional narrative is a redemption plan in the Genesis creation tale, one that offers heavenly life, before or after the so-called fall of Adam. Neither was Abraham promised heaven, but only the land of Canaan. Rome placed all humans under the curse of Adam, in need of a redemptive savior. It was then imperative to produce Abraham as a world-class protagonist to champion the symbolic Noah's Ark and redeem lost souls.

No one seems to know who wrote any of the scriptures, specifically the New Testament. Just little research can clear up the uncertainty of that. Rome is at the scene of the crime with weapons in both hands with an appalling mob-style usage of scripture. Jesus is used in imaginary terms, to befuddle our minds…In the crowd was one with leprosy, and he came to Jesus in adulation, asking to be healed. Jesus put forth his hand and touched the man, willing he be cleansed. Immediately the leper became cleansed of his leprosy! Interestingly, though, Jesus told the man not to tell anybody, but to go show himself to the priest and offer the gift that Moses commanded, as a testimony unto those things.

Shortly thereafter, Jesus traveled into a place called Ca-perna-um, and a centurion fellow came begging him to heal his servant who lay at home sick of palsy and grievously tormented. Jesus told him he can go and make his servant well again. No sooner than Jesus uttered those words, the centurion said to him, "I do not deserve your presence under my roof sir; you can just speak the word and I am sure it will happen. In my field of employment, Jesus, I have bosses and I am boss to those under my control. I give commands to those who take instructions from me, and they do exactly as I instruct them—but you are by far greater than I."

When Jesus heard this man's words, he was touched, and expressed marvel—and he drew his followers' attention to the centurion's great faith in him. And he remarked to them by saying, "Verily I am telling you, I have never found such immense faith round Israel, and I am telling you this, many shall come in from the east and west, and shall sit down with Abraham, Isaac and Jacob in the kingdom of heaven—but the children of the kingdom shall be cast out into outer darkness. There shall be weeping and gnashing of teeth." Then Jesus said to the centurion, "Go your way; and as you believe, let it be done unto you." Now, in that same hour, the centurion's servant was made perfectly whole.

From there, Jesus went to Simon Peter's house and found his mother sick, and he healed her. He then gave out a hint about his economic status, and offered instruction on how to follow his ways.

Then he entered a ship with his disciples and fell asleep, only to be awakened by his agitated disciples as they were shouting out unto him, "Lord save us, we perish!" When Jesus woke up, he said unto them, "Why are you so fearful? Your faith is too small." Then he rebuked the boisterous winds and the sea, and there came then a great calm. This caused the men to marvel and wonder what kind of person Jesus was—even the works of nature listened to the instructions of his voice!

After those happenings, Jesus came to the country of the Gergesenes, and he met up with what we call in our day two "mad men," but in those times they were said to be possessed with devils. As the alleged crazy men came out from among the tombs, they were very fierce to deal with, so nobody would pass by where they frequented. But when Jesus approached these men, they began to say strange things, like, "What have we to do with you, Jesus, you Son of God? Have you come here to torment us before the time? Please send us to be in the herd of swine nearby, so that we may not go floating in mid air." So Jesus permitted the evil ghosts to enter the pigs. After they entered into the herd of swine, they all ran violently down a steep place into the sea, and were drowned.

Rome made Jesus a public nuisance to the society of his day, as indicated in one of his purposeful missions into the city of Ger-ge-senes. At least the citizens there thought so of him, and their reason is worthy of respect. While it was, of course, a noble deed to heal the two men possessed with evil spirits, what good purpose can be found in pleasing devils, at the expense of living people? You see, those swine, allegedly possessed by the demons that perished in the sea, were the agricultural product of locals, and it was the herdsmen who cared for those animals who ran into the city with the breaking news to the owners about what happened to their cattle. They did not like what they heard, because they had lost a lot of money and food with the drowning of their swine. Who wouldn't be angry over the destruction of their livelihood?

The God of the bible says that we should pray to him for our daily bread; he is our provider, not a destroyer. Rome made a mistake by showing Jesus as one who will do even senseless things to show off his power. Jesus is introduced as God incarnate, a great power from heaven, who is supposed to be a provider for the poor, instead of being a destroyer of their valuables.

It makes no sense, and combined with what he did when he left John the Baptist in prison without visiting him, the killing of all the people's livestock, etc., that is enough reason to regard the bible as something perverse, and reject this depiction of Jesus' deeds as belonging to holiness. Rome will look us straight in the face and say, "My friends, God can do anything, even torture, murder and acts of pedophilia."

One thing is for sure, according the scripture, the people of the city wanted to see who Jesus was, but when they saw him, they were obviously angry with him. They did not try to harm him since they were clearly afraid of him, but they kindly begged him to leave their province to prevent more losses of their toiling. Now were the people of the city justified in ejecting Jesus from their coast? Or should they have wanted him to stay? In other words, should they receive him despite the horrible circumstances they suffered? So as not to be condemned in history for rejecting Jesus Christ, as Christians believe they have done today?

Matthew Chapter Nine

Jesus left the Ger-gesenes and caught a ship bound for his own city, Capernaum. As he disembarked from the ship, instantly they brought one sick lying on a stretcher, ailing grievously with the palsy. Jesus was very impressed by their strong faith in his power to heal, so he looked the sick in the eyes and said, "Son, be of good cheer, thy sins are forgiven."

Now there are facts in evidence that Jesus Christ was a high profile figure in Israel, and that his influence was both widely known and an offense to the Israeli authority. According to this gospel, government agents followed him around wherever he went. When Jesus told the sick person his sins were forgiven, certain of the Scribes thought he had blasphemed, for only God can forgive sins. Jesus, by knowing what they were thinking, began to say in their presence, "Why are you pondering evil in your hearts? For what is more appropriate for me to say to the sick? Your sins be forgiven, or arise and walk? But this is all happening for you to understand that the Son of Man has power on earth to forgive sins."

Then in an effort to appease the Scribes, he said to the sick, "Arise, take up your bed and go unto your house." And the sick with the palsy got up and walked to his house. Upon seeing such unmatched power performed by Jesus, the people were overwhelmed as they talked among themselves, praising God who gave such great power to men.

Jesus moved on to his next venue with an interest to enlarge his group. While on the way he spotted Matthew and said to him, "Follow me." And Matthew did. The rest of the chapter establishes a few important things. First, Jesus bolstered his messiah-ship and gave evidence that he did not do miracles in a small corner of Palestine, but rather countrywide, and in the presence of all branch members of the Sanhedrin.

Next, he healed the daughter of one of the rulers by attending the home. A woman with issues of blood was cured, and two blind men who followed and cried after Jesus (they addressed him saying, "Thou son of David have mercy on us) were healed upon the merit of their faith; their eyes received sight. Jesus also cast out a devil that made a man dumb, so that the speechless man spoke. Throngs of people gathered to witness the many mighty deeds of Jesus, even fainting because of the press.

Verse thirty five notes: "And Jesus went about all the cities and villages teaching in their synagogues, preaching the gospel of the kingdom, and healing every sickness and disease among the people. In the glorious ending, Jesus lamented at the host gathered round him because he saw them as sheep scattered without a shepherd. Then he said to his disciples, "The harvest truly is plenteous, but the laborers are few; pray therefore the Lord of the harvest, that he will send forth laborers into his produce."

Given all of the recognition the bible says Jesus acquired for his righteous notoriety performing miracles, why isn't there even one Jewish relative to affirm the account of this chapter? Or one biography to vouch for it? One corroboration that connects these episodes with any of the twelve disciples, or the many others who were committed to Jesus? Should anyone accept that these things are true when they stand alone in four gospels written by the murderous Roman regime? It is necessary that people apply a little commonsense to this, because the names given to the four gospels are on record. This tells us that if they were real people, they would have progenies that should have surfaced. Would anyone like to convince me that there is not even one descendant of Jesus' following around to write about their famous father, mother, brother, sister, uncle, niece, or first cousin?

Some people may say, "What about Josephus? He confirmed Jesus was real." First of all, Josephus is not identified as being a blood relative to any party belonging to Jesus. Secondly, he was not alive in those days. And the third reason to consider: Josephus became Rome's puppet after he lost the final resistance against the Roman army at Masada, across from the Dead Sea. He waived the white flag of surrender, and then took up residency in Rome, where he was writing under the influence of the Empire. Who can trust in a Roman puppet like Josephus' take on Jewish history? Not this author. Josephus lived at a time when they needed Jewish intellectuals to help solidify and launch Christianity. Being in Roman territory, if everyone else failed to authenticate Jesus—Josephus would not.

Matthew Chapter Ten

"And when he had called unto him his twelve disciples he gave them power against unclean spirits, to cast them out, and to heal all manner of sickness and all manner of disease."

So Jesus sent out all of his twelve disciples on a great healing campaign, including Judas Iscariot (Jū′das Is-căr′i-ot). And my contention about this is: Should Jesus have known that Judas was a devil? And that he should never, under any circumstances, grant evil the opportunity to co-mingle with good? Especially Judas with his evangelism work, which would later cause disgrace on the ministry.

As it turned out, this disciple did not hesitate to betray Jesus, and though believers will not allow any speculation on anything Jesus says or does, still logic questions the betrayer's enlistment into Jesus' ministry. I find it appalling to find so many inconsistencies concerning the things they wrote that Jesus did.

The next eventful features of this chapter, found worthy of noting, are the manufactured clauses they have written in the text. I have identified such as Rome having had a need to insert subtle caveats to protect the ridiculous plot about Jesus, and to seal the hoax of Jesus' divinity. It is the medium Rome used to address all members of Adam's sinful race. And when you notice the way Jesus' pronouncements are phrased, you can literally sense threats, warnings and ultimatums, aimed at perpetually tense paranoia. If you do not accept Rome's (not Jews) Jesus Christ as savior and Lord, you are doomed to hell fire and damnation. Based on that heads up, we have come to verses thirty-two through forty, which graphically explains the essence of my expose as follows:

The words of Jesus (subtle caveats paraphrased): "If you identify with me before other people, then I will also proclaim you before my father which is in heaven. If you deny me before others, then I will also reject you before my father, which is in heaven. Think not for one minute that I am come to spread peace on earth, oh no: I came not to spread peace but sword. I am come to set a man in conflict with his father, and a daughter against her mother, and the daughter-in-law against her mother-in-law. And a man's enemies shall be those of his own household.

Anyone who loves father or mother more than me, I will likewise reject, and those loving son or daughter more than me, I will also ignore. Anyone not taking up his cross and following after me will receive no credit from me. If someone lives after the pleasure of this world, they shall lose out on eternal life: but those who live chase for my sake alone shall find life evermore. Anyone who is receptive to you, the same receives me, and when they accept me, they also receive my father who has sent me."

Matthew Chapter Eleven

Jesus ended his disciples' missionary journey, and departed to preach and teach in the cities.

Now, note this twisted logic. Do you remember John the Baptist, who Jesus left, locked away in prison? As never anticipated, John appeared to lose his mental health because of Jesus' desertion of him. He started to think that something was amiss, though it is written that prophets have spoken by the inspiration of God, that he, John, was elected to serve as the forerunner to Jesus, the messiah. So why did he not apparently understand what purpose he was to serve? What really deprived John of his knowing?

Somehow the prison management allowed John to have a connection with his followers, based on what they wrote. He sent two of his disciples to carry a crucial message to Jesus. The nature of the message John sent to Jesus tells much of what he had been contemplating in his mind. For one thing, John had been hearing about the mighty deeds that Jesus was performing around the place, and felt that with such power, Jesus should have had him released.

So reading between the lines, John was disgusted with Jesus and sent to ask him the following: "Are you really the messiah that should come to us, or should we look for the right one?"

Then Jesus responded by telling John's messengers, "You go back to him and show the things that you see and hear of me. The blind receive their sight and the lame walk, the lepers are cleansed, and the deaf hear, the dead are raised up, and the poor have the gospel preached to them. And blessed is the one not becoming offended in me."

When John's disciples departed, Jesus began to confirm that he was a true prophet, to the extent that no one born of women had ever been greater than John. He said John was more than a prophet, because the prophet in Malachi 3:1 spoke about him saying, "Behold, I send my messenger before your face, which shall prepare the way before you." This shows the story cannot be real. God could not do these kinds of disjointed things. Anybody can see that John was fed-up with the loss of his freedom, and that a quandary was injected with John and his sour disposition; while Jesus, the messiah, got angry by his question—Are you the one? Jesus just continued being available to give sight to troves of the blind and other unfortunate people, but no visit for John. All in all, it appears that since John expressed doubt of Jesus, he was penalized, as is indicated by Jesus' statement saying, "Though John is so great, even the least person in God's kingdom will be greater than John."

Jesus came to look even more insipid for the things he said, though he offered some strong words of comfort in the last three verses of this chapter. I for one find what Jesus is about to be too ironic, because if he could not deliver John from prison, then what power did he have to make the following overtures?

"Come to me, all you who have been laboring and feeling overburdened, I will give you well needed rest. Just take my yoke upon you and learn about me, for I am meek and ordinary in heart; and you shall find rest unto your souls, for my bondage is very easy and my load is light."

Matthew Chapter Twelve

Jesus went through a cornfield on the Sabbath day. His disciples got hungry and began to pluck the ears of corn and to eat. But when the

Pharisees saw it, they said unto him, "Look, your disciples do that which is not lawful for anyone to do on the Sabbath day."

It is important to pick up an important clue in this opening, for it has surfaced in other alleged deeds of Jesus. Once again evidence is given of Jesus' popularity, and how government agents watched him closely, but the troubling question is whether such distinguished notoriety existed at all? If any of it happens to be true, one of the elements to explore is to ask whom this cornfield belonged to? Did Jesus intentionally take them into the field for lunch without the owner's permission? It is not made clear why Jesus would be headed to a cornfield while on a missionary trip, with the Pharisees following along like paparazzi. It would be theft to take produce not given by the owners of the field, and that may have been good grounds for the Pharisees to prosecute for unlawful conduct.

Furthermore, based on Jesus' philosophy of fairness, stealing corn from farmers would be contrary to God's holy integrity. Thus, Jesus would never have done that. But then there is also the protrial that has Jesus as an iconoclast, too, because he gave justification for breaching the Holy Sabbath day. I see it as a dichotomy of Jesus' personality, and not understandable. He said, "Have you not heard how David entered into the house of God when he was yet hungry and those with him, how he and his followers eat the shewbread, which was not lawful for them but the priest only? And have you not read how the priest on the Sabbath days profane the Sabbath, and are held blameless? You must know that the Son of man is Lord even of the Sabbath day."

Here it is made plain that Jesus is portrayed as one who gained divine acceptance among his Jewish natives, because of his cosmic mystique; to the extent of performing deeds that make no sense whatsoever, yet accepted as an absolute power from God. One may be able to sort through all of these shenanigans and figure them out, with all of the holy shock and awe Jesus created, but if there be anything true to the story I have yet to realize it.

Right after Jesus shut up the Pharisees over issues of the Sabbath, he went into one of their synagogues, and there was a man with a withered hand. Certain congregants in attendance were fearful that another instance of a Sabbatal breach may occur, so in preemption, they asked Jesus, "Do you think it is legal to heal someone upon the Sabbath day?" And this being his specialty, Jesus pulled from his resourceful intellectual reservoir and said to them, "Tell me this: if one of your sheep happens to fall into a deep pit on the Sabbath day, would you let it stay in it and perish, or would you even get help to recover it?"

While they remained speechless, he put forth more thoughts to them, contrasting the value of an individual compared to a sheep. While they kept still without a rebuttal, Jesus turned to the sick man and instructed him to stretch out his hand. And as the man put forth his withered hand, it became whole like his other.

Now, if you are not a Jew, just try to put yourself in their shoes for a moment, as a child of Abraham. Your historical prophets have told you that a messiah will come to bring change and relief; old things would pass away, and new things would come into view for you. You have wise men confirming the birth of the messiah the prophets spoke of. As a reasonable person, what would your reaction be to the things that Jesus was doing? Would the things recorded in the KJV bible concerning Jesus' miraculous deeds be remotely likely to cause you to reject him?

Upon witnessing the man's hand restored, the Pharisees went out and held council against Jesus, plotting how they might destroy him. But Jesus was informed of their trap and withdrew himself from them. I wonder who told Jesus of the plot, because he supposedly knew all things and needed no man to do secret service surveillance for him.

At the same time, the bible states that great multitudes followed Jesus and he healed all of them, it strangely says that he then cautioned them not to disclose where he was. I do not get it. As long as plenty of people are following him, he could not be kept hidden.

In the biblical narrative there is more interesting caveats for the authentication of Jesus' divinity: "That it might be fulfilled which was spoken by Esaias (E-să´ias) the prophet, saying; 'Behold my servant, whom I have chosen; my beloved, in whom my soul is well pleased: I will put my spirit upon him, and he shall show judgment to the gentiles'." Based on these observations of the biblical narrative, the flames have long died, and attention to them is diminished.

Matthew Chapter Thirteen

Jesus left a residence and went to sit by the seaside, a great multitude gathered together unto him.

Allegedly, Jesus began to address the crowd. And on today's inspirational menu agenda, there were seven unusual and sensational themes. These allegorical virtues herein are very engaging to say the least, and I am willing to say that the portrayal is of heavenly importance, especially to those with a view oriented solely by the King James Bible.

What happens in the biblical narrative here is just rich bamboozle, camouflaged in caveats and acting as sealant to both attract and bond people in conviction to faith in Jesus as an authentic messiah. For example: Jesus is portrayed as working from a blueprint that was drawn up in heaven, setting forth, as it were, a digital sequence in which God's work should be done. As such, Jesus' actions and speech are linked to some Old Testament prophecies:

> "Therefore speak I to them in parables: because they seeing see not; and hearing they hear not, neither do they understand. And in them is fulfilled the prophecy of E-saias which saith, by hearing you shall hear, and shall not understand; and seeing you shall see, and not perceive."

All these things Jesus spoke unto the multitude in parables; and in this instance he used a parable that it might be fulfilled which was spoken by the prophet, saying, "I will open my mouth in parables; I will utter things which have kept secret from the foundation of the world."

I have read this text on numerous occasions, but when I read it more carefully it caused me to feel so outraged I grow weak! Another clue that I have found in the narrative lies in the frequent use of the word "Saint." Take note that all four epistles of the bible are "St. Matthew," "St. Mark," "St. Luke," and "St. John." As an investigator with keen eyes, I spotted that Jews do not carry around anything with "Saint" this, or "Saint" that on it—but who does? The Roman Catholics.

Practically everyone is "Saint" something. If you should ask Jews today about these kinds of issues, many of them don't have a clue. If you are reading between the lines, it may start becoming clear why the narration is riddle with the title of Saint, decorating outstanding Christians. Who would you say is responsible for filling the biblical story with Saint titles, and the alleged rejection of Jesus by the Jews? *Rome.*

You have a thinking cap. I want you to put it on responsibly and let us reason together for the sake of our individual dignity. The big question needing an answer is this: *Who derived the designation that created the two groups, Jews and Gentiles?* Who determined the name 'Jews' for Abraham's progeny? The biblical narrative says that, by destiny, Jesus is Abraham's progeny—meaning he is Jewish. It follows that whoever is not a Jew is a gentile person.

The bible says that Jesus came unto his own and they rejected him as their messiah. Why did the Jews deny Jesus? Wait a minute—that is only an allegation made by a bible produced by the Roman Empire. Strangely, though, no one should ignore the position of today's Jews. When asked about Jesus, they are not aware of such a Messiah and hate to hear the mere sound of his name.

Matthew Chapter Fourteen

At that time, King Herod (Hĕr´od) heard of the fame of Jesus and told his servants, "This is John the Baptist risen from the dead; and therefore mighty works do show forth themselves in him."

For the first time we learn the circumstances under which John was put in jail. It is represented that John got into trouble when he chastised Herod for sleeping with a woman to whom he had no conjugational rights. The woman in the mess was his own brother Phillip's wife. According to St. Matthew's writing, John did not mind his own earthly business; instead he sought to purge sinful men, for God's sake, and interfered in Herod's love life.

For this, he was bound and shut away. While John was locked away in jail, Herod was embroiled in scorn; and things only got worse for John when Herodas' daughter danced for Herod and his illustrious company. Under the sedative influence of wine and drink, and being so pleased, Herod made a gratuitous oath to the girl, "Ask me for anything and it shall be yours!" Upon hearing those words, she ran in unto her mother and gave her the scoop. Herodias told her daughter to ask for the head of John the Baptist—on a plate.

In a veiled recollection, Herod sort of realized that he had ventured off course in his responsibility by making such a pledge to the damsel. But according to custom, it was unbecoming for a King to swear to something and then renege. So it is written that Herod sent word and had John beheaded in prison. His head was chopped off and brought forth in a charger, given to the young girl who in turn brought the bleeding head of John to her mother.

I am livid about this entire convoluted narrative, because I find it patently incoherent. The supposed exchange of messages between Jesus Christ and John the Baptist and the behavior attributed to Jesus are depressingly unrealistic. No wonder they saturated the tale with forewarnings, charging that one should just believe and remain faithful.

It is because time passes and people's interests change; important facts of yesterday become obsolete to contemporaries. It is in the process of time that the atrocities used to introduce and further Christianity were forgotten, and all doubtful authenticity waived. Everything that should have a logical reference to it is replaced with faith and believing, with no scrutiny to support genuineness.

When Jesus heard of John's death, he departed thence by ship into a desert place…and when the people heard where Jesus stopped over, they trailed him on foot out of the city. The chapter ends with other spine-tingling deeds by Jesus, giving relief to many.

But don't all of these mighty works appear to be in stark contradiction to the treatment Jesus gave John the Baptist as he sat in prison?

Matthew Chapter Fifteen

We shall now attempt to digest a few of the interesting excerpts in this chapter, but please do not lose your sense of observation and wonder.

Coming off of one of his most recent feats of calming a boisterous sea, Jesus received great admiration from many people. Now he arrived in a place called Gennesaret (Gĕn-nĕs´a-rĕt) and no sooner than he settled down, word got out that the healer was in town. So right away they brought as many of their sick folks as were possible to be cured by him. No problem—some just wanted to touch the thread of Jesus' clothes, and guess what, that was all it took to get them healed. Whoever exercised strong faith was made completely well by the mere touching of his clothes.

By now we know Jesus was very famous, and it seems that for either love or hatred the authorities, the Scribes and Pharisees, were always in attendance wherever crowds gathered round this Jesus.

When Christians begin to really examine these things, shame will wash over their faces.

And, behold, a woman of Canaan came out of the same coasts, and cried unto him, saying, "Have mercy on me, O Lord, you son of David," (How did Jesus come to be David's son?) my daughter is grievously vexed with a devil…" But Jesus answered her not. Then his disciples came near and begged him, saying, "Please send her away, for she is too much after us." But Jesus responds by saying, "Look, I am not sent but to the lost sheep of the house of Israel." Upon hearing Jesus' reaction, the woman moved forward and showed reverence unto him, saying, "Lord, help me." Jesus stipulated and said unto her, "Listen, it is not right to take the children's meal and throw it out to dogs." She said, "Jesus, your statement is true, but even the dogs eat up of the crumbs which fall from their masters' table." Then Jesus replied to her, "O woman, you have such great faith; as you have asked, be it unto you according to your desire." And her daughter was made whole from that very moment.

There are a few points in this that bear noting. What did Jesus mean when he said he is sent only to lost sheep of the house of Israel? Lost in what sense? That saying, in my view, strayed from the general context of "redemption for all." In that, according to the scripture, Jesus is a lamb that was slain before the foundation of the world, to die for the sins of the whole world. The reasoning on this is that transgressions of the Jews are equal to every human on earth. What substance is there that elevated Jews so that all other people get classified as dogs? Is this fact or fiction? You mean to say that with all the allegations of constant departure from their covenant with God, they managed to remain superior to people who did nothing wrong? Except be born under Adam's so-called "curse."

Could God's favoritism of Abraham have resulted in such bifurcation, creating such a righteous disparity? Jesus actually called the sick woman a dog, in clear daylight—removing Jews from the pool of human sin. And the biblical irony and error got even worse, coming from the mouth of Jesus himself. A distinction is made, which elevates Jews to being a premium people, but non-Jews? Dogs. And now this humble woman, with her ailing daughter back home, retorts in desperation to the celestial savior of all mankind, "But even dogs eat of the crumbs that fall from their masters' meal table."

Readers, I do not believe any part of this story. Do you believe a real Jesus came down from heaven with that?

From this venue, Jesus went forth into Galilee (Găl'i-lee), where he once again climbed into a mountain and took a seat. As he relaxed, a multitude came unto him bringing many that were sick of various illnesses. And he healed them all. When folks witnessed the dumb speak, the maimed become whole, the lame starting to walk and the blind receive sight—they glorified the God of Israel. Jesus also took small amounts of bread and fish from members of the audience, blessed them until they increased to feed all who were present, with leftovers on the table.

After a well-spent day of ministering, Jesus sent the multitude on their way, hopped into a ship and came into the coasts of Magdala (Măg'da-lá).

Matthew Chapter Sixteen: Is Jesus the Real Messiah?

Let me say that I am trying very hard to complete these chapters, because the repetition of Jesus' alleged acts invokes so much ridicule! It is nauseating, to say the least. The rubbish becomes trite after a while, especially after you have been through several of the self-reveling charades. However, I believe some readers may appreciate my persistence since this may be one of the first works to explore the bible in this fashion, many readers may very well find it captivating to follow. Having released my uneasy tension about this, I breathe with a little more tolerance to finish the job, so let's dig into the biblical maze once more.

For incomprehensible reasons, the man, Jesus, the Messianic light of the world, deserving of the trust of all men, suddenly became suspected of being deranged from cultural interests; to the extent that he was kept under surveillance, seemingly around the clock.

The Pharisees and the Sadducees went to Jesus, tempting him, wanting him to show them a sign from heaven. He, knowing their egos, turned to them and said, "Look fellows, when you observe an evening you say, it will be fair weather, for the sky is red. And in the morning, it will be unpleasant today, for the sky is red and lowering. Oh, you hypocrites, you can discern the face of the sky, but fail to understand the signs of the time? A wicked and adulterous generation hounds after a sign, and none shall be given unto them, except for the sign of the prophet, Jonas." And then Jesus walked away from them.

Jesus then tested the disciples' perception about who he, Jesus, was. On this particular question I feel outraged. Why? The biblical narration forgets every single bases of its own record. All Jews in Israel supposedly knew and waited for Jesus, their Messiah, right? To be born of a virgin. Jesus was surely a long-awaited national pride!

Now, while on the coast of Caesarea (Caes-a-rea) Philippi, Jesus allegedly asked his disciples, "Who do men say that I am?" Peter was able to hone his focus and come up with the right answer when no one else got it correct. Then Jesus responded, saying:

> *"Blessed are you, Simon Bajona: because flesh and blood has not revealed this unto you, but my father which is in heaven. And I say also unto you, that you are Peter, and upon this rock I will build my church; and the gates of hell shall not prevail against it. And I will give unto you the keys of the kingdom of heaven: and whatsoever you shall bind on earth shall be bound in heaven: and whatsoever you shall loose on earth shall be loose in heaven."*

Then Jesus warned the disciples not to divulge to anyone that he was really Jesus, and began to tell them classified secrets concerning things to come; how he would face hardships to fulfill his divine purpose on earth. "I must go up to Jerusalem," he said, "and suffer much harm at the hands of the elders, chief priests and scribes. They shall kill me, but I shall come up out of the grave on the third day."

When Peter heard Jesus utter those thoughts, he took Jesus aside and began reprimanding him, saying, "Be it far from you Lord, this will never happen to you." Jesus replied, "Get thee behind me, Satan. You are an offense to me, for you love not things belonging to God, but that are of men." Remember this is the same individual who not too long ago blessed and gave keys to the kingdom of heaven.

It is not forgotten that, according to the scripture, God himself had been speaking to Peter, revealing to him who Jesus was. So how come all of a sudden, Peter became a *devil*? Peter had left his fishing business and forsook everything to follow Jesus, yet he was rebuked and besmirched in this tongue-twisted way! And all for defending the character of Jesus, his master?

The chapter concludes with Jesus exalted as one who must die, but return in glory. But sure enough, so far, none of the titles Jesus gave to

Peter included "Saint;" yet someone later gave Peter this title—but it was not Jesus, or any other Jews for that matter.

Matthew Chapter Seventeen

And after six days, Jesus took Peter (who he had just branded as Satan), James and John, his brother, into a high mountain apart from the rest, and was transfigured in front of them. His face shone as the sun, and his raiment as white as the light. And in the surrounding glory, Moses and Elias appeared unto them, talking with Jesus.

Peter got excited and began to suggest that they make temples to represent these three personages. But while he was yet speaking, a bright cloud overshadowed them, and there came a voice from the cloud, which said: "This is my beloved Son, in whom I am well pleased. Listen to him." When the disciples heard the voice, they fell on their face, and they were very afraid. (Remember a similar depiction of how Roman guards fell as though dead at Jesus' resurrection.) But Jesus said unto them, "Be not afraid, it is alright." And as they blinked their eyes, the other images disappeared leaving Jesus standing alone.

While they were en route from the mountain, Jesus cautioned them not to disclose what they had seen…until after he was raised from the dead.

Why does this Messiah want so much privacy? As though he was a mobster.

The disciples raised the issue of something known in Jewish camaraderie, relative to messianic revelations; and in some sense it contradicts any notion that Jews did not know who Jesus was. They asked Jesus, "Why did the scribes say that Elias must come first?" Jesus replied by saying, "It is true that Elias should first come and restore all things, and I am telling you that he came already and they did whatever they wanted to him, without knowing who he was; and likewise shall the son of man suffer at their hands." Then the disciples put two and two together and concluded that he spoke of John the Baptist! The man he left in prison without helping him, resulting in the loss of his head.

From this point, Jesus healed more of the sick, and Peter, who Rome later call "Saint Peter," was once again back in the spotlight when tax collectors asked him if Jesus paid taxes.

Matthew Chapter Eighteen

Before going further into this content, a caveat crossed my mind. It is about the danger of thinking a thing, past or present, is *real* when it really is *not*. We can avoid wasting our lives by default, just by exercising classic thought management. Let every element of information count for what it is.

We should not be as one who has a vision of eating, only to wake up from sleep to find an empty stomach—this is the reality of Christianity.

Let's continue. At this time, the disciples went to Jesus, saying, "Who is the greatest in the kingdom of heaven?" And Jesus called forth a sweet little innocent child into their midst, and said, "I tell you this, my friends, unless you change your lifestyle to become like little children, you cannot receive entrance into the kingdom of heaven." Then he explained the advantages of childlike life, and the disadvantages of not being as a child.

He charged that when you receive one who behaves like children, you have received him, Jesus Christ; while the opposite works in similar principle with a relevant addendum added: "Whoever shall offend one of his supporters, it is better for such a one to have a millstone hanged about his neck, and be cast into the sea…" And here is yet another nugget that none of us should forget, because it thumps many of the ideas set forth in scripture. Think on what the narrative hints:

> *"For the Son of man is come to save that which was lost. When a man has one hundred healthy sheep, and one of the group goes astray, does he leave those remaining and go after the one that has wandered off? And if by chance he finds the lost sheep, does he now rejoice over the redeemed one in a way he would not do for those who went not astray? I say unto you, even so it is not the will of your father who is in heaven that one of these little ones should perish."*

I am hoisting the flag of caution on this, because I think these affirmatives should be examined and made applicable to the way Mother Nature works. Bear in mind that when we speak of Mother Nature, it is interchangeable with speaking of "acts of God," and the way he causes the planetary powers to operate. If Jesus is real and his words are true, then we should see it in the way the forces of the earth operate.

Jesus allegedly exercised the power of his Father in heaven to rebuke the raging waves that threatened to overturn the boat he and his disciples were on, right? Well, what about the many prayers prayed to God over the years until now? Even devout 'Saints' have prayed but were not protected from calamity! In the last 2000 years, how many Tsunamis, tornados, hurricanes and earthquakes have wiped out hoards of Christians and other religious people, indiscriminately? How many of His children has He allowed wicked prowlers, heartless rulers and harsh circumstances to destroy? Their prayers to gain mercy and miracles did not rescue their lives.

And what about those innumerable souls who have yet to accept Jesus and be saved from hell fire and other acts of God—does he care to save their souls, too, as the bible suggests? These no-shows of fulfillment seem to neutralize biblical credibility. How can it be true that God wants to save all men under these circumstances?

Now—there is no need to make excuses for God, like Christians do; saying that man is too sinful and rebellious, and God knows best, he has a plan. The fact is that scripture makes no stipulations about anything preventing God from protecting people who are predestinated to be saved. Everyone is a child of God, 100% vested in his assured plan to redeem him or her.

Remember the biblical precedent with Abraham and his nephew, Lot? When the Gods did not find ten righteous people in Sodom, they moved Abraham out of danger and dragged even stubborn Lot and his family out of the impending wrath. If God was extending such kindnesses back then, there is no reason the same mercy shouldn't exist for us in our day.

After Jesus outlined the policies of right conduct, like that of a child, he then taught on a very impressive principle, what constitutes an offence by one, and forgiveness by another. Peter came to Jesus and asked, "Lord how often should my brother sin against me and I forgive him, is until seven times?" You can see the text for Jesus' answer to that question. However, let me say this: There are many virtuous things in scripture that people should learn and practice to make their life more enjoyable. I consider myself to be a sophisticated man.

Much of my sophistication, believe it or not, comes from biblical wisdom, but I have learned how to diversify, and not be carried away by those things alone. The idea of a biblical apocalypse is dangerous because it requires faith to give it meaning.

Jesus ended his sayings in this chapter by echoing a very judicious maxim: "So likewise shall my heavenly father do also unto you, if you do not forgive his brother their trespasses from your hearts." Yes…it is good to forgive by following rules of forgiveness, but the 'father in heaven' the narrative refers to, is akin to being hoodwinked and bamboozled.

Matthew Chapter Nineteen

Jesus departed from Galilee, and came into the coast of Judea beyond Jordan. As usual, a multitude followed him, with Pharisees in their company. It must have been a tense time for Jesus, because these Jewish agents were on his heels everywhere he went.

On this day, the Pharisees decided to use something from the Moses canon to tempt Jesus…and this time, may God help him. They said to Jesus, "Tell us, master, is it lawful for a man to put away his wife for every fault?" And he replied unto them, "Did you read that they (let *us* make man in *our* image and after *our* likeness) which made them at the beginning made them strictly man and woman, and said for this cause shall a man leave father and mother, and shall fit tightly unto his wife, and they two become one flesh? In this case, they are no more twain, but one fleshy tissue. What therefore God joined together, no man shall put apart." But the Pharisees retorted by answering, "Master—why then did Moses command that a court order of divorcement be given to put spouses away?" Jesus fired back and countered, saying, "Look—for the inflexible muscles of your hearts, Moses allowed you to put your wives away, but this does not follow the grand design of man from the beginning."

Now, these are very interesting ideas, I give credit to whoever made them up—they are full of high voltage thoughts. When the laws of marriage arrangements are considered, it becomes unavoidable to reflect on the chief proponent and vicar of Christianity, because in Catholicism, marriage is proscribed among all clergy in the church body; and in so doing, constitutes an obvious anti-reproductive situation. Clearly this is very much a willful disregard for God's imperative ordinance for life. Anyway, I meant that as food for thought.

The purported concept Jesus sets forth in this text, about humans obtaining an experience of eternal life by adhering to codes of belief, has no known ancient historical root. Rather, it is found to be contrived material, made up long after man's origin, in midstream, probably within the last 3,000 years. Rome used the four New Testament gospels to discourage the reading of ancient history, while directing mass focus onto the surreptitious extract they have taken from the Sumerian Mesopotamian history. Of course, the prospect of living in heavenly realms with an imaginary God and His son, Jesus…well, it's all too glitzy for humans to ignore!

So they wrote that a host of angels would be there, singing glory, praise and honor unto our Lord, walking on streets of gold and feeding on honey and wine. However, in the eyes of true academic honesty, there is no denial that real history gives no salvation precedents anywhere; but rather a finding that both the Old and New Testaments are spurious at best. It is to be expected that believers and even non-believers will deny obvious facts, in favor of talking points on eternal life, heaven and hell, used to enhance the landscape of the scriptural narrative. For that reason the following is an example of the mindset those who framed the Jesus story wanted ingrained in the heart of converts:

> *Verily I say unto you, that you which have followed me, in the regeneration when the Son of man shall sit in the throne of his glory, you also shall sit upon twelve thrones, judging the twelve tribes of Israel, and every one that has forsaken houses, or brethren, or sister, or father, or mother, or wife, or children, or lands, for my name's sake, shall receive an hundredfold, and shall inherit everlasting life. But many that are first shall be last; and the last be first.*

That is what the Vatican wants people to believe, but it has no foundation. It is pure fallacy. If you have been paying attention to the preceding, the narrative reduced Jews to being everlasting victims; down from being Abraham's chosen seed, to being judged by Gentiles dogs. What happened before your very eyes is this: *Rome's loathing for Jews has placed them exactly where it thinks they've belonged for centuries.*

Matthew Chapter Twenty

> *"The kingdom of heaven is like unto a man who is a householder who went out early in the morning to hire laborers into his vineyard."*

A portion of this text has an elaborate metaphoric style, designed to convey the principles of how the "kingdom of God" works. Jesus brings the disciples up to speed about his lethal fate, saying that his present visit into Jerusalem will reap a betrayal of him into the hands of the chief priest and scribes—who will condemn him to death.

At this same time Jesus consulted with a woman identified as the mother of Zebedee's children. She asked that Jesus bestow preferred status in his kingdom upon her two sons—but of course the request was denied. After that he departed from Jericho, and as usual, a great multitude followed after him. The blind went to him and received their sight.

Matthew Chapter Twenty-one

Verse twenty-three says: "And when Jesus was come into the temple, the chief priests and the elders of the people came to him as he was teaching and said, 'By what authority you do these things, and who gave you this authority?' Jesus answered and said to them, 'I also will ask you one thing, tell me this: the baptism of John, whence was it? From heaven, or of men?'

The text is once again laced with diverse activities aimed at authenticating Jesus' role as the only begotten Son of God. Once the veil is removed, you will see what artistic ability was exercised to make Jesus' tale compelling enough to engage the whole wide world.

Time and again we find Jesus speaks with such a cosmic, sovereign voice, saying things in the following terms so that readers will believe the words of prophets have come to fruition: "The kingdom of God shall be taken from you, and be given to a nation bringing forth the fruits thereof. And whoever shall fall on this stone shall be broken: but on whomever it shall fall, it will grind to powder." Notice along the way, wherever Jesus went preaching, the scribes and Pharisees and other notable Jewish leaders (who we are to believe knew of Jesus' divine mission to his nation and all mankind) were always poised to destroy him.

Though Jesus performed all manners of miracles, it was not enough for them to accept him. Oh, no! They wanted his blood. And this time, when they heard the audacious things he proclaimed, note their attitude towards him: "And when the chief priests and Pharisees had heard his parables, they perceived that he spoke of them. But when they sought to lay hands on him, they feared the multitude, because they regarded him as a prophet."

Matthew Chapter Twenty-two

Once again Jesus opened his mouth in parables, and what he had to say is something that readers should think carefully about. Examine what they alleged Jesus said. "The kingdom of heaven is like unto a certain king who made a marriage for his son and sent forth his servants to call them that were invited to the wedding, and they would not come." So when the wedding was ready, the invitees failed to attend. In response to their ridicule, the king got angry and sent out armies, destroying the murderers and burning up their city. Following that horrible action, the king told his servants: 'Go into the highways, and as many as you shall find bid to the marriage.' So his subordinates went away into the highways and gathered together as many as they found, both bad and good, and the wedding was furnished with guest.

It is critical that we understand the enigmatic meaning of the parable, and I want to touch on two important components of it. First, it is in collusion with the framework that initially established salvation for the Jews, but they refused Jesus, and by that forfeiture, he turned to Gentiles. Second, the part about destroying murderers and their cities is indicative of the manner in which the Roman Empire ran roughshod over the Jewish people for such a long time. These things cannot be from a merciful, heavenly God.

The narrative intends to intimidate people so they think about God just as they think of Rome. We are to beware, for there is a price for rejecting Jesus. That declaration means that it was God who instructed Adolf Hitler to kill off six million Jews for rejecting Jesus.

So is it clear how Rome blended an anti-Semitic undertone into the writing? If we were to ask a reputable theologian to interpret and unscramble the allegory, just to see what they make of it, we should expect that they would affirm it was the way God worked.

After the parable, the Pharisees sent out their own disciples with the Herodians to have Jesus arrested. Then the Sadducees engaged Jesus about issues of the resurrection. They knew their ancient history and renounced the idea that there was really such a thing as a resurrection of the dead. Other notions are included to show Jesus' authority, and in the end of the session, Jesus was elevated because no man could answer the questions he put to them. I am sure these things never made much sense before because they were taken in faith, but having applied scrutiny to what is written, I see Rome is busted—it is all bamboozled.

Matthew Chapter Twenty-three

Then Jesus spoke to the multitude, and to his disciples saying: "The scribes and Pharisees sit in Moses' chair, whatever they instruct you, observe and do; but do not follow their example of hypocrisy, for they preach things they will not do."

Jesus gave a strong monologue, wreaked with disdain for the status quo leadership. He turned their self-righteous way of life upside down with a broad brush of correctness, pointing out specific areas of their conduct, how they aloofly separate themselves from others. He classified them as blind guides, white sepulchers, who tithe but give not into mercy, judgment and faith. He said they strained at a gnat while swallowing a camel.

There is no need for further review on this chapter. It is pretty much the same trite, brainwashing theme, with nothing fresh to dwell on.

Matthew Chapter Twenty-four

This is one of the more serious chapters Rome used to sure up a solid, divine image of Jesus. Among the most amazing things written in this chapter, covering the fifty-first verse, a reference is made to Noah's flood, and it depicts Jesus as one who always lived in the heavenly realms unknown to man. So here is a good question: Where was Jesus at the time of the flood? Was he sitting up in some cosmic residence looking down and witnessing scores of human beings perish?

I have chosen to sift through these texts to illustrate how the biblical writing is no less than a dosage of poison. It is like an ancient grave being walked on over and over without fear.

Matthew Chapter Twenty-five

> *"Then shall the kingdom of heaven be likened unto ten virgins, who took their lamps and went forth to greet the bridegroom, and five of them were wise and the others foolish. While the bridegroom was en route to marry his many wives (though in this case they consisted of male and female genders), some of them forgot and began to pay attention to other matters. But then without any warning, they were called upon to appear for the wedding. The smart virgins kept the bridal dress in readiness, but the other five may even have lost their virginity."*

As usual, I have done some light paraphrasing above, while keeping it in linguistic context. Here is an important question for believers: Why is the person introduced as the Messiah and savior of the world now turned into a bridegroom who proposes to ten virgins? And why does he say so many things in parables? Mind you, these are the supposed sayings of Jesus, which Matthew must have had a recorder to capture them on.

> *"When the Son of man shall come in his glory, and all the holy angels with him, then shall he sit upon the throne of his glory: and before him shall be gathered all nations: and he shall separate them one from another, as a shepherd divides his sheep from the goats: He shall set the sheep on his right hand, but the goats on the left. The king shall then say to them on his right hand, come, you blessed of my father, inherit the kingdom prepared for you from the foundation of the world: for I was hungry, and you gave me meat: I was thirsty, and you gave drink: I was a stranger, and you took me in: naked and you clothed me: I was sick, and you visited me: I was in prison, and you came unto me. Then shall the righteous respond unto me, and ask, 'Lord, when did we see you in need, and offered all these kindnesses unto you?' At that time, I shall say to them, 'Truly I tell you, inasmuch as you have done it unto one of the least of these my brethren, you have done it unto me.'"*

Now it is time for a pause, for just a little reflection on what happened to John the Baptist.

We went over John the Baptist's dilemma, and it aggravated me very much. The question is whether or not my feelings are justified—I think they are. Up until the time that these things were supposedly said by Jesus, he himself had not yet been arrested, and had not yet been in any of the unfortunate circumstances of which he spoke.

But he then made himself a recipient of kindness, by proxy. As he said, "When you do it unto the least of my brethren, you have done it unto me," Jesus is put forth as an example for those subsequently following in his footsteps. Why then did he depart from the place where John the Baptist was arrested and imprisoned without helping him? And why had he not offered any condolences for his death? So why would Jesus preach to his followers of good deeds that he flagrantly failed to do? Poor John…he was treated shamefully by the Messiah, the Savior, the deliverer and Lord. What was gained by John's pain, agony and awful death?

A Jim Reeves lyric is appropriate for his lamentation; I think we should dedicate it to him. Let us all join in our hearts and sing melodiously and mournfully, in loving memory of the greatest prophet ever born of a woman—John the Baptist.

> *"Where does a broken heart go, does it just fade away? Is it lost forever, will it live again someday? How can a broken heart live on with more than its share? When it knows the game is lost and it's hopeless to care? When a heart has taken about all it can stand, is it then protected with God's loving hand? Where does a broken heart go when it dies of pain? Is there a heaven for broken hearts, will it live again? Is it then protected with God's loving hand? Where does a broken heart go when it dies of pain? Is there a heaven for broken hearts, will it live again?"*

Matthew Chapter Twenty-six

The cosmologic mission of the Messiah is winding down, and now in the depths of its twilight, the narrative reaches a crescendo. It packs a full punch, loaded with eternal life—to all who believe in Jesus.

Now the monologue ends with a declaration of how the future experience will be for saved and unsaved people, before he turned his attention to another, more serious dimension of his earthly career. Jesus told his disciples: "You know that in just a few days, there will be the feast of Passover, and the Son of man shall be betrayed and crucified." And while Jesus spoke those words, the chief priests and scribes were assembling together at the palace of the high priest, Caiaphas (Cā′ia-phăs), to discuss how they may have Jesus placed in custody on charges of public mischief—offenses upon which they could seek his execution.

Today there is a degree of hush-hush taboo on the subject of whether or not Jews killed Jesus Christ, their own Messiah. When we read relevant history, we understand how sensitive the question really is, and get the full picture of the Jewish position on this matter. We know that grim political clouds hang over the Jesus tale, and Jewish people. It is then obvious why the issue has grown cold. And I will hasten to say, though I hate to, that no one's interest is best served by engage in public outcry over something so bogus and unjust.

Ironically, in the biblical script, those who conspire to seize Jesus are none other than the Jews. The record makes it clear that they are the ones who initiated the prosecution of Jesus, leading to his demise. And who exactly wrote the account of this Jewish and Roman saga? There is no record that shows the Roman governor Pilate knew about Jesus' resurrection, though he was the sitting judge at his trial. So who was it? Josephus Flavius? He was not around when these alleged things happened, so Josephus could only write from the spurious accounts of his Roman sponsorship.

Nothing plausible about Jesus could possibly be derived from Josephus, who became a traitor to his Jewish roots. Indeed he wrote important things about the Jewish life experience, but given that Josephus defected to Rome and befriended high-ranking rulers of Rome, even adopting the name 'Flavius,' I would suggest that the most innocuous of his Jewish history writings be cherry-picked for authenticity. This was a writer who preferred to seek Roman aggrandizement than remain in suffering, fighting against them.

The next segment starts out with one of Jesus' twelve disciples, Judas Iscariot. He was presumably desperate for some cash, and knew that the anti-messiah elites wanted to put a noose round Jesus' neck, so he went to see the chief priest. After their greetings, Judas said to the priest, "Look, I know that you want him, but you are having difficulty setting him up. I am one of his disciples; my name is Judas Iscariot. I can be your confederate for a fair price." Think about this: Based on Jesus' forecast of his sad fate, we have to assume that Jesus was somewhere watching every move they were making to destroy him. The high priest made an offer and struck a deal with the betrayer, and arranged to execute a furtive plan to capture Jesus.

On the first day of the week of the crucifixion, Jesus organized the itinerary for the days leading up to his destiny on earth. He told the disciples to find a place suitable for eating the Passover meal. And when the time came, he sat down with his dozen disciples for the supper. During the meal, he said to them, "You know, one of you here shall betray me." And while the disciples jostled over who that would be, Jesus would not identify whom he spoke of, but rather moved to authenticate his divine Messiah-ship. He became expressive, saying: "The son of man will go as it is written about him: but woe unto the man who betrays him. It had been good for him, that he had no birth."

Judas then stood up and asked, "Lord is it me who betrays you? Jesus answered him by saying, "You have well said it." But, oddly enough, no one seems to have paid any attention to the exchange between Judas and Jesus, since they just went ahead with their meal. Jesus gave them his symbolic bread and wine. As it was spiritually symbolic at the table, so it was literally of his suffering flesh and spilt blood, in just a few hours. And then Jesus said, "After I have finished this supper here with you, it is the last one on earth, and I will not have another meal with you until we are gathered round the throne of my father in heaven." Then they sang a hymn and exited the room, heading straight for the Mount of Olives.

As they spent some time in the mount, Jesus told them, "Tonight all of you are going to be offended because of me, for the things the prophets wrote concerning me must come to fruition—that they shall smite the shepherd and the sheep will be scattered abroad. But after I am raised from the grave, I will travel ahead of you into Galilee." Then Peter said unto Jesus, "I will die with you, and not deny you," and the other disciples chimed in with the same accord of loyalty.

Jesus then led them to a spot called Gethsemane and instructed them to stay there while he went nearby to have top-secret prayer time with his heavenly father. On the way out, he asked Peter and the two favorite sons of Zebedee to accompany him, and as they strolled along, Jesus began showing signs of sorrow, telling them, "My soul is feeling very unhappy, like death is coming down on me. But you three are to stay right here and watch my back for me." Jesus continued on a little farther, then fell to his face praying, "Oh, my Father, if it be possible—do not let this thing happen to me. There must be an alternative way to fulfill this cause. I know that it is up to you, Father, and not according to my emotions. Let your will take control."

It appears that Jesus did not want to die—which is in no way consistent with what he has been saying all along. Up until now, he spent all of Mathew constantly affirming his special mission on earth, being sent by God. He said that his home was in another world and that he was the only one who could undertake the task of propitiation for sin, which is what made him the Messiah. But, now look! He has misgivings about the whole thing, and engaged in sessions of intercessory prayer to forego the bitter cup and escape his noble destiny!

Without question, the scripted picture makes it clear: *Jesus did not want to lose his life.* And I see no reason for why a man, who was so filled with omniscient wisdom, would then behave contrary to the Divine Plan. I see it as simply a flaw of this fictional narrative, used to trick naïve people, and I want people to examine this very carefully— when it's taken as *reality*, one becomes fully bamboozled.

Let's continue. So Jesus spent about an hour in prayer before checking back on his three disciples to see how they were doing. He visited them twice more, then retreated in privacy to recite the same prayer (and just how did these writers get to know what Jesus prayed about in secret?). Remember it was Jesus' own teaching that said when you pray, use not repetitive statements to God; yet here he is, himself violating that same prohibition. Hypocrisy?

After the third prayer, Jesus came and saw the men weary with sleep, and said unto them, "Sleep on and get some rest, because the time of my betrayal into the hands of sinners, draws close." Then, on second thought, he said unto them, "You know what, gentlemen? Raise up—let us move away from here, for the one who has betrayed me is just round the corner." And just as Jesus stopped talking, Judas came along with a great multitude, bearing swords and staves, with the high priests and elders of the people. Judas acted upon the signal he had given the high priests for identifying Jesus. He walked up to him and said, "My Lord," and then he kissed him. Jesus said to Judas, "My friend, have you fulfilled your mission?" And while the authorities arrested Jesus, certain of the disciples drew out weapons and assaulted the invading team. But Jesus told a disciple to house his weapon, for those who use swords will also perish by them. He said, "Know that I could call my Father in heaven, and he would send twelve legions of angels to deliver me. But now this has to be done, according to words of the prophets."

As you know, I do not believe that there was anyone there to answer Jesus when he prayed, because he had prayed to the Father to spare him from the hour of death—but got no response! See the failed nature of this narrative? Again: Jesus is heard making pleas to God for his life—even though he professed that the prophecies must be fulfilled by him going through all of this.

Jesus then told his captors to set him free, "Do you come out against me, as though I have committed a crime; with swords and staves to arrest me? This is ridiculous, my friends, because I have been teaching in the temple on a daily basis, and nobody tries to arrest me there…But this has to be fulfill for the prophet's sake." When the disciples realized that Jesus was indeed powerless to extricate himself from the will of his captors, they fled, seemingly for fear of their own lives.

Now, the arresting officers took Jesus unto the place of the palace, where Caiaphaus, the high priest with scribes and elders of the people were assembled and waiting to hear the much welcomed news of Jesus' capture. Simon Peter, who had pledged to die with the Messiah, did not run away like the other disciples; he was brave enough to follow along to the high priests' hall, waited inside to see what would happen.

Jesus was presented to the council for a preliminary arraignment. And when they made some trumped-up charges against him, they were somewhat confounded by the lack of evidence. However, they brought in two false witnesses to accuse Jesus of saying, "I am able to destroy this temple of God, and build it up in three days."

Then, the high priest asked Jesus to respond to the charges against him, but he held unto his peace, saying not a single word. The priest said, "I adjure you, by the living God, to tell us whether you are the Christ, the Son of God." (And this is flagrant incoherency, because never before was there any doubt by Jews in scripture about the Messiah; why then would they suddenly question the certainty of Jesus' origin?) The high priest's question drew a resentful response from Jesus. "You have said it, nevertheless, I will tell you: hereafter shall you see the Son of man sitting on the right hand of power, and coming in the clouds of heaven."

This is so clearly fiction. For why would a gracious savior not offer a more informative response, instead of a bluff for those seeking proof of his authenticity?

At Jesus' response, the priest got so angry, he tore the robe he had on. "Jesus—you have spoken blasphemy! What further need have we to bring more evidence? All of you heard him speak blasphemously; so what think you of this?" They answered and said, "He is guilty—death!" They then started to attack Jesus; spitting on him, slapping him as they jeered: "Now prophesy unto us, you Christ—who is it who just smote you?"

Now, while all of this was going on, Peter sat outside the palace and a damsel came by and said unto him: "You were also with Jesus of Galilee." And others also identified Peter as one of Jesus' comrades, but, surprisingly, Peter's gallant energies had disappeared by then. When the last person nailed Peter's identity, by affirming that his very colloquial speech gave him away, Peter began cursing and swearing, saying: "I do not know the man!" Then immediately, a cock crowed, and Peter remembered the words his Master had spoken unto him, saying: "By the time the cock makes his sound, you shall deny that you know me." Peter was fully overcome, and he walked out of the palace and wept bitterly.

Matthew Chapter Twenty-seven

The following morning, everyone woke up to the breaking news: "The Messiah was arrested and his disciples fled." Yes, the Son of man was rendered powerless by the words of the prophets. But there is a mountain of irony to be overcome here: This is supposed to be the long awaited messiah, the Lord of glory who brings everlasting peace for men on earth.

And according to the narrative, the people were blithe and excited on this day. And if you remember the day Mr. Nelson Mandela was release from prison, the international headline news…well this situation with Jesus had to have been, by far, of much greater magnitude. Mr. Mandela was a civil rights activist, a mere human who performed no miracles, nor was he regarded as a divine oracle, yet he received such high-profile attention.

Now, Judas, who had betrayed Jesus, attended the council hearings. And when Jesus could not be found guilty initially, Judas felt condemned, touched with remorse, and repented for what he had done. He then took the coins he was paid back to the high priests. On his arrival, he exclaimed to them, "I have sinned!" then threw the coins on the ground. But the priests would not accept the money, basically saying, "We do not want the money back, it is all yours now. Go and spend it as you please."

The guilt weighed too heavily on Judas after this; he just could not live with what he had done, and so he went and ended his life. Judas' act of evil was not written with a bad ending, because his money was used to purchase an interment lot called 'Potter's Field,' for the deceased without a burial plot in Palestine.

It is still amazing to me that God in heaven would have predestined, or orchestrated, the use of Judas to commit such a wicked betrayal and deliver Jesus into the hands of barbaric men.

The distraction of Judas is now out of the way, and Jesus stands before Governor Pilate. (Take notice of this next exchange. See if you can deduce whether or not Rome/Pilate knew anything about Jesus, his mother, Mary, or what the prophets allegedly said about the Messiahship. If they didn't know then, when and how did Rome receive such knowledge?)

Pilate asked Jesus, "Are you the king of the Jews?" Jesus replied, "That is what you say of me." Then the prosecution team of the chief priests and elders spelled out their allegations against Jesus—but he answered with not a word. Pilate, amazed that Jesus would not defend himself, asked: "Do you care nothing about what they speak against you?" But Jesus still held on to his peace, which made Pilate somewhat of an admirer of Jesus'.

Since this was a festive Jewish season, Pilate thought he had an opportunity in signaling his willingness to free Jesus, who clearly, in his eyes, had nothing of which to be condemned. So Pilate said to the assembly, "You know it is the custom that one of these prisoners be released unto you. Which one of them should I release? Shall I give to you Barabbas, or Jesus, who is called Christ? You know that envy is the reason he was brought before me."

Now, in an eerie turn, Pilate's wife allegedly sent him a divine, cautionary message. She advised him to recuse himself from the case, because she had a terrible dream that day concerning this just man. But all of that did not help Jesus, for the chief priests had clout and persuaded the crowd to request to release Barabbas, the real criminal—but destroy Jesus. So the people said, "Release Barabbas!"

and Pilate replied, "But what am I to do with Jesus, the Christ?" And with one accord the people shouted, "Let him be put to death!"

Seeing that he could not win, for the strong hatred and determination of the enraged multitude, Pilate washed his hands in water before them and said, "I am innocent of the blood of this just person—see you to it." Then the people replied, "Let Jesus' blood be on us, and on our children."

And that's how the chief priests got exactly what they sought, an unjust verdict against the innocent man. (Without a doubt, this narrative is fabricated so Jews would be stigmatized for killing their Messiah, while Rome is cast as negligent and dismissive in the prosecution of Jesus...

And today that is the way the world at large views Jewish people— as those who murdered the one and only savior of mankind, Jesus Christ.)

Another aspect in this case that does not jive is the seemingly unprecedented conduct by judge Pilate. In this whole proceeding there is nothing, nada, zilch, zero in evidence that could give Pilate any indication that Jesus was divine. And from this scene there is nothing to make one believe that Rome, who occupied the country in hostility, was seeking to save souls, least of all Jewish souls—they were too busy killing people.

So has there been any other case where the civilian attendees forced a judge to render a verdict of *their* liking, when the court thinks otherwise? This proceeding of an alleged trial of Jesus is disingenuous at best; it is horrendous. Readers should put Jesus' "trial" through a very meticulous and rigorous analysis regarding what was involved.

Since ancient times, there have always been the same basic procedural rules with respect to court proceedings, for civil and criminal rules. And those core courtroom guidelines are still followed in the 21st century. Today we have two forms of court jurisdiction that decides and hands down decisions. One is a judge, and the second is a jury. Jury's may consist of either six or twelve jurors. The setting of the so-called courtroom as presented in the bible according to St. Matthew, is somewhat different from this, as the courtroom consisted of a flailing crowd, as it were, with high priests acting as prosecutors, and mere spectators as the jury.

According to Matthew, Pilate substitutes his own judgment for the whim of a hateful, wild and undisciplined crowd, which seals Jesus' fate. Again this is just one more instance where a pattern is formed: Rome's diplomatic strategy to blame Jews for their own barbaric deeds. Take note: *Rome shows its representative, Pilate, as someone who did not want to kill Jesus.* So it is my logic that the biblical narrative casts a Jewish crowd in the role of the 'jury' responsible for Jesus' death, while Pilate, throughout time, would be regarded as a sympathetic character.

So with a little intelligent examination of this story, we can see how it is loaded with impeachable inserts, which clearly indict Rome as the chief architect of this Jesus chronicle. Justice was not served when Pilate failed to vindicate Jesus. Instead he washed his hands while delivering Jesus over to the Roman soldiers, to be put to death.

In a modern court the judge has the power to review a jury's decision, to see if it follows the law. And if their verdict is not in accordance with the law, it is called "jury nullification" and is overruled by the presiding judge. Unfortunately, Jesus' tale debuted in an era when there were fewer people in the world, and the level of consciousness was stumpy, submerged beneath artlessness. Therefore, it is understandable how Rome could pull off saturating the populace with Christianity. Well, who has eyes to see, let them see, right?

After the court's decision, Pilate's soldiers marched Jesus to a place where he would be exposed to public shame. (A pause—why are Roman guards escorting Jesus, and not Jewish guards?) They placed a robe on Jesus, a crown of thorns on his head, a reed in his right hand, and then knelt in front of him saying, "King of the Jews!" Then they concluded the session of mockery by removing the robe used as part of their condescending disdain for Jesus, spat on him, and stroked him with shrills. They put his own raiment back on him, and carried him off to be killed. Then it is said that many ridiculous things were done, leading up to the alleged death and resurrection.

The chapter ends with the high priests' efforts to tighten security and prevent anyone from removing the body of Jesus.

Matthew Chapter Twenty-eight

One human leads a herd of cattle into the grassy fields, a reason for the herd of many beasts to follow one person. That illustration brings our attention to why many human beings would follow one leader, under the claim that 'God' sent the individual to lead them. I introduce that thought to illustrate the weight of spurious stories when they are framed in a 'biblical' setting.

Hey, what a story so far! And the best is yet to come—the crescendo that seals the eternal deal. Oh, yes, this chapter is one of the most interesting and tranquilizing of all the things written in scripture, but readers should think at a greater depth, to observe the contents with common pragmatism.

At the end of the Sabbath, as the first day of the week dawned, Mary Magdalene and her colleague, Mary, went to see the sepulcher. Upon arrival, an angel of the Lord came down from heaven and set off an earthquake (the size of which was apparently not recorded for posterity). This angel did not remain obscure to human eyes, but appeared in the flesh. He rolled the rock away from the tomb to let Jesus come out. The ladies claimed they saw the bright countenance of the angel, dressed in snow-white, and saying, "Women, have no fear. I know that you are looking for Jesus, the crucified one, however, he has left, but come let me show you where he was buried…" Then the angel said, "Go quickly and tell his disciples that he is raised from the dead and is gone ahead of them into Galilee.

By the time they arrive there, they shall see him…and one more thing—try to remember what I have told you." Upon hearing what the angel said, the two women quickly departed, their hearts beating with a mixture of joy and fear, anxious to connect with the other brethren and break the glorious news of what had come to pass. But lo and behold, before they could reach the others, Jesus appeared saying, "Greetings," and the women fell to the ground and held on to his feet, praising him. Then he said unto them, "Go and tell my brethren to come into Galilee, and there they shall see me."

At the request of the Jews, Pilate had ordered guards to watch Jesus' grave, because chief priests and Pharisees informed him: "While he was alive, the deceiver said he would rise after three days." So they wanted watchers at the sepulcher of Jesus. And when the earth allegedly shook because of the angel, fear overtook the guards watching the grave and they were shaken and became "as dead men." Whatever that description means, unless they were pretending, I interpret it to mean that the guards became dizzy and fell into some type of comatose mental state. They could not have had any awareness of what took place.

Now, since I see this story as a clever manipulative tool, orchestrated by the ancient Roman government for long-term control of the populace, humor me with a little speculation…The unofficial report of the guards was that the disciples had stolen Jesus' body, that there was no divine resurrection. Why then did Romans build Christianity upon a resurrection story that was not reported to the Roman authority? Could the guards have awakened from their stupor and witnessed the angel speaking with the two women? Did they then rush in to report it, only to be bribed by the Pharisees, to say the body had been stolen over night as they slept?

It is compelling to raise this question of authenticity about the "resurrection," for there is no government report reliable enough to support the idea that Jesus miraculously arose from the grave. In those days, the high priests were the second level of power in Palestine, under Pilate, and they apparently decided that there would be no record of Jesus' miraculous recovery…

So what source were they relying on when the scripture asserts that this resurrection occurred? Did they learn about it from the two civilian women? And would the Roman government accept the testimony of two women over the word of the high priests and soldiers?

Bear in mind that these priests told the guarding officers that if word got to Pilate that contradicted their story, they would back them up and protect them from being court-marshaled. To say that they had been sleeping while men stole Jesus' carcass could've gotten the officers put to death.

Now, does this alone impeach the credibility of the Christian religion, murderously launched by Rome? Surely it does. And one is bound to wonder: *Was the angel's earthquake not also felt in the area where Pilate and the chief priests resided?*

Well, the officers must have just taken their cash and did as they were told. And thus, the claim that the disciples took Jesus' body from his grave is very commonly held among Jews, to this day. But I argue that if it were cultural knowledge among the Jewish people, would it have remained solely among them in perpetuity?

If the guards had reported such divine acts by a Jewish God, it makes more sense that the chief priests would have changed their minds about the situation and become repentant; they would've come into accord with the blessings of their father, Abraham—knowing that

Jehovah had visited them, in the revelation of Jesus. However, their attitude was ignorant and intractable.

Despite the promises of God, Moses and Father Abraham, nothing could convince them. Here again, Rome portrays Jews as fools, not knowing what is good for themselves—and notice how Rome is doing so while occupying their bona fide land. How can one entity violate the sovereignty of other nations while branding its besieged citizens as fools and murders, when they are actually victims?

Finally, after they received the joyous news, the other eleven disciples went on their way into Galilee, at the spot in which they were accustomed to gathering with Jesus. After arrival, they saw Jesus, and they reverenced him—but some had doubt. Now according to the narrative, these disciples supposedly spent more time with Jesus than anyone else, and were well prepared for what was to happen to him, right? So what cause had they to doubt what they were witnessing?

Knowing of the doubts, Jesus told them, "All power is given unto me in heaven and in earth." But after what took place, who should have faith in this so-called power? Not this author. I can see clearly, and I hope I am showing here, just how Rome used this to become the largest political, universal church powerhouse on earth—which is what it intended to establish with all of this.

So Jesus continued, "Go you therefore and teach all nations, baptizing them in the name of the Father, and of the Son, and the Holy Ghost; teaching them to observe whatever I have commanded you; and, lo, I am with you always, even unto the end of the world."

And so this concluded the life and fulfillment of the alleged Jewish Messiah.

It takes just a little sober inquiry to sense that something is not right here in this doctrine. For instance, my wife was raised in one of the most segregated church denominations there is, and while she holds that the bible does offer some value for good living, she admits that, even as a child, there were some biblical statements that did not add up. She wondered about the things the bible said God would and would not do.

A subtle caveat is contained in a saying of St. Paul's. I'll paraphrase: "Now we see through a glass darkly, but when Jesus appears, we shall know him clearly." This mindset suggests that believers are not to be concerned with outrageous or bizarre statements made in the bible.

Seeing "through a glass darkly" means that people should look beyond their lack of knowledge in spiritual things, and wait for glory in the afterlife. Ancient Rome wanted people to accept biblical claims while pumping themselves up with assumptions. Just accept that there are deep, spiritual mysteries written by man in the scriptures, which are beyond the comprehension of other men—but when God and Jesus return, it will all be revealed unto us, in their presence.

There is good reason why the name of Jesus sounds sweet in a believer's ear, but terrible in the ear of Jewish people. Let us not forget: Rome scattered the Jews all around the world so it could establish Jesus on every continent, wherever there were human beings. The sweetness of Jesus' name to believers is purely psychological; it is nothing of objective substance.

CHAPTER FIVE

ROMAN CATHOLICISM

I suppose that I am one of millions who struggles to get a conscious grip on the world around us, to develop a panoramic view of the things that have happened within the last 2000 years, pertaining to Catholicism. I wish it were all as uninhibited as the sun, moon and stars, the oxygen we breathe, the mountains of the earth. But that isn't the case with the things that pertain to humanity. And so thoughtful people are challenged with unraveling the path their ancestry has trod.

The area of religion over the stated period has been blanketed with very colorful distortions. We have a planet full of people, existing much like a beehive, with a Queen Bee as head of the labor force, and the common worker drone bees and idlers.

Interestingly enough, bees are superior to humans, because they abundantly demonstrate peaceful cohabitation, general purpose, transparency and cohesion, and much more, beyond the level of human function. Humans have simply developed too many divergent ideologies and contrived ulterior customs over the years, which has had a major impact on the way society as a whole lives from day to day. We, therefore, repeatedly malfunction in our efforts to progress, leaving us hobbling along with all manners of ailments.

With the lack of public awareness and inquiry into the staples of Catholicism, a cultic operation is free to dominate the areas of public education, the economy, social welfare, politics, and the very ideological heart of civilization. Because of this, I maintain that the origin of Catholicism is pure evil. It has nothing to do with a God of heaven as logical probes of it reveal so clearly.

So since I am a former Christian, I know what it is like to struggle in the pursuit of understanding the origins of humanity, and why these religious conglomerates exist. The real problem exists on the part of those with closed minds. I know, because I used to be one of them, staunchly defending Christianity and the Word of God. I, myself, stood in the mindset that swore to have knowledge of God, when it was really merely a spoon-fed delusional conception. The religious bamboozle made that mindset very comforting for me, in that the psychology was attributed to the "Holy Spirit." Well, thank goodness I had the cognitive coherency to see through.

I know that many Christians are just too ashamed to capitulate, and consider an alternate view, afraid to notice the gross, unsolvable problems with the concept of traditional faith in God, but I own up to my years in wasteful religion.

Our foregoing coverage of the previous bible chapters ties in nicely to the forthcoming references. We've laid a rich, enlightening background.

Christian biblical writings aim to show that Jesus elected Jewish men to his one-man university, where he taught them the nuts and bolts of how the church should function. Should we not then expect the Jewish people to be the ones doing outreach in the world with the glorious gospel of Jesus Christ, just as he commanded they do? The Christian expectation would be to have Jerusalem remain the headquarters of the Christian church—not any other country. For those who are unwilling to indulge in the pretence, we must be ambitious about the things recognized as God's word.

The spirit of this work is not to question the words of a true God. No, quite to the contrary, this interrogation focuses on a narrative written some 2000 years ago, by a former military power that was quite evil. It's an inquiry into the core of Catholicism, to examine the beginning of a church organization, its doctrines and scriptures. A little detective work can do wonders, and in this case, we know that much of our educational substance is of Roman-Greek decent.

For instance, in the calendar system we use the Rome created designation of "A.D.," a Latin abbreviation for "anno domini," meaning, "in the year of our Lord," to reference any time since the "birth of Christ." And take note: it wasn't Jews who made our calendar system—it was Rome.

If this information doesn't send a solemn message to Christians, then what will? It makes sense to believe in things that you are able to understand, but consider this: Beef patties are nice to people who like them…but how does one know whether it's real beef in the loaf, or filth? We have the right to check, to sniff and see if we have mess in there, or real meat.

So the A.D. designation marks a period wherein Jesus was allegedly born; a period that has no specific day of birth, because, indeed, none exists. Have you ever wondered why there is no date of birth given in the bible for the Messiah? The age of enlightenment is calling for some verification of Jesus' birth, the date being primary.

All modern-day Western society live according to the Roman calendar; a time marker derived from military superiority, particularly over Israel. And the borderline between B.C. and A.D. was crucial to the writing of Jesus, thus we were given a subjective time log—and this is how we have come to know the era of the "21st century." Given this perspective, we can count thirty years from Jesus' alleged birth. From various ambiguous accounts, Jesus' actual time spent in ministry ranged from eighteen months to three years of that period. If we say three years, we can then conclude on the alleged birth period as well, and assume that Jesus died when he was thirty-three years old.

We can guess that Jesus' twelve disciples were over eighteen when Jesus called them to ministry. But we have no documentation of Jesus' daily ministry during his lifetime, or even immediately after his "death." So there is reason to question how the recording of Jesus' and others' words and actions came about…and why. How is it that so many years later, the happenings could be documented in such detail, and made available for printing and mass distribution?

To explain the metamorphosis of the gospel, Rome asserts that it migrated from the provinces of Jewish apostles and into the domain of the Romans by divine appointment! Rome says that God designated Rome as the apostles of Jerusalem successor, for the government of the church.

I have done much research and have gathered vital information that sheds light on some essential points. One such source, the Encyclopedia Britannica has been very helpful. The following is drawn from said source.

Saint Peter and Saint Paul

Note: There is a reference about Jesus' interaction with Peter, of which no Roman personnel would have been privy. The allusion is brand new, and only serves to establish a false profile of church sovereignty and authenticity.

According to Rome, Peter was named the rock on which the church was built. And then after St. Paul's conversion, he was grandfathered into the ministerial hierarchy as the thirteenth apostle, but had a higher status then Peter, a man whom Jesus allegedly taught for three years. In short, the book of Acts, and other epistles, recorded the pattern of Paul's many missionary trips with his fellow brethren. And it is made clear that he and his traveling companions always returned to Palestine with a status report.

We read that Paul was ultimately jailed and put on trial by Jewish people who were overzealous in the laws of Moses. Then Paul was shipped to Rome when he filed an appeal unto Caesar.

In the latter chapter of the Book of Acts, Paul's story says, "He was placed under house arrest upon his arrival in Rome, whereas he was granted permission to rent/lease his own house." But there is no biblical reference about what became of Paul and his appeal. Don't you find it rather unsettling how some of these biblical segments just vanish into thin air?

In all of my scriptural exploration, I have never found where we are shown that Peter migrated to Rome; and therefore, I guess the reader is left to rummage around to find out why Rome has no record to show that Peter handed over the heavenly keys of the Kingdom to Roman rule, upon his alleged visit to the empire. But I have found a little background on both Peter and Paul, which is supposed to broaden our horizons on the subject.

Encyclopedias tell us of Peter's first journey to Antioch in Syria, but give no details, which does not jive. The easiest way to efface evidence is to deny that it exists. And as we shall see, Rome provides evidence from thin air when it best serves the interests Rome wants to advance. Whatever jives with its propaganda—even when it involves calling angels down from heaven! Notwithstanding, though, we are offered unsubstantiated evidence of Peter's travels to Palestine and other distant regions. And Peter's own alleged correspondence is offered as proof. Interestingly, though, the strongest evidence of Peter's forays from home comes with his time in Corinth.

One Bishop, Dionysius of Corinth, in circa 2nd century A.D., stated affirmatively that he owed the origin of his authority to the apostles Peter and Paul. Consider that this guy lived in the 2nd century and is claiming that his bishop authority ("See") traced back to St. Paul and St. Peter—how exactly did this happen?

Let's not hold our breath on it.

It is Rome's claim that both of these apostles died as martyrs in Rome, during persecution under Nero. But by way of a disclaimer, the account notes that there is no reason to assume these two apostles were working together, or that their circumstances of martyrdom occurred simultaneously. We are told that there is more evidence of Paul's presence in Rome than of Peter's, but this "evidence" cannot withstand any serious challenges.

They say that the "Prince of the Apostles" was in Rome, emphatically established beyond all reasonable doubt—first by indication in writings by the Roman priest, Gaius, in the late 2nd century (and we still have to ask what we can know about things that happened back in 30-60 A.D.?), from Irenaeus of Lyons in circa 180 A.D., and from St. Clement circa 95 A.D., the first epistle of St. Peter; if we interpret these writings by archaeological evidence of confessio in the basilica of St. Peter in Rome, in the 1940's, we speculate that Peter stayed in Rome a short time if he went near the end of his career...But surely within enough time to establish the center of the Christian church, in what was then the capital of the Roman empire.

Note: Since the scripture also says that Jesus established the headquarters of the church in the land of his birth, why would Peter be authorized to take it elsewhere? Does moving the headquarters from Palestine mean that Jesus' church would no longer be represented in Palestine? There is no record beyond the bible that indicates a functioning operation instituted by Jesus was running from the late 1st - 15th centuries to the present.

With these kinds of unverifiable offerings regarding periods and people, we can give no credit to the period of Jesus and the apostles either. As a matter of principle, decent people cannot believe or trust in murderers and torturers to give them truth.

We cannot say how long Peter had been in Rome before the first harrying of the young church broke out. However, Rome is certain that Peter died in the violent persecution started by the Emperor Nero in 64 A.D. How come? Their biographical account of Peter's lifetime does not pinpoint a date, a time or place where any formal or informal meeting occurred between Peter and any Roman converts, to establish the nucleus of the Christian church in the capital of the Roman Empire.

If Peter had made a sojourn to Rome, it would have been so significant that it would be impossible for them not to have had record of when he arrived, prior to Nero's alleged torturous and lethal persecution. It is this area of Peter's biography that I call the "chamber of fact," and given that everything they've set forth as authentication is nebulous at best, I am well satisfied that they have not offered anything truthful to reinforce the claims that Peter handed over the church authority to Rome.

It's important that we don't dismiss the area of Peter's alleged arrival in Rome. Let us take it seriously, because it is one of the important links in the "Christianity chain of belief."

Now the Vatican's position gives two descriptions of how Peter transferred the church administration over to Rome. One of the instances supposedly took place in his lifetime when he personally appeared in Rome for an unspecified amount of time prior to his death, and the second is that the transfer was done through his successors. Now, it is hard to tell which of the two is their official position.

This part of the discussion is a lightening rod—the root and nucleus of the Catholic bamboozle. The discourse on Peter pertains to the exact time in history where this paradigm/matrix was engineered by Rome; the foundation for the "salvation" ideology. Once again, this is the Vatican's explanation of authenticity via the early successors of "Saint Peter."

> "*Of Peter's first two successors only the names are known, Louis and Anacletus. The third, however, stands out more clearly. This was St. Clement, whose letter to Christians of Corinth, written to settle a controversy among them, still extant.*
>
> *While its tone is one of clarity, rather than of authority, this letter shows that the bishop of Rome considered himself empowered to intervene in the affairs of other community; and the fact that his letter was soon regarded as having almost canonical status is evidence of the Roman bishop's prestige throughout the whole of Christendom.*
>
> *Little is known of the first successors of Clement, though we are better informed on the series of bishops of the Roman church than on that of any other. In Rome alone is the Episcopal succession traceable without interruption back to its apostolic founder. While their dates remain uncertain, we know that Clement was followed in turn by Evaristus, and Alexander I, and others, with all bearing names in Greek.*" –
> **Encyclopedia Britannica**

These claims were never initially challenged, which gave the Vatican freedom to proceed in establishing its powerful organization, a universal religious hoax—a prank that contained all the ingredients necessary to sucker millions into being "believers." Readers should especially pay attention to historical dates, where precedents were set. For example, 64 A.D. was a time of which the Vatican should have proof that Peter did in fact carry out a consignment of the Roman church.

The foundation of this bamboozling was laid by Romans in Palestine with the Jews to foster their pursuit of the polarization of societies all over the globe. Thus, it was crucial they convince people of ties between Peter and Rome. Short of that, no dominance could be exercised.

Since the church was responsible for establishing concepts of monotheism and polytheism, the incarnation of Christ and the Holy Spirit, which are shared by churches all over the world today, can we not recognize how the Catholic church system is the beneficiary of Catholicism? Yes! Of course we can! Again certain dates herein are very important for judging the potency of this story's credibility.

It is helpful to see that Rome has been working on establishing Christianity for *centuries* up to this point. A little research shows that this big project began in the so-called B.C. era, ushering in A.D. and the 1st century, of which they used the "birth of Jesus Christ" as the dividing line between both eras. From the birth of Christ, the project continued onto the enigmatic conversion of Paul in about 34 A.D.

Based on the chronological progression, Peter and Paul were fairly young men at the times of their calling, and they were still actively preaching in 64 A.D., per the Roman presentation.

Rome treated the foundation of this religion with great patience. And as we fast-forward into the 2nd and 3rd centuries, we can see that they achieved colossal breakthroughs.

Emperor Constantine I
(February 27, circa 272 - May 22, c. 337)

For me, Constantine was an alien enabler who just didn't belong in the ministry. The first time I read about Constantine's role in advancing the administration of Jesus' ministry, believe me when I tell you—I saw two worlds collide. Had Jesus' church still been thriving in Israel, it would not have had the same impact on me, because there would be a historical presence of the church among the Jewish people.

Jesus said, "It is written: let him come unto me and drink of the water of life freely." So my depression sets in at the slightest sign of nothing to corroborate Jesus' church functioning in Palestine, as it is written in the scriptures.

Now, we are coming from 64 A.D., when Peter is said to have handed the church over to Rome. But I believe that if the Peter we read about in the bible were indeed a real person, he would have known not to hand holy things over to the Romans. He would know that they would do away with the principles of Jesus; and he would never have assigned it them.

> *"And he gave some, apostles; and some, evangelist; and some, pastors; and teachers; for the perfecting of the saints, for the work of the ministry, for the edifying of the body of Christ: till we all come in the unity of the faith, and of the knowledge of the Son of God, unto a perfect man, unto the measure of the stature of the fullness of Christ: that we henceforth be no more children, tossed to and fro, and carried about with every wind of doctrine, by the sleight of men, and cunning craftiness, whereby they lie in wait to deceive; but speaking the truth in love, may grow up into him in all things, which is the head, even Christ: from whom the whole body fitly joined together and compacted by that which every joint supplies, according to the effectual working in the measure of every part, makes increase of the body unto the edifying of itself in love."* -* **Ephesians 4:11-16**

In all fairness, the explanation given in this scripture is the only map believers should be at to follow; it renders it impossible to have Constantine or Rome in charge of Christendom. I feature these biblical excerpts to engage readers in serious content observation, to draw a line between what is correct and what is incorrect.

Looking ahead, it is astounding to see how Constantine furthered the church's scheme. Judge for yourselves whether or not he, himself, even met the precepts set forth by scripture for following the faith.

Constantine I was raised in a culture of paganism, and he served in the military of his country. He grew ingenious, and someone not to be underestimated. He moved through the ranks and became an army general. In a battle against rival general, Maxentius, Constantine kicked his butt and took his soldiers. This victory occurred October 28, 312 A.D., paving the way for greater things to happen for Constantine. In recognition of the victory, he became the undisputed master of Rome, and from that position, he seemed destined to become the father of Roman Christianity, which at the time was still generic and not yet adopted as the official religion.

Constantine fought against other military subdivisions with great success, but he was more for peace than for war. He sought reconciliation with his enemies, and seized upon the opportunity to use his growing influence to expand Christianity, which, up until then, had been struggling for dominance. And most importantly, Constantine I knew that, Christianity, poised as a universal religion, could significantly strengthen his political base.

After Constantine made a peace treaty with his predecessor, Licinius, in 315 A.D., things went fairly well for some years, until Licinius resumed persecution of the Christians in 321 A.D. as he was, bit by bit, losing political ground. He regrouped his army and stirred conflict twice again against Constantine, and twice he was defeated. In the aftermath of all of this, Constantine reigned as the sole emperor of the East and West provinces of the Roman Empire, and he won the right to preside over the council of Nicaea.

In 326 A.D., Constantine moved the seat of the Roman Empire from Rome to the Eastern province, and before the end of that same year, he held a groundbreaking ceremony that laid the foundation for Constantinople. Now, let's ask: why did Constantine make this move? We know that Rome was a stronghold for paganism at the time, of which all of the hotshot senators were ardent devotees.

But to increase his political power, the expansion of Christianity became Constantine's number one priority. Clearly, he felt it was a time to move most of the world's society in a different direction, and paganism, which consisted of ancient alien Gods, did not have the potential to hypnotize the masses. Worshipping multiple Gods led to many discrepancies, which worked against the federation of groups. So apparently some research was done, revealing monotheism, the concept of one 'God,' as the most advantageous model to use.

So Constantine, the visionary, was born right on time, he knew exactly what to do; and let's remember that Rome had already been working on this venture for a long time, perhaps longer than the public may ever know. And the time had come to meet one of Rome's most ambitious benchmarks.

Given his power as Emperor, Constantine could have used the ways of old—violence and persecution—to wipe out the practice of pagan worship, but he saw this method as counter-productive. So he spearheaded a new and progressive approach, applying agreeable orders and policies of peace and love, all attributable to 'monotheism'—one God of heaven. This new philosophy operated under the operative word: "Ecclesiastic." As displayed at this juncture in history, it appears Constantine was one of the greatest tacticians of his time. He mastered the art of psychological manipulation. He knew he would have to make himself an integral part of the scheme if he wanted it to work, so he devised the ingredient of professing to have received a mysterious conversion to Christianity—very similar to that of the apostle Paul's.

According to Emperor Constantine, the site for the new empire in Constantinople was revealed to him in a dream. And Christian clergymen performed the inauguration ceremony on May 11, 330 A.D. to dedicate the city. But in a frightening turn, the sanctification of the building was not made to God or Jesus—but unto none other than the Blessed Virgin Mary…Hold it, hold on a minute. Hold it right there— can you see the black hole in this set up? The flaw? What did Constantine know about the importance of Jesus' mother, when it was almost three hundred years behind him, when his country was just a hostile power in Palestine? And didn't he live in Rome? Where all he knew was worship unto many Gods? So how did Constantine manage to become so well versed in Christianity?

Leaders in ministries have either gone to seminaries or attended a church for some length of time, taking many theological classes, before they are deemed competent enough to teach or lead a flock of believers.

Evidence shows that Constantine was a recipient of Paul's works when Paul acted as a Jewish traitor and collaborated with the greater power of Rome. But for Constantine to dedicate his building to the Virgin Mary and not to any of the Gods was a huge mistake on the part of the narrative. Nothing so far has shown that Constantine's learning and cultural background exposed him to any in-depth Jewish folklore, and even if he had been exposed to such, it made no sense for him to elevate the Virgin Mary above God.

And what made this all the more contrary in biblical logic was that the Jews recognized neither a Virgin Mary, nor a Messiah called Jesus Christ. Therefore, I feel this proves my stand and shows that Rome concocted this 'Jesus as holy savior' hoax, using the Jew's religious culture of expecting a Messiah as a basis; and if you ask me, of all the places that Rome occupied illegally, Israel remains the most invaluable of them all.

It is duly noted that Constantine's main demonstration of greatness pertained to how he executed the promoting of Christianity. Let it be understood that Constantine did not promote this religious ideology on a whim, but in collusion with the high priest, Pontifex Maximus, of the College of Pontiffs, which was a group of high-ranking priests in Rome's then polytheistic state religion.

Pontifex Maximus gave Constantine the religious power to push Christianity forward upon the masses. He was the religious nucleus with the influence to pave the way for bamboozling everyone into believing it was the "will of God" that the gospel of Jesus Christ be spread upon the world. And the account shows that his own conversion to Christianity was brought on by a mysterious vision no one else witnessed, so there can be no corroboration; and the baptism that new converts usually receive was not done on him until he was near death.

Now, pick up on this: Throughout Constantine's reign, he did more for the advancement of Christianity than the majority of Christians seem to know. And much emphasis is placed on the many sessions of the Nicaea Council, over which Constantine presided, and how it framed the functional procedures for Christendom. Whether modern-day Christians want to acknowledge this fact or not, no one can separate any part of Christianity from the things Constantine I did in the formative years so the world would receive Christian ideology, and adopt its beliefs.

At this point in history, there was no church establishment as we have today. Therefore, Constantine's action, while sick with leprosy, to institute a papal power in Rome is of terrible importance.

Surely, many of you have wondered, as I have—just where did the pope originate? And most importantly, where did the papal political power come from? Well, in examining Constantine's reign, we can see the truth. The historical account shows that Constantine established the papal operation, which proves that the Roman Catholic Church was not a private entity, but a government-sponsored unit used to subtly keep society under raps.

The Vatican lied about receiving the church from St. Peter. Because if they had said it came from St. Paul, the story would not have had any value. They did a very proficient job in creating the story that Paul was jailed when the Jewish people rebelled against him for preaching the gospel of Jesus; and that he lived in Rome serving time in prison for the offence. Do a little research and the story is easily unraveled. The story falls apart because it cannot be proven that Peter was anywhere near Rome during this time so could not be the one who gave them Jesus' church.

Now it is obvious to me that Constantine endowed the Roman priesthood with conflated power so they could use political and ecclesiastical dynamics, not just to preach the gospel around the world, but to execute a totalitarian dominance of it in as many territories as possible. This is the message of Matthew chapter twenty-eight, where the order is given to spread the doctrine far and wide.

Since the time that Constantine made Christianity a legal religion, Rome has used the church as a means for expansion in many other countries, defacing their rough and tough image that came from harsh military might. Then under the guise of trying to recruit souls for the "kingdom of heaven," they were able to carry out something more cleaver even than what cult leader Jim Jones did at Jonestown in Guyana, South America. Using the façade of the church medium, the Inquisition could torture, imprison and murder those who refused to accept Christianity.

In the 21st century, if you could find seventy Christians who knew that the system of belief they observe as "faith in Jesus Christ" had been invented by Rome, then you would've found a lot. They don't want to recognize the glaring truth, because as I said before, the name of Jesus sounds so sweet in a believer's ear. The belief gives them false comfort, you see, and so they despise any contradictory ideas that would rob them of their comfort zone. And I do understand why.

It is not reasonable to be angry with staunch believers, because they need to believe and feel that a God created planet earth with them in mind; that our souls are a top priority in the mind of this God. People conditioned in a culture where Adam sinned and was cursed are psychologically damaged by that concept, and it is very difficult to get them to think in a different way—which is in exact accordance with Rome's objective—and is it working? You better believe it's working. Oh, uh, uh, oh! Is it ever working!

I can't see how it is possible for a loving God to ever 'allow' some 'Satan,' over which He had control, to destroy His handiwork of the human race. Rome did not make it easy for anyone to know or think towards reality when they designed the character of 'Satan,' because in reality, 'the devil' is proven to be nothing more than a thing people *imagine* exists—an implantation of the illusion.

Maybe someone reading this may wake up from the delusion, too, and realize the true understanding of the physical world we are living in, and the adjacent vista surrounding us. Yes, Constantine I masterminded a grand scheme indeed. Think about it: If we were made for such a 'higher purpose,' do you think God would have made so many dysfunctional moves, undermining his own plan? Would He have made such a haphazard decision to wipe man and beast from the face of the earth, as is alleged in the Roman/KJV bible? Only to have the same sin and corruption erupt again? I say no. It doesn't make a lick of sense.

Now, let's turn to the Inquisition…

CHAPTER SIX

⚜

THE ROMAN INQUISITION

Time is one of mankind's best friends, but ironically, in some ways, time can be one's worse adversary, too. It can rob us of vitally important, perspective-shaping information.

Are we inclined to understand what the Inquisition was, or what its purpose was? Its sole purpose was to force people to accept Jesus, otherwise called "the Faith."

Now because so much time has passed since the Inquisition occurred, it's difficult to remove the barriers that hinder present-day minds from being able to grasp the horror of that age. Terror, grim and deadly is really the most accurate description for the "Inquisition," and is specifically applicable to the Roman Catholic Church.

I believe there is no room for argument over who is the author of Christianity—it is the iniquitous Roman Empire. The Inquisition was a time of torture and murder for those who refused to comply with the edict that Jesus Christ was sent by God to save the world from sin.

Now you tell me, did any of the so-called churches named in the New Testament kill or torture unbelievers who did not believe or accept Jesus? There is nothing penned in any of the epistles that even remotely went in that direction. Thus the Roman Catholic Inquisition, for biblical purposes, is blasphemy and criminal. In fact, the gross acts of the Inquisition are bound to shock everyone who truly believes the gospel of Jesus Christ, because we who embraced Christ do so on the basis of grace, mercy, love and peace.

Here's how it all went down. Running out of substance and options, and with no desire to lose their power and supremacy, on or about 1220 A.D., Emperor Fredrick II, convened a tribunal to formulate and establish legislation for violent oppression. With the support of the "man of God," Pope Honorius III and Gregory IX, legislations were made and passed to have ancillary organizations execute the punishment of heretics (non-believers) against the ecclesiastical empire. In general, the legislation provided for penalties of death, banishment and confiscation of property. The papacy created the rules of engagement for the Inquisition, which the practitioners applied arbitrarily.

At first the pope's commissioners on heresy would travel from one place to another, addressing communities. They called upon people to confess voluntarily if they were indeed heretics, and to denounce anyone they knew to be a heretic. They offered amnesty, a grace period of one month to absolve themselves of heretical faults; if confessions were made, no penalty would be given.

This process was aimed at getting as many faith adherents into the newborn Catholic Church as possible. (And it was all about cash and power, not Jesus.)

The actual indictment process executed by the Inquisition was done in private; any defense made on behalf of a defendant was merely perfunctory. But once the time of official pardon passed, the law of the Inquisition was then in full effect. The population would then go through a rigorous purging of so-called heresy, by the enforcement squad, until the mission was accomplished, at which time the squad would leave the country.

We are not to forget these are things the government of Rome did in the name of fulfilling Jesus' command to spread the gospel to the world. And to Rome's credit, the suppressive and gruesome treatment of people was very well thought out, orchestrated by a Roman Emperor and his popes, the holy 'Vicars of Christ.' Quite outrageously, they had the gall to say that God chose the city of Rome as headquarters for Jesus' Church.

By what we have seen in history about Roman guardianship of the church, from its infancy to present, it's clear this was a work of darkness. It is not realistic that the work of God would raise a divine Jesus from the dead in triumphant glory over Satan, only to leave us in the hands of a regime ruled with a deadly iron fist. The evil mission of the Inquisition was in no way compatible with the biblical code of free will, and the invitation to receive Jesus Christ through faith.

The Holy Scripture says, "For the Son of man is come to seek and save that which was lost." That is Luke 19:10. So are we to accept the ways of the Roman Empire, the prosecution, jailing and killing of non-believers as compatible with this sentiment?

"If you shall confess with your mouth, the Lord Jesus, and shall believe in your heart that God raised him from the dead, you shall be saved. For with the heart man believes unto righteousness; and with the mouth confession is made unto salvation." – **Romans 10:10**

I have just found a cryptic meaning in this verse, and the next, which says: *"For the scripture says, whosoever believes on him shall not be ashamed."* Can this be interpreted to mean that when the Inquisition commandos indicted a victim who confessed a belief in Jesus, they would not be punished? But by not believing in Jesus, the treatment received culminated into shame? I just have to laugh at this, although it is not a joke.

A dark aspect of the Inquisition process subjected the more stubborn victims to being handed over into something they called the "secular arm" for punishment—the equivalent of a death sentence, there was no more opportunity to plead for mercy on the subject. You were a heretic, and Rome carried out judgment that you would die.

Oh, Jesus, have mercy, Lord.

The biblical narrative asserts that Jesus was one of mercy and forgiveness, but in Rome, the guardian and executer of Christ's commands, brutality and deadly force were used to compel acceptance of the faith.

The absurd practice of the Inquisition was instituted in many countries, all in the name of our Lord Jesus Christ, and all for economic and political gain. The Inquisition's confiscation of heretical property was very lucrative, and Rome is extremely proud of it.

First, there were *no* consequences, because they made the laws of the land to support it. And on the moral side, today they have Jesus Christ, the Virgin Mary, God, Rush Limbaugh, and President George W. Bush supporting the deplorable deeds.

You see: Jesus blessed the Romans with all of this wealth, yet it was all gained contrary to his Word. Jesus seems to reward others who make efforts to memorialize his name, as well. For example, a taxi driver in Jerusalem will tell you that Jesus blesses him, too, for transporting tourists visiting the area of his birth. But how gruesome was the plight of the so-called heretics at the hands of cruel Romans?

Whenever things done in the dark are revealed, it should not surprise anyone. In an eyewitness record I read of some of these wicked ecclesiastical crimes, dated in 1449 A.D., Jacob Sprenger resided in a German Dominican province. Jacob was an insider of the Inquisition's 'death squad' and disclosed much about the innocent people who had perished. As he put it, "we the Inquisitors" caused them to be burnt to ashes. Even in this deep iniquity there were some acts of discretion, on which great credit is claimed, and to some, it is a big deal. Because as author H.C. Lea states in his writings, few people suffered at the stake in the mediaeval Inquisition, for between 1308 and 1323 A.D., Dominican Order Inquisitor Bernard Gui, delivered only 42 of 930 individuals who had been convicted of heresy. We praise and thank the holy name of Jesus for that! He saved eight hundred and eighty-eight (888) people in the space of fifteen years from a rushed untimely death.

I have not forgotten that I am describing horrendous, hypocritical acts of colossal proportions; but it is 'The House that Rome Built.' And it destroyed anyone who refused to support its economic system.

Only Jews were exempt from this ordeal, for strategic reasons, of course, they were spared. Now, they were not exempt because they were God's children, in fact, they were punished for it! For the claim of being Abraham's seed, God's chosen race. Rome was using their cultural heritage to reap an economic boom—it would not have been a wise thing to punish them for not accepting the hoax of Jesus. Besides, Rome was conscious that it had kicked Jews out of their own land for the same reason people were being killed for not accepting the faith of Jesus Christ. So it was apparently more than reasonable to leave the Jews out of the terror. Oh, Rome was so considerate.

Do you see a problem with the way Rome went all out for the cause of Jesus, while driving Jews from their country for rejecting their own Messiah? When you ask Jews about Jesus, they know nothing about the character. So why did this occupying regime latch onto the Jewish Messiah and kill people to accept him?

There is still much to resolve in this. Let us move on to Spain, for more Roman Inquisition abominations.

The Spanish Inquisition

Anywhere the Catholic Church went, the Inquisition went—and it was no different in Spain. But it appears there were too many Sephardic Jews and practice of Judaism there for full-fledged Inquisition activity. And since the majority of the people began to despise the activities of the Inquisition, its progress began to slow. The atmosphere was not encouraging for the Inquisition's evil and harsh dominance, so instances of violence were sporadic.

In 1233 A.D., King James I published his own edict against heretics, but this promulgation secularized much of the Inquisition's activities, to which people were also hostile. And then in 1255 A.D., the King of Castile, Alphonso the Wise, created independent, secular legislation concerning heretics, and then removed his kingdom from all papal contact. There was competitive religious hatred that sparked attacks on Mohammedans and Jews. This began in the 13th century and became more intense during the 14th and 15th centuries.

The Clergy instigated massacres, and forced baptisms were carried out. After the conquest of the kingdom of Granada and the completion of the conquest by King Ferdinand and Isabella, the Jews and Mohammedans of the area were given the option to choose between conversions to Christianity or going into exile.

They called the precinct that planned and executed, extorted, confiscated, tortured and murdered, the "holy office." I still marvel at how human beings were so many degrees backward that they could've allow such things to happen.

I give you a warning: The feature ahead will present the words of the Vatican, the pope—who placed them in mouth of Jesus, the fictional character.

These are the words of Jesus: "*My peace, I leave with you, my peace I give unto you, not as the world gives, give I unto you.*"

In no uncertain terms can the following quoted excerpt be considered saintly, and a thing that correlates or complies with the words of what would be a 'real Jesus':

> "*Being of an active nature, and desiring some immediate powers as a recompense for their moral sufferings, the Jewish or Mohammedan Conversos soon became rich and powerful. In addition to the hatred of the church, hatred and jealousy arose also among laymen and especially in the rich and noble classes. Limpieza, i.e., purity of blood, and the fact of being an "old Christian" were made the conditions of holding offices. And a combination of secular jealousy, national pride and religious bigotry led to the foundation of an essentially national Inquisition, directed against heretics, and founded without the help of the papacy.*" – **Encyclopedia Britannica**

If anybody tells me that they can see the kingdom of heaven in these operations of Rome, then I would say we need no hell after all. What about Rome's own transgressions against the Holy Bible? Not marrying its clergy, committing sodomy and pedophilia on children, etc.? Well Rome did sanction the bible, and there is no penalty for not obeying anything written therein. Corruption was made clear when, in order to hold office, purity of blood and being an old Christian were required.

It is also made clear in that when you accepted Christianity, doors of success were opened unto you; in essence this was discrimination, technically a societal blackmailing.

According to the Encyclopedia Britannica, for Rome, the Inquisition brought forth "a combination of secular jealousy, national pride, and religious bigotry. This has led to the formation of a national Inquisition, directed against local heretics." But in the New Testament book of Galatians, the line is clearly drawn between the works of the flesh and those of the spirit. For things of the carnal flesh, it cites adultery, fornication, uncleanness, idolatry, variance, emulation, wrath, strife, sedition, heresy, envy, murder and drunkenness.

And the apostle Paul said: "They who do those things shall not inherit the kingdom of God." But the fruit of the spirit is love, joy, peace, longsuffering, gentleness, goodness, faith, meekness and temperance; there is no law against those things.

And those who are of the Christ have crucified the flesh, with its affection and lust. These are the things sincere Christians like to hear, and see put into action. And believe it—if Rome had been propagating this ideology, earth would be a real paradise.

But, as usual, evil easily strives, and the Inquisition eventually took hold in Spain, and as noted, Jews who accepted Christianity in those days, under those circumstances, became wealthy…but those who did not had to depart Spain.

Do you wonder how many Jews around the globe were pretending to be Christians? When in their hearts they were just trying to survive, joining a force they could not beat.

Jews were frighteningly terrified of the monstrous force that was the Roman regime. To them, the loss of their native homeland, being tossed about in ghettos as second-class citizens is unforgettable.

What they were able to accomplish in Spain further displayed that those in power could impose any God they wanted to legislate upon the rest of us—under penalty of death. In every ounce of what the Inquisition period accomplished, we can see that all of society was under siege.

CHAPTER SEVEN

MARTIN LUTHER

€arlier on I discussed how difficult it can be to transcend cultural falsehoods—Professor Martin Luther's life exemplifies this.

Mind you, this was one of the most learned and dedicated individuals of his time, so it was not encouraging to learn of his great struggles with this subject matter, particularly when the truth had been in his life for so long. It shows unequivocally that we really become products of the environment that nurtures us.

Martin Luther had strict parents, whose discipline came primarily through Catholicism, the contemporary of the fifteenth century climate. If you have a little knowledge of Roman Catholic history, you can appreciate what that means. This German statesman was born in present day Eisleben, Germany (back then it was known as Saxony, The Holy Roman Empire). He was a brilliant guy, but disciplined through rather harsh treatment from his parents. According to the Encyclopedia Britannica, *"Luther was reared in the current religious beliefs and popular superstitions, which the parents taught their children."*

In 1505 A.D. Luther was twenty-two years old. He was second place on his master's examination list. It is said that he found pleasure in reading some Latin authors, including Cicero, Virgil, and Livy. He was a well-read young man of great intelligence. So when something was set before him, the very subject of this book, "religious bamboozle," we can see how well a man of his IQ would think outside the societal box, and how close he came to cracking Rome's religious hoax.

Luther's father suggested he go into the legal profession, so he reluctantly began studying law in May of 1505 A.D., only to stop abruptly nearly two months later. Luther had a close encounter with death that nobody knew about…and he believed it to be by the hands of God. He claimed that while traveling to Mansfield, near Erfurt, he was struck to the ground by a flash of lightening during a storm. He then grew fearful of death and vowed to become a monk.

Can you see the origin and nature of such a decision? Based on the superstition and collective beliefs of the time, and a mere fear of death? Luther got the idea about a God who speaks to humans by lightening and thunder through *the church's ideology.* So then the coincidental flash of lightening in the atmosphere that prostrated Luther, and happened in the vicinity of the Erfurt Monastery, caused erroneous beliefs (based on those teachings) to saturate his consciousness.

It's like the first picture to appear on the screen of his psyche was interpreted as some kind of divine message saying, "Luther! You are being called into the ministry!" And this was followed by an instantaneous intuition that he was "called" to be a monk. Captivated by this poignant conversion, Luther immersed himself in the monastery, while his father and friends lamented his abandonment of legal pursuits. They were hurt because it was evident to them that something had swept Luther up into his decision to serve as a hermit monk.

Luther fully embraced his newfound, frugal lifestyle, and denounced the world.

The Vow

Martin Luther accepted the Catholic system's training program, and it serves as a real test of whether it complied with the tenets of Jesus.

The first year in the monastery is called "novitiate," which Luther completed. He underwent a critical, strenuous study of the fundamentals as set forth for admission into what they called "the Order." I guess we should assume that Jesus or Peter wrote this process down on a tablet for the Roman monastery.

The second step is when you are required to take a vow, which is in essence a declarative acknowledgement that you are ready for the job of a celibate priest.

> *"Luther took the vows of obedience, poverty and chastity, and submitted to the drudgery which was an essential part of training."* – **Encyclopedia Britannica**

Well, well, well…now we find a discrepancy. I have not seen one item in the vows that comes remotely close to the precepts contained in the 'New Covenant' scriptures, which comprised the New Testament. And thus it is alien; not a product canonized by the Jesus character or the apostles.

So who established this "Order?"

After taking his vows, Luther was off to a good start, and in 1507 A.D., he was assigned a teacher for a course of theological instruction to become ordained a priest. His studies continued for biblical degrees in areas such as *Sententiarius,* dogmatic theology, which included attending lectures of the theological faculty of the university. (Again, ask yourself who exactly established these curriculums. Jesus? St. Peter?) The curriculum was dense and well expanded, steeped in the arts of many intellectual heavyweights of the time, such as Lombardus, Occam, D'Ailly, Biel, St. Bernard, Duns Scotus, and St. Augustine.

Filled with attained knowledge, Luther began lecturing on Aristotle's ethics, while still continuing with further studies. Then in late 1510 A.D., he went on a church business trip to Rome, and was not impressed with what he saw there. He'd apparently had some grandiose expectations of the place considered to be the 'Holy City of God.' Surprisingly, Luther found a secularized, ecclesiasticism and low moral standards going on in Rome. Really, he could have just made a u-turn and gone right back home, because a community established by the 'most high God' should in no way be devoid of righteousness to such degree.

Conversion

Luther's mental world opened up with an illumination, he saw a contradiction between the things the church taught him, and what it practiced.

Roman 1:16-17 says: *"For I am not ashamed of the gospel of Christ: for it is the power God unto salvation to everyone that believe; to the Jew first, and also to the Greek."*

If you have been following my argument thus far, then it should be clear to you that this verse of scripture is one of the major inserts of the religious bamboozle, and trying to make sense of any portion of it will just drive you mad.

Now, how much mileage could Martin Luther extract from such a verse, on the road to reformation? With every atom of his smarts, he tried to build on the celestial potential written in that scripture and others. He felt confident the bible was really from heaven, and that the power of men must be subjected to the divine nature of God. But much to his chagrin, he would never reach fulfillment, even with the most exhaustive meditation in "the word of God." So Luther became despondent with the teachings, and liable to fits of depression, which attacked him in acute forms at times. His sense of observation intensified, becoming critical of the Roman Catholic order. And alas, this became a recipe for clinical disaster.

So Luther's diminished mental health was caused by the biblical delusion, and he went wading through theological rough seas: contemplating the scope of sin, righteousness, God's judgment, doctrines of predestination and justification by faith. And his state of mind continued to deteriorate. His condition worsened to such a point that he sought the help of senior professors, but to no avail.

What Luther didn't realize was that there was *no* veracity of truth in the paradigm of the vocation he had chosen. And it came to pass that instead of detecting Rome's scheme and withdrawing his dedication to it, Luther ended up helping to proliferate the same confusion he experienced.

Yes, he unwittingly did just that when he used his scholastic power to further cement the madness Rome had created: he wrote a ninety-five page theses on the topic "Abuse of Indulgence." This ushered in his own brand of innovative interpretation and posted it on the door of Wittenberg Church on October 31, 1517 A.D.

The Church's practice of indulgence and penance was ostentatious, and done for its fraudulent purposes. When believers were punished for sinful infractions, payment in cash was one of few ways in which punishment was mitigated. An auxiliary of the Catholic Church held that the practice brought large sums of money into the papal treasury. The crusading spirit weakened when church funds dwindled.

Pope Boniface VIII reduced periods of jubilee celebration, from 100 to 50, and even down to 25 years, just to revive revenue. And in 1447 A.D., Pope Calixtus III expanded the efficacy of indulgence to extend beyond only living offenders; it now included souls in purgatory—another monitory decoy to lure in the bucks.

Now as clear as these things were for one to see and condemn, Martin Luther was unable to make sense of the insanity. It is our obligation to identify the problem and wean ourselves from its grip. I realize that we are dealing with the core of the soul, and outgrowing the teachings of childhood is not easy. But there is no reason to blame ourselves for having fallen victim to the church delusion; or for why some of us question things sooner than others, or not at all.

I feel great sympathy for Martin Luther. Despite his intelligence, he had been brainwashed too much to break free and see the depth of the delusion. The argument on this issue is intoxicating, unavoidable, irrefutable, and extremely compelling. And you discover the strength of it when you step back and observe how a fledgling mind was brainwashed, conditioned into falsehood by a bogus impression of God. Luther struggled with what he accepted for years before he saw a tiny fraction of it differently.

Now, Luther was witness to the liberties the Church took making up and implementing any doctrine it thought would bring loads of dough through monastery doors. They were not creating foolish dogma, but rather well thought out formulas for long-term and permanent control of the populace and financial supremacy. And they cleverly orchestrated it so that the only way someone could find out that it was total rubbish was to become a "heretic" and or "apostate," and we know what they did with anyone who dared speak against "the faith."

It was upon this religious attitude that what I call the "fees for sin" practice was founded, and Martin Luther was a first class victim. Just open your purse and pay a fine, and your sins will be miraculously washed away. It was given the title of 'indulgence,' but the fee absolved all the wrongdoing. The purpose of the charge had little to do with God in heaven forgiving your sin when you paid a fine—it was all about revenue.

The church realized it was a fabulous business idea; it brought in beaucoup revenue to the Pope's treasury. In fact, the success was so impressive that, although it would be a stretch, the church decided to extrapolate the principle, extending it even unto dead folks! Do not laugh, my friends, this is what comprised the early days of Christianity. Yes, you read it right—the church made it applicable to the *deceased*, with the expectation that it could rake in double the amount of revenue when combined with the amounts coming in from living folks.

And it did not stop there either; the pope decided to add a third plan that would allow for the sale of 'permission to commit indulgent acts.' Well, why not? There were oodles and oodles of money to be made in the name of God, right?

This practice endowed the pope with the power to hear confessions and to forgive sins, but on the condition that his forgiveness was restricted to one's lifetime, and would not shield from God's final judgment. But the pope's authority to forgive sin was a violation of Jesus' teachings, was it not? Because Jesus said that he alone had the power to forgive sin on earth, and that authority wasn't even bestowed on Peter, to whom he gave the keys to the kingdom. So the Church invented this process purely as an exercise of taking advantage of the misinformed laity, because there is clearly no substance in the so-called pope's forgiveness of the living, or the souls in purgatory.

So this practice was predisposed to great abuse, inasmuch as the indulgent preachers strived to raise as much money as possible to enhance their own lives, they didn't always make the conditions of holiness clear to their congregations. Of course not. And there were differences of opinion among Church leadership, on both the doctrine and the practice, especially regarding the application of indulgence to the dead in purgatory; not to mention the widespread dissatisfaction over its abuse.

I give Martin Luther much credit for coming to know that problems lurked in the operation of the Church; he was grossly offended by the flagrant contradictions with original biblical tenets. Now mind you, some of the Church's formidable professors wrote elaborate theses on this "fees for sin" doctrine, allowing the popes' wide range latitude in carrying out the process; well, it filled Luther with outrage! He felt compelled to reject the Catholic Church's reprehensible aggrandizement by showing that, according to scripture, only God alone could absolve people of their sins.

And, naturally, his peers then attacked him to protect the Church, namely Professor Tetzel and Dr. John Maier; they both accused Luther of heresy and schism. But Luther was on top of his game, and he soared above their challenges, using his dominant skills of good rhetoric and powerful academic authority for interpretation of scripture. With these attributes, Luther's position garnered enough support to bring significant changes to Europe and many other countries.

His opposition was commendable, but sadly, Luther was only playing right into the hands of Rome. Rome was very smart; they made space for dissention—as long as it didn't destroy the universal view of the absolute doctrine of Jesus Christ. Oh, those poor nonbelievers! They have not accepted Christ—it's okay. They will burn in hell. Let us pray for their souls. May God have mercy on their souls.

And so it came to pass that Luther's interference with the Church's economic plans warranted his replacement. And he was summoned to appear in Rome within 60 days under the accusation of being a heretic, a rebel to ecclesiastical authority. He appeared before a tribunal, presided over by one Cajetan, in Augsburg, in October 1518 A.D. He was told to recant his offensive thesis, but Luther refused, telling them he would only recant if they could prove by scripture that he was in error. The hearing ended with Luther's appeal to the pope, but he later withdrew his appeal from the papal jurisdiction and submitted it to the general council.

It became evident that the Church's doctrine on the "fees for sin" practice was in stark contradiction to Luther's view of scripture and they were irreconcilable. A second trial failed to resolve the matter as well, ending in a gridlock for the most part. Although he would not capitulate, at the insistence of his professional peers, Luther wrote instructions to the pope, charging the abuses instituted by the Church, and affirming that he still recognized the papal supremacy and the duty of obedience to the Roman Church. But, you see? Luther was beating a dead horse here, because he didn't realize the extent of the bamboozling. The pope was like a mafia don!

By recognizing papal supremacy, he was unwittingly pledging continued obedience to the Roman Church system—hypnotized by the whole Jesus story. So he was playing on their created field.

In the interim of Luther's tribunal, his case received a series of reviews under what was called a *bull of condemnation.* It found that there were forty-one errors in Luther's teachings, and they gave him a sixty-day grace period for subjugating himself to the Church's authority, or face serious penalties. Wherein he then stood as a heretic, he could've decided to retract his objections and return to the Church in good standing, or risk being excommunicated, arrested and punished as a heretical traitor.

If anyone thought the Roman Catholic Church was about God and his love, the stance it took against Martin Luther for speaking his biblical truth, as explained above, should, at the very least, cause them to question this belief. Where in the scripture does God ordain man to punish? Does Romans 12:19 of <u>New Testament</u> scripture not say, "*Vengeance is mine; I will repay, saith the Lord*"? Please, please, please!

I'm so sorry that an educated man like Martin Luther didn't realize that the writings of Jesus' crucifixion and resurrection were being used as a hoax. Unfortunately his parents were church fanatics and that must've seeped into his pores as a young boy…it scatterbrained him. Even with his elite academic achievements, he was still crippled. He should not have stopped at challenging the Church's failures to comply with scripture; he should have gone all the way to challenging the very authority of the pope as well.

Now, in Rome, one called Professor Eck decided to assume the responsibility of prosecuting Luther, and during the next hearing, he asked Luther to identify some books as his own writings, and after Luther claimed ownership of books, the prosecution asked whether he intended to recant their blasphemous message. And again, Luther argued that they needed to prove by using scripture that his writings were in error. When they used the scripture to prove same, he would be the first to cast his books into a fire. Being unable to meet this challenge, the Church officials grew angry at his claim of elite scriptural knowledge above and beyond the Church; and they resented Luther's demands for straightforward answers as the condition upon which he would recant his position.

The Encyclopedia Britannica quotes Luther as having said:

> "*Unless I am convinced by the testimony of Scripture or by an evident reason (ratione evidente)—for I confide neither in the pope nor in the council alone, since it is certain that they have often erred and contradicted themselves—I am held fast by the Scriptures put forth by me, and my conscience is taken captive by God's word, and I neither can nor will revoke anything, seeing that it is not safe or right to act against conscience. God help me. Amen.*"

The trial ended in 1521 with the pope excommunicating Martin Luther and the emperor condemning him as an outlaw. By his effort here, at least Luther created an opportunity for people to have more biblical freedom to worship—without having to pay for spiritual slipups. But I must say that, notwithstanding Luther's arduous and exhaustive scholastic work, he made no progress in dissolving Rome's biblical fallacy. So basically, Luther's adamant resistance further advanced the Jesus hypocrisy.

He made the fundamental mistake of recognizing the bible as the revealed 'Word of God,' escalating a definitive ideology of an invisible God who created man, judged him sinful, and then sent Jesus Christ to die for his sins.

Luther's Legacy

Though the infallible credibility of the Roman Catholic Church suffered a serious blow from Martin Luther's assault, it did not lose much of anything. It merely had to tweak its operations and hope no more bombshell troublemakers cropped up to completely destroy 'The Faith.'

Ultimately, Luther created what is today known as the Lutheran Church, with offshoots of broad based evangelical churches. I suspect that Rome saw the whole thing as its legacy and cherished the sentiment; the sweet smelling flower of a religion most of humanity liked to savor.

Martin Luther is dead and gone after wasting his life in Roman bamboozle, he did not have the advantage of even great insight, but you do—stop wasting your time in the service of false sacredness.

CHAPTER EIGHT

THE DEAD SEA SCROLLS

ℜome's gliding wheel of bamboozle continues to turn rapidly with The Dead Sea Scrolls.

You may soon be scratching your head in confusion with this chapter—but try to remember that a good sense of history keeps people from avoidable confusion. Many people have only heard in passing about the information you are about to read, and little or no attention is paid to it; others have heard nothing.

Well, I have discovered that the Dead Sea Scrolls attest that Rome was nothing more than a mafia government pretending to be benevolent to people, and close to God. The history of the scrolls, and the people to whom they belonged, lived in the time Jesus and his disciples are said to have existed.

Note this miniature preamble of what Jews feel and think concerning Jesus:

> *"The labors of twenty centuries of pious churchmen have so completely obscured his genius and his humanity that it is well-nigh impossible to extricate the historical Jesus. Jews have known little of him and have wished to know less. Throughout their long history he was not, to them, the Prince of Peace, messenger of goodwill. In his name every conceivable outrage was perpetrated on the despised and cursed race that gave him life. When the crusaders set fire to Jewish villages, plundered Jewish homes, and outraged Jewish daughters, it was in the shadow of the cross they bore. Hounded from one land to another, burnt, hanged, spat upon, compelled to live in filthy ghettos and to wear degrading badges, denied the right to exist as human being, to work as others worked, to play as others played, in no country, in no age, at peace, all because of Christian bigotry, it was impossible for Jews to regard the prophet of Nazareth as other than the scourge of God, a fiend*

unmentionable." – **A History of the Jews by Abram Leon Sachar**

Once again, Christians, who do you believe tells the true story about Jesus, the Messiah? Well, if you are still cynical and undecided over the evidence, just read on, clarity could come along the way. I am convinced, as I am about to explain, that it was because Rome knew the New Testament was rife with conflicting and contradictory information that it sought to censor almost every publication of the Scrolls' content. Rome could not have that information undermine the Jesus story; the truth revealed in the scrolls could cost them centuries of ill-gotten gains. They relied on the ages of slumbering ignorance by Christians—this wise thinking kept Rome and the Vatican in business.

Hot Scrolls Report

By a stroke of good luck, these intriguing documents were found, and the process of publishing the material fell into the hands of a man who became the cat that guarded the milk, so to speak. I'm referring to the Vatican's Roman Catholic Father Roland de Vaux, who headed the international team that undertook the academic processing of the Scrolls.

As a participant in the affair, one Mr. Yigael Yadin, gave a piece on the 1967 events to British writer David Pryce-Jones, covering how the Scrolls project started, along with some insight into Father de Vaux's personality. Now things got off to a bad start, because he said de Vaux hated Jews with a strong passion, and without good reason. He was furious that the scrolls had fallen into the hands of the Israelis because of their recent war victories.

But this state of affairs was misleading, at best. Because regardless of the change in jurisdiction of the documents, the Israeli Department of Antiquities decided to leave Father de Vaux in charge of the Scroll project, with the stipulation that he expedite the process. I think this was a big mistake on the part of Israel. Why? We shall see.

An international committee of scholars was assembled to handle some eight hundred Scrolls, under Father de Vaux. De Vaux was apparently cloaked in a charming façade, which enabled him to form alliances among committee members, which supported his ulterior motives. As previously mentioned, the Catholic Church is owned by the equivalent of the Italian mafia—the Holy Roman Empire. He was a man who hated Israel as a political entity, and was inwardly anti-Semitic; he resented Jews attending his lectures. He was found to be ruthless, narrow-minded, bigoted and ferociously vindictive. Clearly this was not the appropriate individual to choose to handle these explosive Scrolls, but he was the chosen one.

Based on what we've seen thus far, this whole venture could not possibly be about authenticating Jesus being born in a manger, but it was certainly purported as such. As we proceed with this autopsy, let's keep weighing the matter of who has more credibility here; who do you believe? Jews or Rome? Let's see if this Father de Vaux's character exhibited the behavior you'd expect from a minister of Jesus Christ.

In 1953, de Vaux was president of the Rockefeller Museum's board of trustees. He made requests for nominations to be drawn from various foreign archaeological schools such as American, German, British and French. Funny enough though, the Hebrew University there had more well-trained staff to help out with the Scrolls, yet they were passed over by de Vaux—and no Israelis were invited either.

Do not separate the Roman Empire from Catholicism—remember that Constantine I, Emperor of Rome, was the first to interweave political secularism and ecclesiastical operations to rule people. So de Vaux was by no means working for the cause of Jesus Christ's Church as many believed. He was really there to protect the interests of Rome's work of fiction, put together as the holy bible.

He could not allow any member of the Israeli team to unravel the hoax of Christianity. In that endeavor, he chose as confidant Professor Frank Cross from McCormick Theological Seminary in the state of Chicago, then working with the Albright Institute in Jerusalem. The scholars nominated to the process were allowed to take on tasks that dealt in the subject matter of their areas of expertise. The distribution of work to the scholars was in no way arbitrary, but was given unnecessary supervision by de Vaux and Professor Cross.

Now here is a noteworthy point: Dr. Claus-Hunno Hunzinger was assigned a particular text known as the "War Scroll," with other materials transcribed on papyrus, not on parchment. For some mysterious reason, this guy left the team quite suddenly and was subsequently replaced by yet another French priest, Father Maurice Baillet. (I would give anything to know why Hunzinger left the team immediately after being assigned those materials—could he have discovered something sinister about de Vaux?)

Another nominee was Father Josef Milik, a close confidant of de Vaux who received an especially important corpus of material. It contained a number of Old Testament apocrypha. It also included pseudepigraphical writings–texts in which a later charlatan commentator gave authority to his words by attributing them to earlier prophets and patriarchs. Most importantly, these materials consisted of what was called "sectarian material," significant writings related to the community at Qumran, their teachings, rituals and disciplines.

The team proceeded well enough with de Vaux and his accomplices, until a British nominee, Mr. John Allegro, joined the team in Jerusalem. Suddenly de Vaux's world went into a tailspin, his dream turning into a nightmare, simply because Allegro happened to be a serious scholar, and of a non-religious ideological thread. He was working on his doctorate at Oxford, and was the only philologist in the group who had five publications in academic journals. In so far, he was unquestionably the most qualified in this field among his peers working on the scrolls. The others were on entry-level experience with the texts, basically trying to make a name for themselves.

Allegro—oh, I love his attitude—was assigned biblical commentaries, which turned out to be "sectarian material," the same kind allotted to Father Josef Milik, the Polish priest, and of course, you remember the previous emphasis I placed on the ones he got. This was a body of so-called "wisdom literature": psalms, hymns, exhortations and sermons of moral and poetic character. It just so happened that more explosive materials were given to Allegro than to any other member of the team—he had more experience. What made it interesting? Allegro, by inclination, was a real maverick, having no qualms about interrupting de Vaux's consensus with the other guys, which of course would later play a role in his expulsion from the team. John Strugnell, who at the time was enrolled in a doctorial program at Oxford, would replace him.

I feel it is imperative for zealous believers in Roman Catholicism and Christianity to pay very close attention to the behavior of monk de Vaux. Noting his conduct is crucial, because his actions, when observed, are one hundred percent antithetical to the apocryphal gospel of Jesus.

The entire stockpile of material was arranged in a large room, called the "Scrollery," and everyone had the liberty to drift about to see the progress of their colleagues, and could even help each other based on individual expertise.

Because he didn't play along well with the plan to manipulate the materials, Allegro became a pariah thanks to de Vaux's conniving strategy, but he remained adamant, until the time of his death, that vital and controversial material was kept on ice. And he was not alone. Another self-willed scholar who later joined the team reported that he received instructions in the 1960's to "go slow," to proceed in a half-hearted manner, "so that the crazies go away." De Vaux apparently wanted to avoid any embarrassment to the Christian establishment, because that is exactly what the Qumran material was capable of doing. It seems De Vaux used every trick he could to stall the processing and publication of the scrolls.

Every description I've read of de Vaux's supervision of the scrolls reveals secularized prestige, deviousness and devilish monopoly, nothing sacred about the process. And the atmosphere he created at the Rockefeller and the Scrollery room was very elitist and exclusionist; so much so, that it was clear to those on the periphery that a dishonest operation was going on.

If I've shown nothing else thus far in this book, I have definitely shown that ecclesiastical abuse by priests is not at all an unusual occurrence; hardly surprising to find this type of thing took place in the Roman Catholic domain—after all, the Empire defined itself by means of well thought out schemes, and abusive subjugation. Every move de Vaux made with the scrolls was to cover up schemes to maintain control of the people. And although he took the position of not wanting to embarrass the Christian community, it was more an obsession with protecting the power of the Roman Catholic establishment.

Let me illustrate why it is evident that the processing of the Dead Sea Scrolls was unnecessarily prolonged over decades. Note a stark contrast with a similar project overseen by Father de Vaux's counterpart, Professor James B. Robinson from Claremont Graduate School in California. He directed a team that translated texts found in the Egyptian desert of Hammadi.

After the texts were handed over to his international team in 1966, draft transcriptions and translations were made available to scholars within *three years*! And by 1973, the entire Nag Hammandi library was drafted in English, and in circulation among interested researchers. By 1977, all Nag Hammandi codices were published, making a total of forty-six books plus some unidentified fragments. Therefore it took Professor Robinson eleven years to have the whole Nag Hammandi scrolls translated and in print. In direct contrast to de Vaux, there were no reports of Robinson having some ax to grind over the texts he supervised.

Father de Vaux's international team formed in 1953, with the stated mission to publish all scrolls found at Qumran, a series to be issued by Oxford University Press entitled: *"Discoveries in the Judaean Desert of Jordan."* In two years, the first volume was released from what was officially designated as Cave 1, but the second volume didn't emerge until six years later, in 1961, and it had nothing to do with the Qumran text at all. In 1963, a third volume appeared, which dealt with scrolls from about seven of the Caves.

> *"In the meantime, however, the bulk of the most copies and most significant material—the material found in the veritable treasure trove of Cave 4—continued to be withheld from both the public and the academic community."* **- The Dead Sea Scrolls Deception by Michael Baigent and Richard Leigh**

We now know that the gem of the scrolls was found in Cave #4, for over time, small tantalizing fragments made their way into scholarly journals.

But it wasn't until 1968 that the official publication on Cave #4's contents appeared, and it's worth mentioning that it was a small portion of information; which would probably never have been published had it not been for de Vaux's defector, John Allegro.

The delay in the processing of the Qumran material continued until folks began to notice the length of time between published volumes. Curiosity bells went ringing. Critics began voicing serious concerns and speculating about the reason for the delay.

To sum it all up, here's the gist of it: It took Professor James B. Robinson and his team eleven years to complete the Nag Hammandi scrolls translation project; while on the other hand, thirty-eight years passed since de Vaux's international team began working, but from 1953 to 1991 only about twenty-five percent of the whole collection had been completed!

Father de Vaux used time to sedate everyone, thereby offsetting the full effect of the incriminating scrolls right into oblivion. The Romans had planted the artificial ideology of Jesus, near the latter end of the B.C. era, and the Qumran folks were residents of Israel when Jesus and his disciples supposedly roamed the streets of Jerusalem. But de Vaux was charged with keeping the root firmly in place. He realized the value of the Scrolls collection, and to protect the church's interest, Cave #4's materials must never be published. Should that information be published, the ubiquitous religion established by the Roman Empire would come undone. Over two millennia of the most lucrative entrepreneurships would disappear. Yes, it would evaporate because everyone would come to know that there was no such thing as a Jewish messiah called Jesus Christ who raised the dead, walked on water, turned water into wine, etc.

We are circa 2010, nearly half-a-century since the Scrolls project began—who has been talking about the importance of the Dead Sea Scrolls? Or even the subject in general? No one. Christians are still looking for Christ's return.

An interview by Professor Robert Eisenman, a biblical historian and scholar, was published in the New York Times in the early nineties and confirms that one of the reasons they were able to carry out the suppression of some of the Scrolls was because of the many eager students who were more than willing to sit in prestigious academic chairs. De Vaux had his pick, with all the wind blowing in his direction.

In an interview with the New York Times, Frank Cross, one of de Vaux's appointees, agreed that the processing of the Scrolls had been slow, and gave two reasons for it: 1) most members of the team held full-time teaching jobs and could only get into Jerusalem to work on the Scrolls during summer holidays; and 2) the materials that have yet to be published were badly fragmented, making them difficult to organize, much less translate; he referred to them as the world's most fantastic jig-saw puzzle.

If we rate Cross' explanation from one to ten, with one being no belief, and ten being full belief, I give it a whopping one! Why? Well, his responses are clearly rubbish. Remember, there were highly qualified Israeli scholars that monk de Vaux refused to let dust the Scrolls, much less translate and assist with them. These were qualified and willing helpers yet the Scrolls sat for so many years, waiting for sporadic summertime attendant students? Come on, seriously? The excuses offered by Frank Cross are depressing when all things are considered. And only in extreme, fanatical religious faith can his explanations be accepted.

Another significant aspect is how de Vaux could so easily publish misleading information. Robert Eisenman tells of the sophistry employed to feed the public with rubbish.

From what I've learned, Eisenman was the first to defect the team, and give vital insight as to de Vaux's machinations. And the serious question remains: Why after decades have Cave #4's documents not been released? Do you think Father de Vaux would behave in such an underhanded manner for nothing? No need to speculate about his motives; we've had at least two insiders (the witness of two people is true in most instances) who tell us plainly what really went on among the team members.

They would have us believe that these materials are redundant, repeats of the Old Testament scriptures we already know, perhaps with some minor alterations, but nothing radically new. They want us to consider the material insignificant.

I feel it is a real tragedy that, since the Scrolls were revealed, Christians continue to hold firmly to a belief in Jesus, and are still preaching the "gospel" of an assumed Apostle named Paul. Evidence should not be taken with a grain of salt.

Where is civilization headed?

Allegro the Maverick

John Allegro was the only member of the team to publish all the work assigned to him and, thus far, the only one to break with the team's conspiratorial deception, insisting on telling the truth contained in the scrolls, to the best of his knowledge.

Allegro was the one on the "Lord's side" here—yet the church sought to destroy him and cover up. An examination of Allegro's eloquent delivery on the subject of the scrolls shows that he was very competent, the most qualified of the group. There is nothing in his portfolio that remotely implies he had any aberrational bent, or was someone who sought selfish admiration, or had esoteric interests—zilch, nada, zip.

I feel so much respect for Allegro, and envy the opportunity that was presented to him. He was a gallant guy fighting with what he had, but because a polarizing secular/religious environment surrounded him, he was totally victimized by it. There should've been a different outcome, even unto the death! Read on for a good look at what happened.

Not Everyone Sleeps

In 1955, author Edmund Wilson wrote a lengthy article to the New Yorker raising suspicion on the Scrolls process, which alerted the public something was wrong.

> "As early as 1955, Wilson detected a desire on the part of the "expert" to distance the Qumran scrolls from both Judaism and Christianity." - **The Dead Sea Scrolls Deception by Michael Baigent and Richard Leigh**

It seemed to him that the "experts" were protesting too vehemently, and this aroused his suspicions. He noted that as soon as one set out to study the controversy caused by the scrolls, there was tension, which indicated an ulterior motive.

He also observed that the scrolls were vital to shedding light and making a connection between rabbinical Judaism, as it was budding in first century A.D., and how it juxtaposed with the earliest forms of Christianity; there was a noticeable reluctance between Judaic and Christian-oriented scholars to delve into the connection. One would like to see these problems discussed, he said.

> "If in any case we look now at Jesus in the perspective supplied by the scrolls, we can trace a new continuity and, at least, get some sense of the drama that culminated in Christianity…The monastery [of Qumran]… is perhaps, more Bethlehem or Nazareth, the cradle of Christianity." - **The Dead Sea Scrolls Deception by Michael Baigent and Richard Leigh**

The people to whom the Billy Grahams of the world preach the gospel are the ones who are most deserving of the efforts to support inner confidence once they have accepted the faith.

But in de Vaux's treatment of the Qumran Scrolls the contrary is true, as it reverberates in the following statement: "For it was Wilson who gave precise and succinct expression to the very issues the international team endeavored so diligently to avoid." - **The Dead Sea Scrolls Deception by Michael Baigent and Richard Leigh**

Rome: Not Afraid to Kill

Let's not leave any stone unturned on this issue. The episode that took place between John Allegro and de Vaux's international team is crucial. Allegro tried to shine a light on a centuries-old truth being hidden by Rome. Present day society suffers greatly as a result.

Arnold A. Rogow:

> *"As long ago as 1817 important privileges were conferred by law on those Jews who consented to embrace Christianity. Land was gratuitously bestowed upon them, where they settled, under the name of The Society of Israelitish Christians."* – **Jews in a Gentile World**

It was for the cause of Christianity that Rome destroyed Israel in 70 A.D. and displaced Jews around the world. And this ultimately led to six million of them being victims of Hitler's gas chambers.

Now, let's examine some of the reasons they wanted John Allegro's blood. In this saga, Allegro was made into a victim, and de Vaux was the victimizer, representing the Catholic Church. Though times have progressed and become more civilized, we can agree that things are not as they were back in the 13th and 14th centuries, when the social environment allowed for the Inquisition to adjudicate murder. However, we have not made the kind of progress that is needed.

Modern intelligence has retained all of the evil products (imaginary God, Jesus, Mary and purgatory, etc.), and the Roman Catholic Church still dominates world religion—they are still in business.

The trouble started when Allegro made comments to one of the pack, John Strugnell, who had ministry ambitions. I think Allegro made a tactical mistake opening himself up to John without reservation. But he should not be blamed, though, for trusting because he was unassuming of any ulterior motives. He peeked Strugnell's interest and invoked his religious bias when he said:

"Recent study of my fragments has convinced me that Dupont-Summer is more right than he knew." He naïvely jesters and said: "Should not worry about that theological job, if I were you: by the time I have finished there won't be any Church left for you to join." - **The Dead Sea Scrolls Deception by Michael Baigent and Richard Leigh**

Such a statement by Allegro was tantamount to playing with fire, but he never knew it.

Allegro aired a television special on the Scrolls in the U.K. in 1956. After the show aired, the headline read: *"CHRISTIAN BASES SEEN IN SCROLLS"* followed by:

"The origin of some Christian ritual and doctrine can be seen in the documents of an extremist Jewish sect that existed for more than 100 years before the birth of Jesus Christ. This is the interpretation placed on the "fabulous" collection of the Dead Sea Scrolls by one of an international team of seven scholars...John Allegro...said last night in a broadcast that the historical basis of the Lord's Supper and part at least of the Lord's prayer and the New Testament teaching of Jesus were attributable to the Qumranians."

At this point in February 1956, serious damage was done to Christianity, and it was like the roof had been blown off the house. Even if Rome had to kill this guy, they had to do something to restore confidence in the minds of die-hard Christians. So they warned that there would be opposition to what Allegro had broadcast. And it's laughable that three American religious leaders, not members of the Scrolls team in Jerusalem, came forth to refute Allegro.

There objective was to dispel any ideas that linked the Qumran sect to the so-called Essenes' of Christianity. De Vaux received complaints with requests that he do something about the state of affairs.

Allegro was the first to write de Vaux on February 9, 1956 about the brewing conflicts. He had heard that two of his colleagues were preparing rebuffs to his statements and, wanting peace and calm, he made it quite clear to de Vaux, *"I am not waging any war against the Church, and if I were, you may rest assured I would let any loopholes in...I stand by everything I said in my three talks but I am quite prepared to believe that there may be other interpretations of my readings."*

De Vaux responded the following month, warning Allegro of serious rebuttal, and a letter to The Times in London, signed by all members of his international team. Their letter arrived on March 16, 1956, bearing four signatures, including de Vaux's. Indeed Allegro had never intended to hurt his professional credibility, only to be left standing forlorn, with the truth in hand.

In essence, the team asserted that based on the scrolls inventory in Jerusalem, they were unable to see any validity in the "findings" made by Mr. Allegro. They essentially made the brilliant, intellectual John Allegro look like someone who was having a nervous breakdown:

> *"It is our conviction that either he has misread the text or he has built up a chain of conjectures which the materials do not support."*

Not Without a Fight

Allegro, facing the viciousness of his fellow scholars, shifted into self-defense mode, and came out swinging. Oh, I love it! In a letter to The Times, Allegro replied in his own defense: *"In the phraseology of the New Testament in this connection we find many points of resemblance to Qumran literature, since the sect also was looking for the coming of a Davidic Messiah who would arise with the priest in the last days. It is in this sense that Jesus 'fits into a well-defined messianic (not "Essenic" as I was wrongly quoted...).' There is nothing particularly new or striking in the idea."*

On that declarative point, Allegro's position was well-founded, and put de Vaux's position in trouble, but the gallant was not through flexing his muscles. It is said that they squabbled this way until March 8, 1957, when Allegro took on scholar Strugnell. Allegro knew he had a smoking gun and just needed at least one more confederate, which would boost attention, and likely usher in a new generation that no longer wondered whether Jesus was real.

> *"You still do not seem to understand what you did in writing a letter to a newspaper in an attempt to smear the words of your own colleague. It was quite unheard of before, an*

unprecedented case of scholarly stabbing in the back. And, laddie, don't accuse me of over-dramatizing the business. I was here in England...Reuters' man that morning on the phone to me was classic: 'But I thought you scholars stuck together...' And when it was realized that in fact you were quoting things I never said, the inference was plain. This letter was not in the interests of scholarly science at all, but to calm the fears of the Roman Catholics of America...And what it all boiled down to was that you guys did not agree with the interpretation I put on certain text—where I have quite as much chance of being right as you. Rather than argue it out in the journals and scholarly works, you thought it earlier to influence public opinion by a scurrilous letter to a newspaper. And you have the neck to call it scholarship. Dear boy, you are very young yet, and have much to learn."

This volcanic lava burned Strugnell's conscience. His scroll production quality could not compare to that of John Allegro. The nature of the information being hovered over and protected by the international team came to light in the following attack letter:

"In June 1956, for example, a Jesuit commentator published in the Irish Digest an article entitled, "The Truth about the Dead Sea Scrolls." He attacked Wilson, Dupont-Summer, and especially Allegro. He then went on to make the extraordinary statement that the 'scrolls add surprisingly little to no knowledge of the doctrines current among the Jews from, say, 200 BC to the Christian era.' He concluded in a positively inflammatory fashion: 'It was not from such a sect that "Jesus learned how to be the Messiah"...Rather, it was from soil such as this that sprang the thorns which tried to choke the seed of the Gospel."- **The Dead Sea Scrolls Deception by Michael Baigent and Richard Leigh**

The bamboozling was at its highest temperature, and Allegro was too cognizant of what de Vaux, et al. was safeguarding, and he committed in his heart to stop the conspiracy to perpetrate a contrived religion.

Now, although he was bruised in the first round of the dispute, Allegro still pursued the issue over what is called the "Copper Scroll" found in Cave #3 at Qumran in 1952. Two sections of the fragments comprised the Copper Scrolls, which were not opened for three and one half years. Both fragments were received in Manchester in January 1956, were hastily opened and expeditiously translated. One piece contained a list of secret sites where the treasure of the Temple of Jerusalem was allegedly buried.

The translations piggybacked the fragments and were sent immediately into Jerusalem—but the "expeditious effort" was thwarted by deliberate delays. Yes, hesitation to publish these scrolls involved three primary concerns. First, if the Scrolls' information were to be made public, and leads of the hidden treasures were circulated, interested parties may go after it, and most of what may be found could disappear into the black market. Second, de Vaux and his team worried that the treasure spoken of in the Copper Scrolls may indeed exist, as tangible treasures verses imaginary ones.

And if it turned out to be real treasure, the Israeli government would certainly assert a claim, which could kindle a political crisis. The third concern was that the treasure, if real, would have theological ramifications as well…

De Vaux and the international team wrongly depicted the Qumran community as an isolated, closed society with no political aspirations. Furthermore, if any connections were established between buried treasure and the Jerusalem Temple, all hell would break loose. If Qumran proved to be an accessory to an enlarged magnificence, it could compromise the very origin of Christianity. No doubt de Vaux would have a stroke if these Copper Scrolls referred to a *real* treasure, in that it would have to be a fortune removed from the Temple in 66 A.D.

Revelations like this would've also destroyed the "safe" dating and chronology the international team recognized as a large part of the Scrolls. Expectations among the members of the team were high. John Allegro was in the process of publishing a book, a general introduction to the Qumran material. It was scheduled for release with Penguin Books in 1956, and was expected to incite great interest by revealing the existence of the Copper Scrolls and their significance. But the book was aborted in consideration of the possible detrimental effects of its release.

Allegro cooperated amicably simply because the "prestigious" international team would diminish the importance of the Scrolls through sheer fabrication; after all a scholarly confederacy had formed to undermine truthful revelations.

Jozef Milik, a polish biblical scholar, was the man to whom these particular Scrolls were entrusted. He began releasing statements devaluing their significance.

In a letter to another colleague in April 23, 1956, Allegro expressed his irritation about what was happening. It's a pity he didn't know that he was communicating with yet another backstabber; he naively believed they were on the same page. Allegro took jabs at Milik, saying: *"Heaven alone knows when, if ever, our friends in Jerusalem are going to release the news of the copper scroll. It's quite fabulous; just imagine the agony of having to let my [book] go to press without being able to breathe a word of it?"*

Nothing new was generated from this letter, though it was a calculated attempt to blow a disruptive wind; but nothing was stirred, so Allegro seemed to become a bit pessimistic, figuring that de Vaux's manipulation of the team members ran deep, so he tried to circumvent further plans for delaying the material.

He sent a letter with a diplomatic message to the man in charge of the Jordanian Department of Antiquities, Gerald L. Harding; who was also a colleague of de Vaux's. Tapping into a common concern for the international team members was a good tactic to turn the currents in Allegro's direction. In that vein, he suggested to Harding that when the Copper Scrolls were released reporters would descend *en masse*; that rather than face that potential situation, it would behoove the team, and everyone involved, to close ranks and adopt a "party line" front to the media.

I imagine that as he waited for Harding's reply, Allegro must have been thinking, *As a non-Christian, why am I having to fight with the holy people about the release of information that can confirm Jesus' resurrection and faith?*

As you can guess, de Vaux put Harding on notice about Allegro, the supposed heretic. And so it came to pass that on May 28, 1956, Harding wrote back as one having an anointed tongue; as one blessed by Lord de Vaux himself, saying: *"The treasure listed in the 'Copper Scroll' didn't appear to be connected with the Qumran community at all. Nor could it possibly be a real cache – the value of the items cited was too great. The 'Copper Scroll' was merely a collection of 'buried treasure' legends."*

But can we believe anything coming from a person whom de Vaux had filled with warped and distorted information?

Some four days later, on June 1st, the official press release regarding the Copper Scroll was issued, which echoed Harding's declarations. Allegro was flabbergasted, and expressed his reaction to Harding; he wanted to keep the lines of communication open. He discouraged a few others from the gossip that the Roman Catholic brethren of the team might be hiding something contained in the Copper Scroll that the public had a right to know.

Allegro held out hope that Jozef Milik would release the official translation of whatever they intended for the Copper Scrolls, as Allegro's book was to be published thereafter. But unexpectedly, and without good cause, they postponed it again, which seemed like yet another contrived delay.

Then Allegro was asked to delay the publication of his long awaited book. Who made this request? One of de Vaux's team surrogates, whose name remains anonymous for legal reasons, which suggests there would've been undesirable consequences if the unnamed didn't capitulate to de Vaux's wishes.

Knowing that they were up to no good, and being the kind of person Allegro was, he published his book anyway. But the book didn't have the kind of impact it should've had since the translation of the Copper Scrolls did not precede it. The team had now closed ranks against Allegro, using reverse psychology by blaming him unjustly for the delay! Under this sham, the team claim for themselves grounds to effectively alienate Allegro, at a time when they badly needed a legitimate excuse to cover up their underhanded actions.

It would be two years after the release of Allegro's book, in 1962, that Milik's translation of the 'Copper Scroll' would appear.

It is clear from all angles that John Allegro had de Vaux on the ropes—I wish I'd been at his side back then. What could I have added? I would've given him some spiking rhetoric to really expose the teams' suppression of information.

It was still inconceivable to Allegro that he would never again be accepted back into the fold after all that had happened. He was quite naïve to the dark underbelly of Christianity, so he returned to Jerusalem, right back into the Scrollery room to work on his materials, and for a time it seemed he was reconciled with the international team members. But Allegro would soon come to realize that de Vaux was incensed against him for so-called opposition to the work of Jesus Christ.

With inspiring energy, Allegro arranged a television appearance on the BBC about the scrolls. The plan progressed well, with the blessings of the Jordanian curator in charge of the Rockefeller Museum. But one more person of interest needed to be on board, and that was the sinister de Vaux. Would he give his approval? Well, he gave the following paraphrased response: "*I called a meeting with my scholars, and they agreed to have nothing to do with anything you have to do with.*" He further said, "*I cannot stop you from taking pictures of the monastery at Qumran, but you will not be given access to the Scrollery or the Museum generally.*"

Two things jump out at me from de Vaux's statements. First is the revelation that he and his Christian scholars disdained Allegro so much they wanted nothing to do with him, and for obvious reasons; had it not been for him they would have suppressed even more information.

Secondly, de Vaux himself wanted as little of the Scrolls' information made public as possible. He was gasping for breath as it was; the public had already been alerted to too much. But for the most part he kept his calm because, contrary to what he wanted the public to believe, he knew for certain there was no God looking down from heaven watching the sins he was committing. He knew there was no Judgment Day in his future, where he would have to answer for them and face eternal damnation. And he had to be pretty sure that the Jesus belief had been rooted deeply enough in societies around the world, in government policies and churches, to withstand any evidence to the contrary. He knew the belief was strong enough to weather the storm.

De Vaux would discover, though, that he did not have complete control of everything in the world, as he could not prevent Allegro's BBC show from going forward. The team tried to influence Awni Dajani, curator of the Palestine Archaeological Museum, to have Allegro dropped from the cast! And they anonymously left a £150 payoff in exchange for not photographing the Amman Museum.

John Allegro invited Cross to be on the program as well, but after consulting with de Vaux, he refused.

So my readers, what do you make of all this? Is there indeed a straight gate or a narrow road whereby one can enter into the kingdom of heaven? If so, will Father de Vaux and the Christian scholars reach God on such a road of purity?

John Allegro grew so sick of the corruption that he decided to use whatever influence he had left to attack the team about specific problems. On this occasion he targeted whatever information he believed Milik, Strugnell and Starcky were sitting on.

> *"From the way the publication of the fragments is being planned, the non-Catholic members of the team are being removed as quickly...In fact, so vast is Milik's, Starcky's and Strugnell's lots of 4Q [Cave 4 material], I believe that they should be split up immediately and new scholars brought in to get the stuff out quickly...a dangerous situation is fast developing where the original idea of an international and interdenominational editing group is being bypassed. All fragments are brought first to De V. or Milik, and, as with cave Eleven, complete secrecy is kept over what they are, still long after they have been studied by this group."*

In 1956, literary critic Edmond Wilson favorably reviewed Allegro's popular book on the Scrolls, and expounded in his own publication on the issue. He said that the Scrolls were no longer a mere question of "tension" and "inhibition," but assumed proportions of a cover-up and scandal. Wilson brought to light the confession of a Catholic scholar who observed that earlier on, it was an official policy to award biased scholarships in order to minimize the importance of the Scrolls. By the mid 1970's, biblical scholars were speaking openly of it as a scandal as well, such as British scholar, Dr. Geza Vermes. He also published statements of deep consternation on the matter of how long it was taking the team to publish the Scrolls. On the thirtieth anniversary of their discovery, he said:

> *"The world is entitled to ask the authorities responsible for the publication of the Qumran scrolls...what they intend to do about this lamentable state of affairs. For unless drastic measures are taken at once, the greatest and the most valuable of all Hebrew and Aramaic manuscript discoveries is likely to become the academic scandal **par excellence** of the twentieth century."*

De Vaux and his international team paid no attention to Dr. Vermes' call. And he called them to account again for their negligence, but this time he did it in the *Times Literary Supplement*. Vermes recounted key points of the initial exposé and expressed regret that they failed to respond to his plea, and added: *"And the present chief editor of the fragments has in the meantime gone on the record as one who rejects as unjust and unreasonable any criticism regarding the delay."*

Readers, see if you can understand and feel my pain, sympathize with my frustrated and anger over this matter, and the way it has affected world society.

After thirty years, folks were still trying to obtain information as yet unpublished. No excuse for them not being in the public domain after so long can be valid. How important is this information? Many may wonder why people should have it in the first place. Well, it is of an untold value to the millions of people living their daily lives in bondage to the belief that by living under specific rituals, they are connected to God. Thousands of clergymen are sitting in million dollar homes, bought with the sacrificial giving of very poor believers—in the name of Jesus Christ.

So do they have a right to know the truth? Of course they do, whether or not they would act upon it by discontinuing their contributions to churches, that's their prerogative. But without question, people have an autonomous right to be informed on the matter.

Look, the scrolls and the interest therein trace back to the root notion that Jesus was God, the Messiah and Savior. To me, the Scrolls debacle drew a line in the sands of time, and too many people are overlooking their significance.

There is much at stake here, because the governments of the United States and Great Britain, among many other countries, are run on Roman secular and ecclesiastic ideology, under the idea of a non-factual God story used to woo people under a spell. Allegro's fight was a sign that the Roman Catholic Church is not real, and everything in history confirms that this entity is full of petrifying sores, the inventor of a Jesus epic that is completely bogus. Jesus Christ as savior of the world is a Roman forgery. Power-thirsty Rome seized upon an opportunity to fashion the Jesus icon.

For his persistence over the years that he tried to bring the Scroll's information to the public, John Allegro was a true hero, a man who had championed a worthy cause on behalf of humanity. One year before his death in 1987, he affirmed that the international team's delay with Scrolls was 'pathetic and inexcusable' and made no bones about how for years his colleagues had put their feet up on the Scrolls:

> *"There is no doubt ... that the evidence from the scrolls undermines the uniqueness of the Christians as a sect ... In fact we know damn all about the origins of Christianity. However, these documents do lift the curtain."*

My heart swells when I read these words. John Allegro fought the good fight and has my deepest respect. Bless his soul if it lives.

Father de Vaux's treatment of John Allegro in the handling of the Scrolls process speaks strongly of this truth. Nothing more needs be said.

CHAPTER NINE

❧

WHO WAS BISHOP JAMES?

The New Testament portrays the apostle James as gentle and dutiful, entirely concerned with matters that pertain to believers and to the kingdom of heaven. The five chapters of his Book are replete with trite generalities, exhortations about grace, wisdom, endurance, and temptation, the tongue of fire, the world of iniquity and lust. These sayings are attributed to someone called James, but in all good conscience, any talented writer could have written these things, at any time in antiquity, right? How could we tell the difference?

I declare that there is no power in assumed faith that makes up for all the missing information on these biblical images—they need to have detailed and real biographies. For these biblical caricatures to carry any significance as people who actually existed, they must be authenticated. This is established by proper name, place and time. A verifiable identity has never been established for biblical icons such as James, in whom we are asked to believe wholeheartedly.

We have never had one vouchsafe authentication for James (except for a slight reference to him being the Lord's brother in the gospels) or any other epistle of the New Testament. And so far, only the Catholic Church is certain that James and the other biblical authors wrote these so-called scriptures.

The overall image painted of James is low-key. He's fashioned as a mature bishop over the church flock. His presence and influence is reflected in a rebellion that broke out in the Antioch church, referred to in the Book of Acts 15:13–21.

Before I share an excerpt of James' dictum with you, please bear in mind the problems surrounding this individual, and what must have been the reason for Father de Vaux's being hell bent on censoring the Dead Sea Scrolls. Listen to the tone of James' letter, in which he addressed the issue of people not obeying the rituals of Moses:

> *"And after they had held their peace, James answered, saying; Men and brethren, hearken unto me: Simeon has declared how God at the first did visit the Gentiles, to take out of them a people for his name. And to this agree the words of the prophets; as it is written, after this I will return, and will build again the tabernacle of David, which is fallen down; and I will build again the ruins thereof, and I will set it up: That the residue of man might seek after the Lord, and all the Gentiles, upon whom my name is called, said the Lord, who doeth all these things."* - **Acts 15:13-17**

With that said, James concluded that no one compelled Gentiles to keep the laws of Moses, because God, so to speak, ordained their exemption, in the words of the prophet, from keeping those laws.

James said such a thing? If all were indeed well with the record, and if the things attributed to James in the New Testament were consistent with the events of the time, what need did de Vaux have for inhibiting qualified scholars from even seeing the Dead Sea Scrolls, not to mention transcribing and publishing them?

The information found there is crucially relevant to the accounts of early Christianity; specifically as it pertains to the church hierarchy, its orthodoxy and practices. It all links profoundly to the Qumran brethren.

So on this basis, I find the apostle James to be no different from a cartoon character, and all scripture attributed to him completely unfounded. We don't need to wonder why there is no biography to be found in James' portion of the New Testament. Why? Because Rome covered up information in the Scrolls that filled this vacancy, essentially reducing biblical ferocity.

This makes the New Testament a terrible embarrassment, like a decomposing wound that one must place an antiseptic cloth over to hide it from public view!

And now we know whom Bishop James, the Lord's brother really was: a fictional medium.

The Religion of Hallucination

As I go along, I see more and more revealing evidence of a religious scam. It is very difficult to understand how the story of Jesus Christ could be untrue, because many of us have grown up with it as a clear fact of history. But as I've been saying, we need to seek verification of history, and that requires our serious attention.

Let me show you how clear it is in my view right now, at least by making one broad point: Christianity was specifically designed to use psychological means as its modus operandi, to create a "hallucination" of the mass consciousness. Hallucination means to have an apparent perception, as by sight or hearing, for which there is no real external cause—illusion or false notions.

There are trillions of things that everyday church people can't explain; it is all a phantom. Rome's mantra is "see a little or you won't be able to see at all." Under such a mental state, one is inclined to become quite scrumptious; unable to get enough of what you can't explain, and in most cases you don't desire to comprehend it. Think how easily we become blind, gullible and then deluded, because our minds are programmed to hallucinate false notions as though they were real.

The nature of a hallucination is that you don't know you are hallucinating. When you realize it, you are no longer hallucinating and the spell is broken. Make sure you are not hallucinating. Be sober. Process these issues correctly.

I know this is all very hard to swallow—it might feel strange, because we have been so enamored with religious faith, never having an inkling that we may not be seeing things as they really are.

Let me just say this before moving on to the great Apostle Paul: Usually when we think of a hallucination, we think of a person being close to a comatose or catatonic state, but taking direct note of the definition, it describes a mental disorder that affects functional people. A hallucination is a type of disorder that sober people should beware of, because it happens to normal folks almost daily. Just think of the many times that normal men single or married (even men of the cloth) murder or do bodily harm to a spouse or girlfriend in the heat of the moment. It's as simple as straying on thoughts that are false.

How many times have we gone to church and left under heavier spells than before—oh, it happens everyday! And there are countless examples I could cite to highlight the linguistic sense of the word, but I think the point is clear.

The Charismatic Apostle Paul

I want to call this guy Dr. Saul of Tarsus. His name was changed to Paul with Christian conversion, a pattern, if you took notice, which started with Father Abraham.

All of Christendom reveres Paul as the greatest apostle, because he handled himself as one with superior wits much beyond his peers. He was grandfathered into the apostleship according to his sensational conversion story in the narrative. Saul of Tarsus was not of the group Jesus had ordained.

Paul is described as both refined and idealistic in his vision of the church. He had a passionate fervor of benevolence. He could delineate ideas without distorting proper context, and was apparently well poised and very compelling.

Upon inspection, we can see that the things Paul was most adamant about, the things he used as justification for departing from the laws of Moses, were the very reasons for the problem Rome knew the Dead Sea Scrolls could impeach—undermining the very words of the great Apostle Paul.

Now the Scrolls inform us of Jews who sided with the Roman Empire's occupation of Israel, including the priesthood element—and this understanding places Paul's role into context for us. This is where it becomes clear how Rome used Jews who were interested in making life easier for themselves to advance its ambitions.

This is a key discovery. It gives great insight into, and unravels, Rome's biblical scheme.

In this spirit of cooperation, Saul of Tarsus feigned his defection from a prestigious position, as officer of the Sanhedrin counsel, and became a so-called born again Christian. This was a guy who was a shrewd double agent diplomat.

I once wore an assumptive, faith-believing fedora, holding the great Apostle Paul in the highest esteem. Well, I no longer wear that silly fedora. I have great justification for changing my previous view and acceptance of the Apostle Paul—let me show you.

To remind you, we have good grounds upon which to question the literal reality of Adam's fall from grace, and the divine plan to redeem his children from the resulting curse. The specialness of Abraham and his lineage is basically an empty myth, along with all the prophesies, doctrines, etc. Man is not born a sinner! This is a default belief we must scrutinize and see why it has taken root in our consciousness.

The character called Paul, once an ardent follower of the laws of Moses, suffered a psychological eclipse suddenly while on the road to Damascus—purportedly powered from above. He then awakened from his trans-like state of mind to find he was blind. Through psychic communication, his name was called in a warning tone, "Saul...Saul," and when he answered he was told, "It is me, Jesus, you are persecuting; it is hard for you to fight against me." Paul replied, "What now, Lord, am I to do?" And Jesus gave him instructions to proceed to a city in Damascus, at which point further instructions would be given to him.

Take note that he was sent to the city, but not to a designated address. However, Jesus spoke to Ananias, the blessed one, and sent him to go in search of Paul at a specific house in the city. (We do not know how Paul knew to go to this house.) Ananias then told Jesus that he was afraid of Paul because he persecuted those who called on his name.

But in a surprising twist, Jesus admonished him saying, "Fear nothing. Paul you are a chosen vessel unto me (of course, it is really unto Rome) to carry my name before Gentiles and kings, and the children of Israel.

The narrative then charts that Ananias found Paul at the house, laid hands on him and filled him with the Holy Ghost. Instantly scales fell from his eyes, and his sight was restored! Paul arose and was baptized. Paul had purportedly gone three days without a meal before his arrival, and so he grabbed a bite to eat.

After a few days with the brethren in Damascus, he entered the synagogue and debuted his preaching career, proclaiming Jesus Christ was the Son of God.

Can you smell the recipe to make converts for posterity?

When you read the writings said to be that of Paul's, it clearly reveals undercurrents of problems with the rank and file of the church hierarchy. The Community Rule found in the Qumran scrolls, revealed things that Paul's writings hints at, but glosses over.

In the first book of Galatians, Paul talks about how his conversion happened—and it's a carbon copy of the Qumran Sectarian Community document. Another interesting observation is seen in Jesus' ordination of twelve disciples. And after Judas fell out, the other apostles got together, cast lots and chose a replacement.

Now, out of nowhere, the man who was Saul of Tarsus, and later turned Paul, self-gratuitously crowns himself as of the Apostles of Jesus Christ! He stealthily joins the twelve, becoming known as the thirteenth apostle, not disciple. As such, we can question how a man who was never included in the original group with Jesus suddenly became equal to the twelve graduate apostles? This Paul character just seized an Apostle rank on the basis of a mysterious encounter, a subliminal chat with Jesus. Further, Paul subjected himself to the Qumran Community for three years for freshman orientation.

Now here is the smoking gun. The New Testament presents a quandary by showing Jesus as not being political, but as being a spiritual revolutionary; as the prophets foretold that God would do strange things through the coming messiah—and that the Old Covenant, Moses' law, would be done away with.

Now the New Testament gospels presented Jesus as one who scoffed at the Jewish status quo regarding practices like observing the Sabbath day, the death penalty for adultery, etc…The New Testament also indicates that there was a team spirit among the apostles and disciples. But I find Paul's quandary with the church leadership and general clergy body contradictory to the already stable unity among the apostles and disciples.

I think this constitutes a snafu in the biblical narrative, evoking a few questions: 1) should all of these hand-picked and ordained dignitaries of Jesus embrace Moses' law, which contradicted what their Messiah taught them? Let's hone in on this: Peter, James and many other believers were of Jesus' stable, they received the New Testament fulfillment tenets and knew the doctrine Jesus left them to preach very well; 2) how could it be possible that Jesus would reveal different tenets to an outsider named Paul (formerly Saul) over matters of keeping the law Moses gave?

Under this condition, the Roman Catholic Christian church is wiped out completely—with no antidote available to save it.

To those who may oppose my view of Paul's hypocrisy, I say this: if there is proof that Paul was not working with Rome, then my assertions have no stance. But if the evidence points to his being a spurious conversion, with Paul's final residence being in Rome (where people were subsequently tortured and killed to believe his doctrine), then my analysis and encapsulation proves sovereign, with the proper historical records serving as the final tribunal.

By now it's become common knowledge that when resistant Jews turn into Christians, wealth begins to flow their way. There is an obvious reason for that, and if you've still not seen it, don't worry; the realization may appear sooner or later.

Digest the following clue: Under Judaism, God punished Jews by not watching over to protect them, so many factional forces ran roughshod through their country…but under Christianity, as long as they accepted, or at least accommodate Jesus' nativity scene (wearing a cross would be good, but not mandatory; and proselyte? Even better), God watched over them night and day; he'd now hear their prayers, bless and heal their lands.

Figure out the irony.

Paul's Condescension

One of Paul's most notable attributes is the way in which he maneuvers ideological minefields. Have you ever noticed this? Well, if not, come with me to Galatians 3:1-3:

> *"O FOOLISH Galatians, who have bewitched you, that you should not obey the truth, before whose eyes Jesus Christ has been evidently set forth, crucified among you?*
>
> *This only would I learn of you, Received you the spirit by the works of the law, or by the hearing of faith?*
>
> *Are you so foolish? Having begun in the spirit, are you now made perfect by the flesh?"*

Then the oratory continues, bearing down on the authenticity of faith in Jesus Christ. And of course, his argument is both appealing and convincing, as it appears everyone likes to do his own thing; self-will is comforting, as opposed to being controlled by the laws of Moses.

It is then illogical to argue against such appealing statements, even when they oppose Jewish belief. It took a long time for this incredible plot to unfold, but as the axiom goes - God does not sleep. And even the great apostle Paul - a cunning craftsman on top of his game - can be busted. Indeed, God does not sleep.

Note an excerpt found in a Newsweek piece by historians Michael Baigent and Richard Leigh (portion in bold for emphasis):

"Does Paul, then, belong in the company of history's 'secret agents'? Of history's informers and 'supergrasses'?

These are some of the questions generated by Robert Eisenman's research. But in any case, Paul's arrival on the scene set a train of events in motion that was to prove irreversible. **What began as a localized movement within the framework of existing Judaism, its influence extending no further than the Holy Land, was transformed into something of a scale and magnitude that no one at the time can have foreseen.**

The movement entrusted to the 'early Church' and the Qumran community was effectively hijacked and converted into something that could no longer accommodate its progenitors. There emerged a skein of thought which, heretical at its inception, was to evolve in the course of the next two centuries into an entirely new religion. What had been heresy within the framework of Judaism was now to become the orthodoxy of Christianity.

Few accidents of history can have had more far-reaching consequences."

Paul is just a pretentious figure, working the Roman machine of manipulation. And it only matters in our lifetime, because once we are deceased, based on what history tells us, nothing matters.

CHAPTER TEN

✢

THE HOODWINKING CHURCHES

We have seen the basic foundation and origin of the Church. Now let's take a look at the Reverend Billy Graham, a classic example of how the blood of Jesus neither heals, nor washes our sins as white as snow.

Billy Graham

"William Franklin Graham Jr. (born November 7, 1918), better known as Billy Graham, is an Evangelical Christian. He has been a spiritual adviser to multiple U.S presidents, and was number seven on Gallup's list of admirable people for the 20th century. He is a Southern Baptist. Graham has preached in person to more people around the world than any Protestant who has ever lived. According to his staff, as of 1993 more than 2.5 million people had 'stepped forward at his crusades to accept Jesus Christ as their personal savior.' As of 2002, Graham's lifetime audience, including radio and television broadcasts, topped two billion." **Source**: www.en.wikipedia.org

According to The New York Times:

> *"On Friday, Mr. Graham, 83, apologized for his words captured on audiotape 30 years ago. The conversation was among 500 hours of Nixon tapes released last week by the National Archives. Most were recorded from January to June 1972.*
>
> *'Although I have no memory of the occasion, I deeply regret comments I apparently made in an Oval Office conversation with President Nixon,' Mr. Graham said in a statement. 'They do not reflect my views, and I sincerely apologize for any offense caused by the remarks.'*

> *In the conversation with President Nixon, the evangelist complained about what he saw as Jewish domination of the news media.*
>
> *'You believe that?' Nixon asked in response.*
>
> *'Yes, sir,' Mr. Graham said.*
>
> *'Oh, boy, so do I,' Nixon said. 'I can't ever say that, but I believe it.'*
>
> *'No, but if you get elected a second time, then we might be able to do something,' Mr. Graham said.*
>
> *In his recent statement Mr. Graham distanced himself from those comments, and said his legacy was one of working for stronger bonds between Jews and Christians.*
>
> *'Throughout my ministry, I have sought to build bridges between Jews and Christians,' he said. 'I will continue to strongly support all future efforts to advance understanding and mutual respect between our communities.'*
>
> *The friendship between Mr. Graham and the president began in the Eisenhower administration, when Nixon was vice president.*
>
> *Later in the conversation, when Nixon raised the subject of Jewish influence in Hollywood and the news media, Mr. Graham said, 'A lot of Jews are great friends of mine.'*
>
> *'They swarm around me and are friendly to me,' Mr. Graham said, 'because they know that I am friendly to Israel and so forth. But they don't know how I really feel about what they're doing to this country, and I have no power and no way to handle them.'*
>
> *Nixon replied, 'You must not let them know.'"*

Do you think Mr. Graham, in his wildest dreams, ever thought this conversation would ever become public knowledge? He was speaking freely, from his heart some 36 years ago, and while understandably his memory dulled, he now admits to making those statements! But then says right to our faces—it does not reflect his views. That is preposterous! His response is puerile, and is not to be taken seriously.

It does not matter how long ago he said it. It is vivid, and that line of thinking was not impulsive, but rather a settled perception and conception of the way he saw Jews. By following the context of Bamboozled!, you can see in Mr. Graham's statement about wanting stronger bonds between Christians and Jews, the direct Roman intent to impose a bogus Jesus story on Jews, and the rest of the world.

What then? Has Mr. Graham been through some magnificent transformation that led to a radical new conviction where Jews are concerned? If so, what would've caused his view of Jews to shift? Did Jews change their monopolizing ways over the media? Or was Graham's view of them wrong to begin with? After all, he still preaches the palpably bogus gospel of Jesus.

To have a minister of Jesus Christ chatting in such ways, with the president of the free world, disparaging a people that he preaches and identifies in scripture as God's chosen ones, is a gross mockery of the nature of the gospel he preaches.

Could Mr. Graham feel that way and be friendly with Israel at the same time? It sounds contrary to me, and later to have the gravitas to dissolve the acrimony of his true feelings toward the Jewish mentality.

Well, this author can tell you why the number one Evangelist speaks with such confidence in exonerating himself: Imagine, Billy Graham has been duping millions of people for probably more than forty years, with his impressive posits of Jesus Christ, resurrection, love and forgiveness, and has cultivated the public's perception of him as the modern-day 'chief of evangelists.' Nothing he says can be seen as rancor.

But I have no doubt that, within his heart, Mr. Graham knows the things he preaches about Jesus are patently false. There are accounts that show Graham is squarely a charlatan who, like the character of the apostle Paul, is two-faced; and when they are caught in unbecoming acts, they lie their way out, as it appears to be with Graham's situation as cited below from Wikipedia.org:

> *"In 1994, H. R. Haldeman's diaries revealed that Graham had taken part in conversations speaking of Jewish domination of the media. The allegations were so at odds with Graham's public image that most did not believe his account, and Jewish groups paid little attention. Graham released a statement denying that he talked 'publicly or privately about the Jewish people, including conversations with President Nixon, except in the most positive terms.' He said, 'Those are not my words.'"*

There is an interesting story concerning Mr. Graham and a brilliant companion of his that I am about to introduce. If anyone has profound knowledge about the Reverend Billy Graham, it would have to be his partner in religious fallacy and deceitful conduct, right?

Most people would be surprised to know this, but the duo allegedly co-founded a ministry and preached in the bogus name of Jesus for quite a while before the relationship ended in a bizarre twist of fireworks. Read on, my friends.

He Knows Graham Better

> *"Charles Bradley Templeton (October 7, 1915 – June 7, 2001) was successively a Canadian cartoonist, evangelist, agnostic, politician, newspaper editor, broadcaster and author. At the age of seventeen, during the Great Depression, Chuck Templeton (as he was then known) got his first job as a sports cartoonist for The Globe and Mail. This would be the first of many careers. Templeton was diagnosed with Alzheimer's disease in the latter part of the 1990s and died from complications of the disease in 2001.*
>
> *In 1995, he published, A Farewell to God: My Reasons for Rejecting the Christian Faith which put forth his arguments for agnosticism, while also depicting the Reverend Bill Graham as a fraud who didn't believe in his own crusade. In the latter part of the book, Templeton includes several quotes that have been described as 'devastating' to Graham and his career of evangelical teaching, setting up the case that the latter was simply caught up in a lucrative way to make a living."* **Source**: www.en.wikipedia.org

Based on his résumé, I find him competent enough to tell fact from fiction.

Is the Reverend Bill Graham a fraud who doesn't believe in his own crusade? I say yes, beyond even the shadow of a doubt. Mr. Templeton does not seem prone to making a living by slandering his former partner, who he'd apparently lost respect for. I have more regard for Templeton than Graham, because the latter is implausible, as proven by his own words, and by eyewitnesses such as Mr. Templeton.

This may sound strange to some readers, but I believe that Billy Graham's consistent preaching of the Roman hoax speaks to his seared conscience. He is a subtle con artist who managed to suppress the knowing of his act, with no remorse or shame, as he watched billions of people trot down the isles to receive a Jesus who does not really exist. On the other hand, Mr. Templeton's conscience got tired of misleading others, so what did he do? He ceased and desisted from the bamboozling.

There is no doubt Mr. Graham, rapaciously acquired millions or billions of dollars from the pockets of the saved and unsaved. Try to recall what Billy Graham has been preaching all these decades—he preaches that either people repent, or face Satan in hell. Graham has gotten the whole world of his followers afraid of going to meet the devil with his pitchfork, standing at the gate of torment.

Friends, we must now face the hard facts: if we had known what church was really all about, our feet would never have entered the doorstep! All they have ever wanted was your money and control of your mind!

I will share something with you concerning what church is about, but I must warn you - it is very unpleasant. Many will instantly think of excuses, but I assure that there are no exceptions...

In the late part of the 1930's to mid 1940's, a man named Simone was an espionage agent; he had multiple connections with several government dignitaries from a few prominent countries. This excerpt is taken from a 1952 court trial transcript, where the defendant was one, Rudolf Slanski, who pled guilty to all charges.

One of the schemes Simone was involved in was to aid in the success of America's imperialist domination. As I understand it, the scheme secretively involved sinister ploys of treason, sabotage and espionage when necessary. Simone tells of a U.S. overseas agency, an organ of the U.S. Jewish capitalists, that was financed by a man named Bernard Baruch.

The agency was said to be the most important link with the U.S. Zionists and Jewish nationalist in the United States and cooperated closely with the State Department. Through this agency the U.S Psychological Warfare Board spread outrageous lies and slander against the Peace Camp. Simone told the court that he knew of the operation before pledging collaboration with the British Intelligence Service in Paris in 1939, in the office of agent Paul Willert.

In this trial, Simone was asked to tell about the U.S. Psychological Warfare Board, and what he said will shock you...He said that the members were officials of the State Department, War Department, the

Catholic and Protestant churches, and Jewish organizations! The Board arranged murders, sabotages, and diversionary activities in China and other areas. They were in the business of eliminating anything in the way of the U.S. Imperialists.

Let the chips fall where they may, so much for religion and the church, right? And don't overlook the connections with Billy Graham's 'behind closed doors' talk with Present Nixon and all of the other presidents, for decades.

Jailed at Church

Having accepted Jesus as my Lord and Savior at the age of seven, I always had a great desire to fully know and understand His word. To that effort, I wrote a letter to Dr. D. James Kennedy in 1985. He was the founder of 'Evangelism Explosion International' and senior minister of Coral Ridge Presbyterian Church, located at 5555 North Federal Highway in Fort Lauderdale, Florida.

At the time, I was an ardent believer in the Christian faith and enjoyed healthy, interactive discussions about scripture interpretation and practice. I was in my religious prime then, coming down the other side of the mountain, from which I had recently discovered a significant distinction between the Old and New Testament covenants. So my letter to Reverend Kennedy addressed two biblical issues: 1) the doctorate designation that Kennedy and many other Christian ministers attained as apparent credibility enhancers, and 2) the clerical robe many ministers wear while holding church services.

I noted to Kennedy, that the New Testament (New Covenant) gives no title such as 'doctorate' to be born by church ministers, and that robe wearing was only under the Old Testament (Old Covenant), where permission was given for the priests to wear robes. I supported my argument by citing relevant scriptures. At first, I received only a generic response from his office, so I had to persist and push to get Kennedy's own words in response to my questions.

In his response, Kennedy offered not a single biblical citing to support his position on the objections I raised. Here is what he replied:

> *"Concerning the wearing of a clerical robe, many protestant ministers have felt for centuries that the Geneva Robe, as it is*

called, adds a certain dignity and decorum to the service which otherwise might not be present.

Regarding the use of titles, many unbelievers like to accuse Christians and Christian ministers of being uneducated ignoramuses whose views on any matter are not worthy to be considered. The indication of academic degrees obviously silences this objection and hopefully removes a stumbling block on the part of some in listening to the Gospel."

After that reply, some of my friends and I started visiting Kennedy's church, whereupon one Sunday three of us sat down in a session with the reverend. This was clearly a man whom always operated at the top of his game, but in the session with us, he did not have his way at all, and it was clear that he felt somewhat diminished with the outcome of the session.

Subsequently, we continued visiting and became acquainted with the Coral Ridge style of worship. Now, I was very serious about the word of God, and I looked at every aspect of the church's operation from the perspective of scripture.

Some three months later, on March 3, 1985, my good friend and brother in Jesus, Lorenzo Walden, and I attended Sunday service as we had been for the prior three months. But on this day, things went wrong after the service.

Unbeknownst to us at the time, some members with whom we had interacted lodged complaints against our presence there, as a result of our biblical discussions. So on that Sunday in March, Lorenzo and I sat in different service venues, and at the close of his service, Lorenzo attempted to complement the hosting pastor, Richwine, on the wonderful sermon he delivered that morning. Richwine had had a prior discussion with Lorenzo and things hadn't gone so well for him. So with that backdrop, he got short-tempered, rejected Lorenzo's complements, and asked him to remove himself from church property.

Over on my end, something was cooking, too, with my host pastor. I was asking of him the same questions I'd sent in Kennedy's letter, to see what he thought. After he attempted to answer one of my questions, he brought me over to Pastor Richwine for him to take on the next one.

As we approached Richwine, he saw me coming and came forward to offer me a handshake, then he exclaimed briefly in an obstinate tone, "Your friend came yelling at me after service, and I asked him to leave. I am telling you also, if you do not intend to come here, sit and be taught, do not come back."

I retorted, "I came to church, and this property I am standing on was bought with God's money, so how can you make such demands on me, Pastor? "Rich," I continued, "Are you telling me this is a church, or what? Or did you buy this place as a home for you, your wife and children?"

Now I am above lying about what happened that Sunday, and the truth is that I persisted for the pastor to give me an answer to what I believed fell in line with the Pauline Gospel. And clearly it was the position I took that got me into trouble—because Richwine called the police to take me away!

Yes, my readers, the cops came, and because at the time I viewed the bible to be true, I thought they had no right to remove me from the house of God for simply seeking answers to biblically laced questions.

When the sheriffs asked me to leave, I ignored their voices and continued my beckoning to Richwine. I would not budge, because I was not being disorderly, just being straightforward on matters pertaining to Christian principles. They realized my determination and so arrested me after instructing me to leave the Lord's house several times, on the second floor of the building.

As we descended to the first floor, Lorenzo appeared and took my bible from the cop. Then they ordered him to get off the premises, and while he and one of the cops strolled to where his pickup truck was parked a few yards away, a second cop followed behind them. In just about thirty seconds or less, I looked and saw the two cops having a scuffle with Lorenzo! They wrestled him to the ground and handcuffed him, then placed the both of us in a squad car and locked us up for trespassing.

We were arraigned in court, pled not guilty of the charges, and for the next nine months Coral Ridge Church sent Richwine and another resident pastor to assist the State of Florida's prosecution team. Lorenzo and I had separate trials, and represented ourselves as pro se plaintiffs.

Lorenzo was first to go on trial, and his case was tried January 26, 1986 (and on January 28, 1986 the space shuttle *Challenger* blew up.) He won a not guilty verdict from a jury of six, on charges of trespassing, and trespassing after warning.

For my trial, I embarked on a discovery process that included taking the deposition of Dr. Kennedy himself. After two days of serious direct examinations and cross-examinations, the jury found me guilty of one trespassing charge.

During my case, Kennedy never appeared at one preliminary hearing and came very close to being arrested by Judge Skaff, but Kennedy had Tom Bush, a very competent lawyer, to squash the subpoena served on him.

Coral Ridge Presbyterian Church is one example of the bamboozling church culture I have shown, which cajoles attendees to join the church, but you are not permitted to question or express disagreement with what they teach. The minute you do so, their invitation to enter the "house of God" is rescinded, and you are no longer welcome there.

I give my word of advice, do not attempt what I did in my ignorance, by adopting an attitude like mine when I attended their services—it lands you in the county jail.

Have you ever read that Jesus or his apostles called in the cops when holy disagreements occurred?

See, Rome easily gets away with doctoring up the writings of the bible, because 2000 years later, no one is interested to see the inconsistent and warped scriptures as nonsensical.

What is it going to take to wake us up and shock our brains into realizing that most men of the cloth are actors? They give the public a common façade that looks like sincerity and faithfulness towards Jesus Christ, but behind closed doors, they delve into all manners of evil concupiscence and sleaze. And the reason for their pompous behavior is because they know most people respect and accept anything that comes from their mouths concerning Jesus.

So that on a Sunday morning at church, while Lorenzo and I were interested in the right way of Christ, Coral Ridge Presbyterian Church was only interested in keeping the church economy flourishing. How to do that? Just keep the congregation well sedated and shielded from the light of real understanding.

Why weren't we commended for our zeal in the word of the gospel? Instead of rejected by Reverend Kennedy and his flock? They were *relentless* in their pursuit of the state's prosecution against us, which lasted close to one year.

If you are having any doubt that this church represents pure greed and evil, and nothing to do with the holy word of God, there is more than enough evidence on public record offering transparency of the case. Their hypocrisy is directly illustrated in their own given testimony, as extracted from Kennedy's 'Perpetuation of Testimony Deposition,' taken on October 29, 1985 in Fort Lauderdale, Florida.

There I was, now in court, fighting for the right to be in church and vigorously participate in church liberty. I was in a confrontation with the State of Florida, because the church treated us as though we had trespassed on a private residence! And turned us over to man's law.

I defended myself because, according to the bible, Jesus told me that he would teach me how to do it. Of course, under the circumstances, the prosecution's case against me was a loser, but in a bamboozled court system, there was little going my way. Though I had no legal knowledge whatsoever, I was not the typical person in the street; I was armed and challenging, and would at least put on a darn good show.

At the time of the arraignment, the judge seemed intrigued by my personality and graciously offered me guidance in finding the church charter.

Keep in mind - I had never done anything like this before. This was the first time I would be taking a legal deposition, but under bamboozled thinking, I believed that Jesus would give me a tongue no man could resist or combat. (Feel free to have a good laugh at that if you like.)

The judge ordered the hearing take place in his chambers to supervise the legality of my questions to Pastor Kennedy, because his attorney, Tom Bush, objected to Kennedy's deposition being taken by me, and suggested I get a real lawyer.

On the day I deposed Dr. Kennedy, present in chambers were Judge Skaff, his clerk of the court, two assistant state attorneys, Kennedy's attorney Tom Bush, my brother in Christ, Lorenzo Walden, and me.

Since I believed Jesus would inspire my thoughts, I entered the hearing looking for deliverance via a linguistic frame of mind. I was up to the challenge, and never in the least intimidated by a lack of knowledge about judicial proceedings, nor by the abundance of legal minds round the table.

So now the excitement is about to begin. The judge did some preliminary housekeeping and finally swore Kennedy in. And it commenced as follows:

The Court: "Now you may proceed. And you've got to ask questions that are relevant or pertinent to your case. Do you understand that?"

Aldred: "Yes."

The Court: "All right. So if the attorney objects, listen to the objection, I'll try to explain it to you and we'll proceed from there. Okay? Okay. What do you want to ask him? Go ahead."

Now, to establish my commonsensical legal foundation, I asked Kennedy if Coral Ridge Presbyterian Church was registered with the State of Florida to operate as a corporation. Sure enough, he said, "Yes, it is."

I thought to myself: *Good, one down and two to go.*

Next I asked him to tell the court what the intent of the church's charter was. Then, the prosecutor, Ms. Beckert, objected on the basis of relevancy.

Her objection was overruled - the good doctor had to answer. And his answer was a most fascinating one. He said: "The purpose of the church is to proclaim the gospel of Jesus Christ; to fulfill the great commission, and to teach people the teachings of Christ concerning their life here and their life hereafter."

Can you see how those two answers from Kennedy worked in my favor? The rest became history—I was then privileged to proceed with the questions I wanted to ask him. I wanted to show that Dr. Kennedy was a charlatan, and that he was not really serious about the sayings of Jesus at all. My questions were designed to unravel him.

I asked: "Did Christ say you should prosecute people for trespassing?" Prosecutor David Hodge, who prosecuted Lorenzo, chimed in with an objection here.

"On what grounds?" asked the court.

Hodge replied: "This is not material to the charge of trespassing. The person is charged with trespassing at the church, which is a registered corporation. And Christ is not the person that can take away the permission to be in the church. It is the people that are in charge who have the authority to take away the permission to be in the church at that time. That would be an irrelevant question, not about Christ, but about—excuse me. I object to relevancy and materiality. Whether or not Christ says that we should prosecute people for trespassing is not relevant to this charge. The issue is whether or not the permission to be in the church was withdrawn by the people who have permission to withdraw that permission."

"Do you agree," asked the judge, "that the rules of criminal procedure provide that the discovery depositions follow the rules of civil procedure? Do you agree with that?"

Hodge replied: "Yes, Your Honor."

"Do you further agree that the rules of civil procedure provide that you do not necessarily have to ask questions that are relevant and material, but which might lead to evidence that is relevant and material? Do you agree with that?"

Hodge: "I agree civil rules say that."

But Hodge continued to make useless stipulations, trying to sway the Judge, arguing that the discovery rules did not apply to perpetuation of testimony, but to no avail. The judge became weary with repeating the same points to Hodge, and finally declared that rules and evidence of materiality still apply.

Hodge conceded: "Yes."

The judge replied: "I will overrule the objection."

So I survived that round also, which qualified me to receive an answer to the question from Kennedy.

The judge repeated the question to refresh Kennedy's memory, since Hodge had caused a distraction.

Kennedy replied: "May I ask a question before I answer that?"

"Well, I would rather you spoke with your attorney," the judge replied. "You really should not ask a question. See if your attorney can help you, perhaps, with phrasing your answer."

"It is not about that question," Kennedy retorted, "it is about this whole proceeding, something that I do not understand."

The judge deferred Kennedy again to his counsel for guidance.

Now, Kennedy had a PhD. So I wondered what he was up to on this particular biblical question...

Kennedy continued: "I want to know exactly what this gentleman is charged with and by whom."

The judge then tossed the charging papers toward Kennedy and exclaimed: "Pardon me for throwing it."

Tom Bush, Kennedy's attorney told him: "Doctor Kennedy, he is being charged by the State of Florida with violating the law of the State of Florida against the dignity and peace of the State of Florida on the 3rd day of March, 1985—I will read you what the charge says specifically.

'Did, having been authorized, licensed, or invited, enter or remain in a structure or conveyance to wit: a church located at 5555 North Federal Highway, Forth Lauderdale, Florida, and then being warned to depart by the owner or lessee of the premises or by a person authorized by the owner or lessee, to wit: Mario Diaz, for your information, that is a police officer, I believe. The said defendant did refuse to do so contrary to a particular Florida statute which is known in layman's terms as trespass after warning.'"

Then Kennedy said: "Okay."

Then the judge told him: "Okay. Now, you want to answer his question about, correct me if I'm wrong, Christ's teachings including the prosecution of trespasses of His church?"

Kennedy: "The New Testament says that we are to obey all the laws of men for the Lord's sake. It furthermore says that authorities are not a terror to good works, but to evil works, and says if we obey the authorities we need not be afraid, but if we do evil, then indeed we should be afraid of the authorities because they are ordained by God to maintain righteousness and order. Christ further taught, He said, agree with an adversary quickly while thou art in the way with him lest any time the adversary deliver thee to the judge, and the officer deliver thee to the judge, and thou be cast into prison. So Christ very clearly taught that, one, we should obey the lawful authorities of the State."

I found it alarming that this preacher continued by saying that I was at fault to argue with his subordinate about Jesus' word. His testimony basically was that by refusing to leave the church premises when asked to, I caused my arrest, in that I disobeyed the State law; and that general teaching in the New Testament supported my arrest under the circumstances.

With my next question, I challenged him with a New Testament scripture. I asked: "Does first Corinthians six of the New Testament say that Christians should not take other Christians to the law because Christians have more intelligence to take care of matters between themselves?"

Attorney Hodge objected to relevancy, saying: "And I would also point out this is the State of Florida versus Mr. Aldred. We're not dealing with the issue of whether a Christian is charging another Christian in this case. So therefore it's not relevant."

The judge tersely told Kennedy to answer the question.

Kennedy replied: "The matter that he quotes there in Corinthians assumes that the individual is willing to be subservient and submissive to the authorities in the church. And it is discussing a situation where two members of the church have a disagreement over a matter, and in saying that they shouldn't go to the civil court."

He then went on to misrepresent the exact circumstances that led to my being accosted by the police. For one thing, Dr. Kennedy was not present, but he testified with hearsay stories. I call him on the fact that he signed an affidavit that said he had no personal knowledge of the case, so how could he testify to facts he had no knowledge of?

He then said that, on his way to the hearing, he'd asked someone to explain what happened to him, so he was speaking from that source."

I pressed him on the matter of the church being registered to do the things of Christ, yet he was failing to forgive as Christ commands. I implied that he wasn't behaving in good faith when he signed an affidavit barring me from ever returning to the church. I pressed him on Christ's admonition to forgive seventy times seven, and asked whether or not he should practice that.

No sooner than I posed that question, prosecutor Lisa Beckert and attorney Hodge objected simultaneously, and they lost again because the judge instructed Kennedy to answer. And he admitted that Christ said that.

I then asked him: "Are you paid by the church?"

Beckert: "I'm going to object to that. That is irrelevant. It's not material to the case at all. The defendant is charged with trespassing. The question is just out of line."

Mr. Bush stepped in: "Maybe if it was paraphrased, are you employed, or something?"

Judge: "I think it has to go to credibility. So I think I'll overrule the objection; just tell the doctor to answer it if he can."

Kennedy replied: "Yes, I am."

The judge wasted no time: "Next question."

I asked: "Are the other ministers paid by the church?"

Kennedy: "Yes, they are."

I then asked him: "Was an arrest appropriate to my participation at your church, and was the arrest a performance of Christ's kind and loving duties, since you say the church is registered to proclaim the gospel of Jesus Christ?"

Oh, boy! No sooner than I posed the question, Ms. Beckert attacked with an objection, saying: "I object to the form of the question, again to the relevancy of the question, the immateriality."

Well, of course, the judge asked Kennedy: "Are you able to answer that?"

And he replied: "Yes, sir."

The judge: "Would you, please."

Kennedy then went into a rambling oration, knitting together several elements. He went into when he met Lorenzo and me, saying he was sorry for our predicament and how he tried to shake our hands prior to the hearing, but we refused, something he found interesting. He also explained that he had met with us for a long period of time before our arrest, spending a number of hours talking with us after having held two services; and he said that I, the author, became very obnoxious with him.

He admitted to having no knowledge of what his church deputies had done to us. He said that after a wearisome dissertation with us, trying to explain their position, he concluded that they tried to treat us correctly.

(You may have noted that the assistant state attorneys were objecting to my questions without any assessment as to whether they were proper, but this next question was tailored to pose a more serious biblical hurdle.)

I asked Mr. Kennedy to give a biblical example where Christ had turned an offender over to the government for prosecution. And of course, this drew a swift objection from Ms. Beckert on grounds of materiality, relevance and hearsay.

The judge then probed me for relevance to the case. After I refined the question to the judge's satisfaction, he agreed and tried to pose it to Kennedy himself, saying in other words: "Would Christ want Kennedy or the other elders in the church to prosecute a trespasser?"

David Hodge chimed in: "Calls for speculation, Your Honor."

Judge: "Well, I am going to direct him to answer."

(As you can observe the prosecutors just could not get their minds around the fact that the church registration had one particular intent and purpose: providing services allegedly of Christ's command—at least I knew that much.)

With that kind of "gotcha" question, I think Dr. Kennedy felt the dramatic scriptures forcing him into to the corner of shame, and so he was compelled to modify his position by expressing empathy for us, his victims, saying: "I did not personally prefer any charges against these men." But he had had months to have the charges dropped and had failed to do anything about it. As far as I am concerned, had he not been faced with the legal obligations to account for the purpose of the church's registration, there never would have been any sympathetic words on his lips.

At that point, it seemed the judge felt empathy for him, being a man of the cloth, and an academic doctor, so the judge offered: "Well, one of your elders did."

And Kennedy said: "Yes."

The Judge said: "Was that against Christ's teachings? I guess, is what he said."

At this point, Dr. Kennedy become a bit brusque in speech and began saying things that were clearly irrelevant to the question put forth. He accused me in particular of acts I had never done, ending with the fact that they had instructed me to leave church premises, and so did the police, but I failed to do so. "It is the State of Florida that is pressing the charges against him and not I, myself."

Throughout all of that, he evaded the actual question, but the judge followed up and asked: "How about Christ? Would Christ have prosecuted trespassers? In his time? Would he have done that in your opinion? If you can answer."

Kennedy said: "I recognize it's speculative, hypothetical." The good doctor then began weaving yet another theological, interpretative web, making everything nebulous. The more he bobbed and weaved, the worse things got for his prestigious preacher image. He reiterated that the question called for great speculative inference, in what things Christ may or may not have done. He cited an instance where people were buying and selling in the temple and Christ did not merely turn them over to the authorities, but made a whip and drove them out. And so he believes Christ's action there justifies his use of the police to arrest us.

Kennedy is all about bamboozle, and that is seen clearly in the way he struggled with the last question—interpreting the scripture to cover his hypocrisy. Now make no mistake, the good doctor lied in all of his accusations against me, and it was quite simple to grasp the encounter between pastor Richwine and me, which occurred when the service was long ended, with only a few brethren standing round chatting. There was no evidence presented to show that I engaged in conduct other than a peaceful assertive quest to have information relevant to the gospel of Christ, to which Richwine failed to address.

When I underscored he was not present at the incident, he again admitted he was repeating hearsay because he had not seen what happened.

In Kennedy's testimony, he alluded to one of his colleagues, James Richwine, who had authorized my arrest. Richwine was in charge of the singles fellowship division of the church. I had attended one of his services prior to the Sunday I was arrested. I would describe him as a soft spoken but obstinate and despotic character. Interestingly though, I believe that this gentleman, from a secular point of view, was quite a civil person, knowing right from wrong. But I doubt he understood anything about literal history, nothing outside of scrambled and deluded bible snippets, and articles in Reader's Digest (he mentioned reading RD a lot during his own questioning).

However, as is usually the case with many of the well intended, he too was destroyed by church operations—which gainfully employed him. He made a living teaching people Roman Catholicism, the bamboozle you and I were brought up in.

And, as with Mr. Kennedy, Richwine could not deal with the simple, relevant questions I was asking, because it would have shown default in their church operation. So the alternative was to brand me a troublemaker and expel me from church property to shun the embarrassment.

Their treatment of us was not an appropriate use of their ministry's duty based on scripture, and he did not realize the seriousness of his actions until I called him to the witness stand and he got a hint. Judging from his answers, he must've wished the whole thing never happened.

Under direct examination, pastor Richwine told the court that I affected some of his fellow ministers and people in groups he was responsible for. He said I had an agenda for attending the church, wanting to push forth a particular point of view that they as a church did not teach, and that I sought to force them into conversations and illicit verbal consent and agreement with my view.

He disclosed that this distinguished style of mine became the topic of discussion at their weekly staff meeting. And the staff came up with a plan to accommodate my continued visits to the church; I was to break from such a gripping style of argument, and just sit and be taught. If I wanted to discuss something, then I could make an appointment to speak with a pastor in the office.

At the end of prosecutor Beckert's direct examination of Richwine, you could almost touch her sense of confidence that she was nailing down a conviction of trespassing against me as she expressively asked Richwine: "Reverend, do you see the man that trespassed on your church here in the courtroom today?"

"Yes, I do."

"Could you please point him out, and describe what he's wearing to the jury?"

"Sure. He's sitting at the table there wearing a yellow and brown jacket with a white T-shirt."

"And Reverend, what County and State did all these events occur in?"

"Broward County, Florida."

"Judge, I have no further questions."

And then it was my turn to take vengeance on my friend, Richwine. Poor soul, I couldn't imagine that he was so uninformed—I was flabbergasted!

He repeated my first question about being employed by Coral Ridge Presbyterian Church word for word before answering. And the answer he gave to my next question, regarding the church being registered with the State, spoke volumes: He actually admitted that he never knew the church had a legal status with the State of Florida. And if you want to snigger at this well respected reverend, go ahead! Remember: these people are exploiters, just pushing the envelope as far as they can, hoping we will never discover what they are doing. The more I embarrassed Richwine with barrages of incriminating questions, the more the jury became infuriated with *me*.

It was basically like this: Who do you think you are, speaking to the man of God like that?

Now, can you picture what was going on here? During this whole thing, I was as genuine a Christian as anyone could possibly be—yet a church that supposedly stood for Christ was doing all these things to me! If Christ is real, one thing was surely evident—this church had *nothing* to do with him!

When I showed Richwine the Coral Ridge Church article of incorporation for identification, he did not have any knowledge what the document was, and I don't think he was feigning ignorance, either. It reflected very poorly on him as a minister of the church, and he must have felt humiliated. Richwine's apparent ignorance in this regard shows he was really no different from the way I believed for half of a century. But I had found too many stark contradictions between what the church practiced and the biblical canon, so as I had done with Kennedy, I thought it was a good idea to establish a common consensus on the issue with Richwine, to reconcile his church conduct with God's word.

I started with basic questions such as what the definition of the word 'church' was and then what it meant to him. He replied: "No, I don't know what the definition is in church." I wondered why it was so difficult for the pastor to give even the dictionary's meaning of church, but from watching his body language, I believe he saw his dilemma.

The judge permitted me to read the dictionary definitions to Richwine, and then asked him if he agreed that those were the recognized definitions of church.

After several attempts to evade acknowledgement, I was quite amazed when he flatly denied the definitions by saying: "None of those are complete. They're all part, all portions of what a church can be."

Me: "Which one of these definitions would closest represent your definition of church?"

Richwine: "None, not my definition."

Me: "What is your definition?"

Richwine: "A church is the body of Christ gathering together, either in a local place or throughout the world. It's the people. It's not the building."

I then asked him to tell the difference between the definitions I'd read to him and the ones he'd just offered. He then asked me to read them over again, and then said the closest would be "collective body of Christians extending around the world."

We had a repeat of that exchange regarding the meaning of the word 'religious.' Truly, Richwine seemed completely out of touch with general vocabulary! It was a pitiful sight to see. Knowing how I had devoted my entire life, for so many years to this corrupt organization, in the belief it was the way to get to heaven.

The reason I won the court's rulings on my questions being material and relevant was because the church, by its articles of incorporation with the state, owed people including me an obligation of accommodation as long as conduct remains in the interest of biblical issues. Our conduct at this church had been totally appropriate, as we were simply trying to investigate and pursue relevant discourses with the church leadership, and that must be allowed, because that is what they have registered to do as a church.

Richwine was collecting a paycheck to win lost souls, and did it so authoritatively—but what was the matter with my soul? I saw a man on the witness stand in front of me, very adamant about representing Jesus, the savior of the world. I had no doubt this man could have been of some secular use, but in my view, his engagement in the bogus ministry deserved ridicule.

At this juncture in the testimony, I was making him look stupider than ever—he was acting as though he could not read well, just so he could evade the more incriminating queries.

Finally the judge took us to a sidebar to resolve the linguistic issue and I continued my barrage. Richwine was incredibly stubborn and refused to concede that it was wrong to conduct religious business, a biblical church, as people ran secular businesses.

Coral Ridge was busted, because of the statements written in their articles of incorporation. They received permission from the State of Florida to operate a non-profit business, and the law requires they abide by it or their certification would be revoked.

I believe the judge knew that by virtue of the church charter, I had not trespassed at the church. And so when the prosecutors made fruitless objections over the course of Richwine's cross-examination, the court overruled them almost every time—not bad for a common person, I think. The key to my having been able to hold my own during the trial was my reliance upon, and use of proper reasoning, and linguistic principles—and that was the destruction of the church's credibility.

If anyone intends on going to heaven, the entrance better not be through Coral Ridge Presbyterian's church doors. I mean, you would never reach heaven, because this so-called worship center is by no means an entrance.

I tried to leave no stone unturned while questioning Richwine— and he helped me show that the church was no more interested in Christ than Satan himself, only for business as usual.

For the jury, I even directed Richwine to article 3 of the church's articles of incorporation, which stated in part: "The general nature of the objects of the Corporation is to be a local Church of the denomination known as the Presbyterian Church in the United States, subject to 'The Book of Church Order of the Presbyterian Church in the United States."

With that backdrop, I asked: "Do you know what the church function is as indicated in the charter?"

Prosecution: "Judge, the State is going to make an objection again, based on relevancy to the case at hand."

Court: "Well, I think it's relevant...I'll permit it, overrule the objection."

Yes, I obviously lacked legal proficiency, but the point here was this: I was making a legal connection by using the basis for this church's very existence! And to have ministers and their attorneys going awry on the meaning of words and basic court procedure really sucked.

Now given the facts of this so-called trespassing charge, had I had my own attorney, the case may not have made it to trial—so the State and the church benefited from my lack of legal knowledge.

When I asked Richwine where he got the authority to preach, he said from the bible. I then asked him what kind of bible he used. The prosecutor objected but the Court overruled.

Richwine: "The church has no official bible." He then named about five different versions that he used.

Judge: "Do all of those bibles carry the same basic evangelic message?"

"I think they do."

Me: "Is the church specifically governed by the teachings of Christ?"

Richwine: "I'm not quite sure what you're asking...Yes, the supreme authority over the spiritual matters of the church is Jesus Christ."

I could see that at this stage of his testimony, he was kind of disoriented, and it would become quite obvious in my next question. "If there were no bibles around, would there be churches?"

"Yes. Without bibles there would still be churches because churches existed before until the bible was written through divine revelation of Christ."

Me: "You have just testified that your church is governed by Christ's teachings, so where would the teaching of the church come from if there was no bible around?"

The prosecutor was objecting to this line of questioning, saying it's speculative and not relevant to the case, but the judge overruled the objection.

Me: "Would the situation of having no bible permit anyone to create their own morals?"

"No, I would not agree."

"Well, there is a bible now that gives instructions, and people are still in disarray, so if there were no bible, wouldn't there be much more chaos?"

"No, it may be. I'm not saying it won't be. I don't agree that it absolutely follows that it would be."

It goes without saying that the testimony of Pastor James Richwine grossly disparaged Christianity. And I would like to reiterate that at the time of this trial, I only felt something was wrong with the operation of the church, nothing beyond that. It wasn't until years later that I started reading up on history and came into the knowledge of more. There was much more behind what I had experienced with the church.

Looking back on portions of Richwine's testimony, I can now see red flags raised, touching on the Apostle Paul's credence in all of Christendom and the credits to his alleged writings. And it is no wonder that when the Dead Sea Scrolls revealed that he was very much a fifth-columnist espionage, having forsaken his Jewish roots to work as a secret agent for the Roman Empire—Father de Vaux had to hide as much as he could of the incriminating material.

So interestingly in my trial, I was arrested for staying on the church property when asked to leave. Discourse between church members and me had outraged church leadership and set them on fire! In an exchange with an individual over Oral Roberts hospital, I made a remark that this person must've been demon possessed to call Oral Roberts hospital "The City of Faith." Well, the church loyalist was so hurt, he reported me, and led to our visits being a hot topic during their weekly meeting discussions.

Well, I have to admit that had I known the very *bible* itself was the source of bamboozle, I would not have wasted time doing that sort of thing.

Now, back to Richwine's fascinating testimony. Driving my point home, I asked him to say whether or not Paul was wrong to blind the offenders. He then stipulated between a master and servant saying: "Jesus could do anything he chooses, because he is sovereign, so to speak, he could see through to man's heart." He could not tell whether Paul was right in pronouncing blindness on adversaries.

I tell you, boy, oh boy, this was a sweltering one for Rich to explain! He had the burden to show how Paul could be performing duties under the anointing of the Holy Ghost, yet the very act is found to be wrong. Richwine abstained from endorsing Paul's vicious (alleged) behavior; perhaps he feared the effect it may have on him.

What bothered me in this experience was my ignorance on this portion of world reality, and by that I mean, there was nothing anywhere in my mind suggesting that the very bible was a book designed to run a societal scheme—one that even transcended the courts.

I must admit that, at times, I did have a slight flash of suspicion that I was just wasting my time. But I was going through all of it because I was sincere. I felt I was emulating the apostle Paul by representing myself (although there was one significant distinction between Paul and me—he had a PhD, I had a GED). But I took the bible at its word. Jesus was savior of the world, and I wanted to vindicate the truth of the scripture and prove that this church was a hoax, and that it was time we let God's word be true and expose Dr. Kennedy as a liar.

You can believe my tenacity and passion came from a genuine intent to let God's Word be true. And I think it is transparent from the above exchanges that if the gospel represented salvation to men, it was I who stood up for the purity of it, and definitely not the so-called Reverend James Kennedy. If that guy had been following the commands as written in the gospel, I would not have found myself in court. So I had to go after his credibility, declaring him a hypocrite by using his own words. This was a hot pursuit, using commonsense as my weapon to shame this Reverend the best way I knew how.

The Perils of Krentel

Now anyone who knows about dramatic scripture, specifically the New Testament texts, knows that it is held up as the fulfillment of Moses' law, and that it is the canon that governs Christian conduct, right? Well, I think you will find the following especially interesting.

Meet Reverend Steve Krentel, assistant pastor at Coral Ridge Presbyterian. A big six-footer, he's someone you would expect to see playing in the NFL, but instead he chose the church ministry as his profession. According to him, God called upon him to serve people by preaching the gospel, so he had an impressive resume, including two masters and, at the time of his testimony, he was working on his doctorate in a ministers' program. Krentel was quite knowledgeable in the collegiate system of duties within the Presbyterian Church, and he was quite expressive.

Although James Richwine was the one who initiated my arrest, Steve Krentel played an integral part, as he signed the police report and affidavit barring me from any further visits to the church.

As one who was so highly trained to handle Jesus' gospel, teaching people how to accept and walk in the faith, his role in having me arrested showed he had no right to be preaching anything; therefore I wanted to appeal to his conscience, hoping he had a soul.

On cross-examination, Krentel testified that he was aware of the waves Lorenzo and I made in one of the church groups when we had participated in weekly bible study, prior to the arrest.

Me: "When you learned that church members were having a problem with my participation, did you seek me out to talk about it?"

Krentel: "The matter was not under my jurisdiction, it was under Reverend Richwine's. The body of elders discussed handling the situation if you continued with the argumentative ways by contacting the police department."

Me: "Is there a biblical procedure that gives guidelines on how to handle situations such as the one I posed there?"

Krentel: "We do things by the book."

Well, let's see what he meant by doing things by the book, or scripture. Let's see what Steve Krentel thought was just.

Although he had given his credentials on direct examination, I wanted to emphasize it as a predicate.

Me: "Are you a minister of Christ?"

Krentel: "Yes, sir. I believe that's what I've been ordained to do."

Me: "What is the appropriate biblical procedure for handling my case?"

Krentel: "The bible really doesn't say specifically how that communication needs be done. There needs be communication to the person that there is an offensive situation. After that warning, then there's a clear injunction that we can either ask that person to leave or we can, in essence, leave that person. You go to the person and you let them know the problem. If they're still hesitant, then you can take a second witness and have the matter confirmed. If they still reject that effort, then you can put them out of the church."

He went on to explain that since I was not an official member of the church, greater patience was not offered for the problem I posed. He basically said that I was not qualified for any biblical treatment, because I was not known to be a brother in the faith, or a member of his church.

(Mind you, the state prosecutor objected to almost every question I was asking, on the grounds of relevance, and the judge overruled them all. It really made me wonder about the sense of relevance the prosecutor had! Since the court had established the basis of the case in Kennedy's deposition, I could not understand why the assistant state attorney continued make inappropriate objections. These guys didn't have a registration to operate a bakery shop, or any other business; they were exclusively registered to preach the gospel according to Jesus Christ and save souls. They existed to advance the Word of God. All my questions were based upon that. They were in no way immaterial to my arrest that Sunday.)

According to Mr. Krentel, the only thing that mattered was that we were instructed to leave the church premises, and not leaving entitled them to throw us in jail.

Now, I can hear some Christians saying, "Well, we would do the same at our church." But your church should be able to stand up to reasonable queries of its practices without resorting to locking up anyone who does not simply nod and say, "Yes sir."

So instead of apologizing for his un-Christian-like behavior, Steve Krentel basically swore that the bible gave the church the right to jail people—I found this very insulting. And I had Krentel on a collision course with his fake cloak bible, because whether he knew it or not, he was alienating himself from the "inspired word of God," with a clear denial of its very principle, but he was blind to that, you see.

In defending his position on my arrest, he gave some general citing of scripture from either Thessalonians or Timothy saying, "There are several epistles where he [St. Paul] put the people out of the church, to warn the heretics."

He then gave an analogy: "Just like if I went to The Church of Latter Day Saints, but went to a Mormon Church and didn't believe what they said so argued with everybody there, they would kick me out of the church, too. They'd say, don't come back. That's something that's normal within every church, and the Bible gives you some authority to do that."

Then I decided to have some fun with Krentel. Let's see where it goes...

Me: "How can you tell that you are not a false prophet?"

Prosecutor: "Judge, the State would object based on relevancy. Based on the fact that this has nothing to do with the trespassing charge. It's not probative, it's speculative."

Judge: "It's probative to the extent that if the defendant was arrested for calling someone a false prophet, he's certainly entitled to. It's overruled."

So Krentel gave his answer: "I don't think I'm a false prophet, my name is not written in the bible, it doesn't say I'm a false prophet."

Me: "Tell me, in your own words, some of the things the Bible says I am to look for in a false prophet."

And for the first time since he took the stand, Pastor Steve Krentel seemed to be wounded through the heart, and he made it known.

Krentel: "I would just like to say, this personally offends me as a minister. I don't know if it's proper to say that. This really offends me."

Judge: "You're entitled to say anything you want to."

Krentel: "I think that's very offensive."

He went on to give some Roman Catholic recipe for defining a false prophet.

Krentel: "The way we look to identify false prophets is whether they claim Jesus is God. If they don't claim that he is God, then we know there's a certain sense of falseness to their testimony."

He seemed reluctant to give us any more characteristics of false prophets. Perhaps because they were too incriminating?

The Judge pushed ahead to fill the obvious vacuum. "He means a false prophet. You can take every facet of Christianity, and if you say you disagree with it, does that make a false prophet?"

Krentel: "Excuse me?"

The Judge repeated himself, and at that point Krentel seemed to be beside himself, appearing to be out of his league. He began stuttering.

Krentel: "Let's go back to the Mormons. Mormons call the people who don't believe in Mormonism false prophets. Anyone who doesn't agree with those particular principles...Are you talking about the Bible? If you want to believe the Bible, it's there for believing. Okay?

Nobody is forcing anybody to believe the Bible. If you say that the Bible is false, then you're a false prophet. Okay?"

Me: "Once you have registered with the State to teach the Gospel of Christ, shouldn't you follow it specifically, line by line?

Krentel: "I don't know if the State does that, but whether or not that's true or not, sure. That's what we're there for."

Me: "Does Christ command shepherds of the flock to protect the sheep?"

Krentel: "Yes, Christ says that."

Me: "Do you believe that you did that for me?"

Incredibly and laughably, Steve Krentel, the ordained minister who acted in Christ's stead exclaimed in obvious frustration: "I'm not Christ."

At this point, I figured I was pushing him over the edge, which was where he rightly belonged. I was not letting up, I pressed on: "Did Christ tell you to do the same?"

Krentel: "Yes, he did."

Me: "Did you do it?"

Krentel: "Did I do what?"

Me: "What Christ says."

Krentel: "Yes. I protected the sheep that we are responsible for."

Now, I went in for the kill.

Me: "Are you saying that you protected those who support your salary?"

Krentel: "I don't agree with that. It's subjective and questions my motives as a minister...It's saying I do my job based on people who are willing to pay my salary. The answer to that question is no."

This guy was caught in the act of dishonesty, and now had to lie his way to some semblance of justification. Nevertheless, the judge brought my point to the forefront—indeed, Steve was protecting the people who provided church revenue from which he is paid an income.

Me: "Should a Christian minister seek to prosecute someone who came to church to talk about the word of God, to fellowship?"

Krentel: "I don't know the situation you're referring to, it is a general situation, and so I can't answer that...I won't call what you were doing at our church fellowshipping."

Me: "Do you want to see me imprisoned?"

Krentel: "No."

Me: "Don't you consider that as a minister of Christ, you *are* putting me in prison?"

Krentel: "I have nothing to do with this; you have called me as a witness. We turned the situation over to the police because you were not willing to be in orderly conduct, and were not willing to listen to any of the admonishments or encouragement to behave properly. Okay?"

Of course, he maintained that I caused the situation that forced them to call in the police. Why didn't they just walk away from us and end the conversation? Was it *really* necessary to call the police? Or were we hitting too close to home with our questions?

You be the judge, my dear readers.

My basic interest in that fun-filled hour was to have that minister openly confounded, for the present time and for posterity. Our last exchanges underscored the extent of the religious bamboozle and hypocrisy I would later discover the full extent of. I am very proud of my effort. My job was well done.

When confronted with being the one who signed warrants for our arrest to State custody, when neither of us had actually done anything beyond the scope of the church charter, this fellow Krentel proved to be totally befuddled and confused. Did he really have no clue what I was getting at? He *must* have been pretending.

Because, you're to understand—we did nothing out of the ordinary on March 3, 1985.

CHAPTER ELEVEN

⚜

NEW WORLD ORDER

Do you approve of the state of human society in the world as it is today, or should it be improved? I think very few of you would say you like it as it is today. But would you like to be the ruler of a nation, or of the whole planet?

I once shared my worldview with a Jewish acquaintance of mine, and the first thing she uttered was, "That would be a dictatorship." But as I further explained the basic principles of what I envision, and gave her details about how a world government could be, cohesive and cogent in design, she responded very favorably to my proposal.

What I shared with her was my view that there could be a pragmatic world hierarchy, made up of an Emperor and Deputy. To serve in one of these global posts, individuals must be over fifty-five years of age, pass a rigorous psychological test, have a university education, and come from a good family background, as cool and gentle as Mother Theresa. How does that sound to you?

Under this system there would be no superpower countries like the United States, Russia, etc. Serving under the Emperor, would be a World Committee (WC) that handles all global affairs, though each country would trade and be competitive in their operations, business is conducted under one centralized economic regulatory system. Every country would be equal, and there can be no war of one country against the other. There would be just one world army and naval force to address any uprising anywhere on the planet by outlaw groups, although structures would be in place to discourage any desire for rabblerousing.

There would be zero tolerance on crime. Every person would carry a global passport and be known as a citizen of planet earth.

Since sexuality is imposed, of course, by nature, it is necessary to have a global policy that addresses sexual relationships accordingly. Recommendations would have to be made to deal with the people in relationships that contradict the natural reproductive order.

As preface to this issue, let me share a little of my experience as a youngster growing. I remember hearing about men who loved other men intimately, though I did not hear about it often, and I didn't know such things happened with women, too. I later found references to it written in the bible, showing that same-sex proclivities have been around for ages. This caused me to take a more reserved attitude toward folks in that situation, because it was obvious that there was more to it than meets the eye.

Please pay as close attention as possible to this important matter: You are aware that the Roman Catholic Church has an edict that holy matrimony is prohibited for its clergy, right? But we know that it does not work for them, because so many of the priests devour alter boys, they are raging pedophilias. It's so bad the courts are handling lawsuits left and right, which threaten the solvency of some archdiocese.

My Lord, if the Holy Father and his priests are both suspects and convicts due to sexual incontinency, and more specifically, acts of homosexuality, then by all means, sinners should be judged using a much lower standard, as they do not have the holy spirit like Catholic people.

In my view, there is a simple perspective from which to view this matter, and I see no reason to even agonize over it much. Under my aforementioned concept of centralized globalization, any behavior considered to be aberrant and subjective in nature would never be accommodated and therefore, while these people must be accepted in society, special recognition is not warranted for their existence. They are simply global citizens without any distinctions.

To be universally honest about sexuality is to recognize that sexual emotions started out with male and female copulation. The world system would leave same-sex people alone to pursue their intimacy privately amongst themselves. Their plight cannot be comparable to heterosexuals. The latter does not publicize their sexual preference, so in no case should same-sex individuals publicize theirs.

My global philosophy is based upon the pattern established by the observed laws of nature. No one in his or her right mind can overlook the facts as they are on the matter. Just ask yourself and the billions around you by what means you or they came to earth? The answer will be simply: mom and dad. It is not going to be 'dad and dad' or 'mom and mom.'

Now, I mean no dishonor to the ever-increasing population of people who are living outside the natural arrangement of the glandular designation of male and female. But any ideal society would, in my view, be crossing the line of disrespect for nature itself if it sanctions such unfruitful endeavors.

Government has to be concerned with the increase of the population, not personal sexual pleasure. If every relationship were to consist of just fun without any offspring, then there would be no human world. I offer these explanations to benefit those who previously thought differently.

Life is perpetually a male and female invention and there is no substation, or any fluctuation in that operation. Therefore, biological snafus in DNA that result in defective sexual orientation, are to be looked upon as unhealthy states; a clinical matter.

Under a global policy, there would be research and provisions in the area of prenatal care that looked into the genetics and development of babies, so any defect(s) could be spotted and addressed early. Nature creates man to be masculine, loving women, and creates women feminine, loving men. This is the very basis of all animal and human life forms and should be respected as such in an ideal world.

CHAPTER TWELVE

U.S. CONNIVANCE WITH ROME

Throughout Christendom there is but one government-authorized bible—yet there is no unity in its interpretation, though the scripture instructs only one gospel is to be taught. In spite of this, we have always had many different churches teaching differently—and they bask in the liberty to do so. What sense is there in teaching things the scripture never even implied, and honoring those interpretations?

Then there is the government's indulgence in war, the destruction of other people, and more violence than you can imagine everywhere—can you dig it? People tend to forget that this government is one nation under God—and there should be peace on earth through the gospel of Jesus Christ.

And few citizens are willing to protest or criticize their government's acts of war, except in severe cases, and then they can pay a dear price. A prime case in point is the sultry singer and actress, Eartha Kitt. Her career spanned six decades, dancing, acting and singing on stage, in movies and on television. She survived an unhappy childhood as a mixed-race daughter of the South, and made headlines in the 1960's for denouncing the Vietnam War during a visit to the White House. The Secret Service and FBI then reportedly investigated her, and understandably so, her career would have been even more illustrious had the government not resentfully dug into her innocent life in that fashion.

America may be thousands of miles from the Vatican's house of abominations, but there is something significant that has formed: an unholy alliance between the Pentagon and the Vatican. As the saying goes: "You know a person by the company he keeps." The close friendship between the U.S. and the Vatican isn't a situation of strange bedfellows. No, it's more like blood brothers—just consider Rome's foreign policies over the past centuries; and the U.S. for the last 230 years or so. And while the grasp for wealth is an effective distraction from the U.S. foreign policy, it takes no time at all to glean the coalition between both countries—right in line with the biblical Abraham and Moses' political philosophy.

Rome writes a bible people think is God's Word, in order to give credence to vile political conduct. Thus is the origination of an imaginary God, with the tendency to destroy rebellious people and nations.

If you have been asleep to this, I am letting you in on the secret: the Papal of Rome is the God of whom the King James Bible speaks. The kingdom of God is the Vatican City. I suppose the Popes of the past may have been eating name brand or generic ambrosia, as they monitored the barometer that gauged the effects of their apocryphal faith on the people. You may take this for a joke, but rest assured, what I am saying is a fact.

Let's ask George W. Bush what he and Pope Benedict discussed at the Vatican in 2008, when they had a leisurely walk on the super exclusive 'holy ground' that common people are not allowed to experience.

It behooves citizens of the Unites States to understand that although it might feel good to live in a superpower country, think of the dangerous times ahead. You can hear commonsense yelling that a real God would not allow Rome to use a Holy Office to operate an Inquisition of murder, torture, imprisonment and ostracizing innocent people in the name of Jesus Christ; something George W. Bush, Catholics and Christians to this day aid and abet. Why do I say that? The answer is very easy: Thou shall not eat meat offered unto idols, according to St. Paul.

Do not think for one minute that the U.S. government gives a damn if you die of a drug overdose; it does not matter if peer pressure drives you to suicide, or if homosexuals believe their malfunctioning bodies are blessings from God. Do you think they really care if you become a serial killer to get attention? Or if young boys shoot up their schools and murder their classmates just to be in the media spotlight?

The U.S. government and its cohort, the Vatican, couldn't care less that pedophile priests are victimizing innocent boys. No, it's enough to simply have it settled in the court of law, on a case-by-case basis, you see.

And have you ever heard a pundit on T.V. or radio blast the U.S. for their negligence in these matters? No—because it comes with the territory. And they will retort, well, that's what courts are for!

But where are their God, Jesus and Mary? Who loves and watches over us? My goodness! Where are they when these things are taking place? America, oh America—the home of the brave, and land of the free!

The headquarters of the U.S. government is located at 1600 Pennsylvania Avenue NW, Washington, DC 20500. Contact phone numbers are: 202-456-1111, switchboard: 202-456-1414. This may be one of the most renowned addresses in the world, a superpower residence. And built with slave labor.

Once again I will remind you, that the government in general, big or small, plays a vital roll in the everyday mobilization of society, but historically, in a number of ways, the government has been the people's most feared enemy. Government = phantom. Remember that.

When people run for government offices, they tell voters they are seeking the job because they want to serve the community, but the darling truth is—they are mostly just about their own economic situation, and self-adoration, of course. So to get your vote, they appear to be one of us, and of course, they were one of us, and maybe had good intentions, as well. But once they got your vote and won, and are now in government employment, they join the ranks of the lobbyist and special interest crony system. We see it happen all the time.

When pundits reviewed George W. Bush's tenure in the White House as he finished his term, they didn't have much praise to offer Bush. On Sunday mornings' "Meet the Press" on MSNBC, it was agreed that Bush neglected the economy at home, while initiating the war in Iraq, which was viewed as clearly unnecessary. They agreed that he had had a huge lack of oversight with Wall Street, which sent it plummeting out of control. There was no money to fund much-needed domestic programs for U.S. citizens at home, yet he was able to invest billions in the Iraqi war.

And you are hard pressed to find a man who has Christian values and principles on his lips more than George W. Bush. You draw your own conclusions.

CONCLUSION

✢

Once you have digested the foregoing information, you are bound to have a reaction, and hopefully you will emerge feeling more affirmed in the way you see things.

I purposely set out with malice against the false history that has been imposed against mankind for centuries. I consider myself to be a natural global philosopher—I am not tainted, and I have zero tolerance for the corruption of society. So my aim is to throw out a comprehensive net over what afflicts us.

I've explained why it's so hard to see what Rome has done with Christianity, how they managed to turn many intelligent people into imbeciles. The well-intended Martin Luther attests to that.

But, the good news is, not everyone is beyond redemption. I encourage folks to strive for self-dignity, get a hold of yourselves and step away from the flight of the imagination, illusive visions, and false faith. Embrace reasonableness and pragmatism. Elevate your focus and wake from the spell of enticing and cunning preachers.

The presentation of this book is designed to offer something that is stimulating, intriguing and addictive. You must be itching to find the true meaning of life itself.

I have great confidence that the natural energies of the information herein, will cause the mind of readers to leap for joy for the outpouring of the knowledge that delivers them from lifelong deception.

Bamboozled is not just a catchy word. Its use in the context of this book represents the precise state of the world—and more specifically of Rome, the U.S. and the United Kingdom—governments that have calculably forced the subliminal image of a false deity upon their people.

Remember what is going on in the relationship between President George W. Bush, and Pope Benedict. There is an abundance of proof that the United States Government is in full cooperation with the

Vatican, in the advancement of religious bamboozle. From day one, they work together in the interest of narrowing people's imagination.

Remember how I told you, the task is accomplished with use of churches, seminaries, public and ancillary schools, you name it. To the Romans, all humans are not equal, there is one superior race, or you could say one more advanced bloodline.

Only one thing can stop the madness and the delusion of an invisible God—the history of man's early ancestors. It's just a shame that we are so very reluctant to devote time to learn about where we originated. Let's change that, friends. Let's open our eyes.

Barack Obama won the presidency, and what have they said about him in regards to his race? Of course, they say, this is the first black man to become president of the United States of America, but what does this mean? It means that these guys are not really equal to Caucasians—and there is nothing that impairs the plain and simple implications that hold the U.S. as guilty of hypocrisy as Rome.

I raise that point to show that our present social, religious, and secular situations are nothing but Roman ideology being played out in the West. You can see connections with these issues in what we know about the Puritans and Pilgrims, and their offspring; because they came directly from England with Roman Christianity in their hearts. And these were the founding fathers of the United States of America—Caucasians who were white supremacists!

Do you see what I see?

They relegated and killed the Indians, the indigenous people of America.

Psychologist Dr. Jerry Bergman wrote the following of David Duke, one of the most prominent white supremacists in America: "Duke also repeats all of the arguments commonly published in the standard biological literature until the American civil rights movement—such as claiming that differences between the major races include not only skin color and hair texture, but also brain size, cranial structure, intelligence, musculature, hormonal levels, sexual behavior, temperament, dentition, and even personality."

Understand that the KKK's thinking was drawn directly from the book of Genesis, directly from the creation story—and this is information that Rome, Britain and the United States do not want people to realize.

Racism is associated with our human alien ancestry. When earth's ruler, Enlil, hated human interbreeding with their heavenly bloodline, he sought to wipe human beings from the face of the earth. According to the Sumerian history, he exposed them to a furious weather system. And so Rome who is full of racist hatred, uses Genesis to perpetuate similar treatment on those it holds to be inferior.

So we must conclude that David Duke and the like were simply products of the Roman confusion. And as I have said, if the government were to take full responsibility for the horror done under slavery, it would have offered all citizens psychological treatment; some counseling to acclimate and centralize our system of thought and our attitudes. For that reason, I have to forgive Duke his misunderstanding in this regard. It's not his fault. It's coming from a long line of corruption.

As far as Roman Catholic racism is concerned, Jews and Blacks are not yet free, because political procedures have been put in place to affect their way of life, for many generations. The key to such deserved freedom is for people to stop supporting the Roman homemade religion, which promises great rewards in an afterlife. People are entitled to live fresh and free now. Not fearing a Rome-created God and waiting for the other side to receive their rewards.

I shall close with a salute to Hugh J. Schonfield, author of, *The Passover Plot*. You may be interested to pick up a copy of this book after this blunt excerpt:

> *"In approaching the historical Jesus no question of his deity arises, since before the paganising of Jewish belief in the development of Christianity no authority identified the Messiah with the Logos, the eternal Word of God, or conceived the Messiah to be an incarnation of God.*
>
> *The right understanding of Jesus commences with the realization that he identified himself with the fulfillment of the Messianic Hope. Only on this basis do the traditions about him become wholly intelligible. We have to accept the absolute sincerity of Jesus. But this does not require us to think of him as omniscient and infallible.*
>
> *With the birth stories of Jesus, and of John the Baptist also, we pass directly from the world of sober reality into the world of fairy-tale. The presentation of what takes place does not distinguish at all. Between the factual and the legendary, and*

no criteria are provided to enable us to separate the one from the other.

But apprehending both the heroic and the theological intentions of the nativity stories there is no call whatever to suppose that his arrival in this world of ours was in any way exceptional or attended by any supernatural occurrences. He was as completely human as every baby, the oldest child, as we have said, of a Jewish artisan named Joseph and his wife Miriam (Mary), inheriting his form from their stock and his portion of their character and disposition."

We are not groping in the dark here, friends.

TABLE OF AUTHORITIES

Encyclopedia Britannica
The American College Dictionary
The Sumerians: Their History, Culture and Character by Samuel Noah
Kramer
Internet Page on Sumer
The 12th Planet by Zecharia Sitchin
Daily Life in Ancient Mesopotamia by Karen Rhea Nemet-Nejat
A History of the Jews by Dr. Abram Leon Sachar
The Dead Sea Scrolls Deception by Michael Baigent and Richard
Leigh
The New York Times - Graham
Wikipedia - Graham
The Case for Christ by Lee Stroble
Emergence of Society by John E. Pfeiffer
The Jew in a Gentile World by Arnold A. Rogow
The Passover Plot by Hugh J. Schonfield

ABOUT THE AUTHOR

At the tender age of seven, Timothy Aldred accepted Jesus Christ as his Lord and Savior. After more than fifty years in the dark, he discovered the light of mankind's true origins. Today his life is dedicated to sharing the truth as passionately as he once shared the lie.

Timothy can be contacted via his Web site:
http://www.timothyaldred.com

Sumerian Civilization → 4000 B.C.

Mesopotamian Civilization → 5000-3500 BCE

Egyptian - 3100 BCE

Enlil Son - Nannar (Sin) moon god

Enki Son - Marduk

70619031R00144

Made in the USA
Middletown, DE
15 April 2018